With special thanks to:
Harm Binnenkade, Dale Ellenbogen, Anita Hermans,
Svea van den Hoek and Jaysen Scheepers

YouTube.com/teamexercises

www.teamexercises.info

facebook.com/teamexercises

instagram.com/teamexercises

Scan this QR code to go to YouTube.com/teamexercise

Printed by Amazon.
ISBN: 9798652213091

"Individually, we are one drop. Together, we are an ocean."
– Ryunosuke Satoro

101 Team Exercises

to improve communication and cooperation

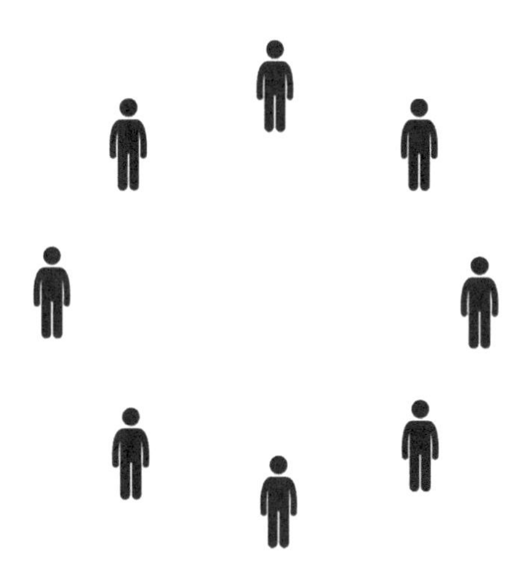

by Herman Otten

Categorical Index

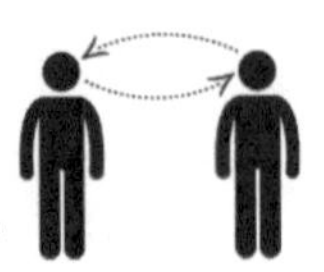

Communication exercises

3 - Make believe story 16-19
9 - Read each other 40-43
15 - Positive gossip 64-67
19 - Truth and fantasy 80-83
21 - Whispering 88-91
22 - Drawing 92-95
25 - Role play game 104-107
31 - How to play werewolves 128-131
35 - Scene of thoughts 144-147
42 - What happened? 172-175
43 - Is this it? 176-179
49 - Transferring 200-203
54 - Questioning 220-223
56 - For or against 228-231
59 - The dictionary game 240-243
60 - Positive communication 244-247
61 - Find the object 248-251
63 - Copy the building 256-259
64 - The word game 260-263
65 - The numbers game 264-267
66 - Filler words 268-271
67 - Who are you 272-275
75 - Acting 304-307
81 - The riddle 328-331
83 - The bluff game 336-339

Insight exercises

4 - Line up 20-23
7 - A step forward 32-35
8 - Getting to know each other 36-39
10 - Stereotypical thinking 44-47
23 - Similarities and differences 96-99
24 - Crossing the line 100-103
26 - Form, a group with 108-111
27 - Stop, start, continue 112-115
28 - Catch the pillow 116-119
30 - Selling each other 124-127
33 - Contact 136-139
34 - Circles 140-143
38 - The key ring 156-159
39 - Points for improvement 160-163
40 - Who stands where 164-167
41 - Musical chairs 168-171
47 - Team constellations 192-195
50 - Yes, maybe, no 204-207
51 - The wishing well 208-211
53 - Distance 216-219
55 - Change 224-227
69 - If you really knew me 280-283
79 - The timeline 320-323
82 - The four elements 332-335
88 - The right answer 356-359
94 - The perfect team member 380-383
95 - The moment I knew........................... 384-387
98 - Music.. 396-399

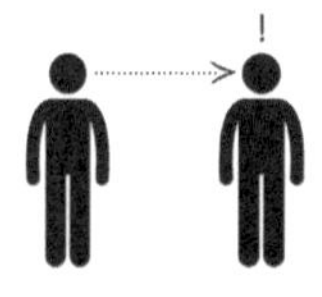

Feedback exercises

5 - The characteristic game 24-27
12 - Describe each other 52-55
14 - Back writing 60-63
16 - How do people see you 68-71
18 - The first thought 76-79
32 - Seeing, thinking, feeling 132-135
68 - Negative to positive 276-279
70 - Instructive feedback 284-287
73 - Animals 296-299
74 - Values 300-303
80 - Gifts 324-327
86 - Like, like, like 348-351
90 - Admiring 364-367
99 - Projecting 400-403
100 - Self evaluation 404-407

Extra exercise

101 - Create your own workshop 408-411

Cooperation exercises

1 - Counting 8-11
2 - The ball game 12-15
6 - The human typewriter 28-31
11 - Forming shapes 48-51
13 - Eye contact 56-59
17 - Blind guiding 72-75
20 - Zip Zap Boing 84-87
29 - Trust fall 120-123
36 - Moving in the group 148-151
37 - 1, 2, 3 152-155
44 - Brainstorming 180-183
45 - The empty chair 184-187
46 - The drawing 188-191
48 - Decision making 196-199
52 - Counting down 212-215
57 - Strings 232-235
58 - Photos 236-239
62 - The maze 252-255
71 - The puzzle 288-291
72 - The catching game 292-295
76 - A million dollars 308-311
77 - Mingle 312-315
78 - The orchestra 316-319
84 - Calling names 340-343
85 - Thinking outside the box 344-337
87 - The newspaper 352-355
89 - The shoe tower 360-363
91 - Simon says 368-371
92 - Classifying 372-375
93 - Imagination 376-379
96 - Making a team logo 388-391
97 - The lunch game 392-395

Cronological Index

1 - Counting 8-11
2 - The ball game 12-15
3 - Make believe story 16-19
4 - Line up 20-23
5 - The characteristic game 24-27
6 - The human typewriter 28-31
7 - A step forward 32-35
8 - Getting to know each other 36-39
9 - Read each other 40-43
10 - Stereotypical thinking 44-47
11 - Forming shapes 48-51
12 - Describe each other 52-55
13 - Eye contact 56-59
14 - Back writing 60-63
15 - Positive gossip 64-67
16 - How do people see you 68-71
17 - Blind guiding 72-75
18 - The first thought 76-79
19 - Truth and fantasy 80-83
20 - Zip Zap Boing 84-87
21 - Whispering 88-91
22 - Drawing 92-95
23 - Similarities and differences 96-99
24 - Crossing the line 100-103
25 - Role play game 104-107
26 - Form, a group with 108-111
27 - Stop, start, continue 112-115
28 - Catch the pillow 116-119
29 - Trust fall 120-123
30 - Selling each other 124-127
31 - How to play werewolves 128-131
32 - Seeing, thinking, feeling 132-135
33 - Contact 136-139
34 - Circles 140-143
35 - Scene of thoughts 144-147
36 - Moving in the group 148-151
37 - 1, 2, 3 152-155
38 - The key ring 156-159
39 - Points for improvement 160-163
40 - Who stands where 164-167
41 - Musical chairs 168-171
42 - What happened? 172-175
43 - Is this it? 176-179
44 - Brainstorming 180-183
45 - The empty chair 184-187
46 - The drawing 188-191
47 - Team constellations 192-195
48 - Decision making 196-199
49 - Transeferring 200-203
50 - Yes, maybe, no 204-207
51 - The wishing well 208-211
52 - Counting down 212-215
53 - Distance 216-219
54 - Questioning 220-223
55 - Change 224-227
56 - For or against 228-231
57 - Strings 232-235
58 - Photos 236-239
59 - The dictionary game 240-243
60 - Positive communication 244-247
61 - Find the object 248-251
62 - The maze 252-255
63 - Copy the building 256-259
64 - The word game 260-263
65 - The numbers game 264-267
66 - Filler words 268-271
67 - Who are you 272-275
68 - Negative to positive 276-279
69 - If you really knew me 280-283
70 - Instructive feedback 284-287
71 - The puzzle 288-291
72 - The catching game 292-295
73 - Animals 296-299
74 - Values 300-303
75 - Acting 304-307
76 - A million dollars 308-311
77 - Mingle 312-315
78 - The orchestra 316-319
79 - The timeline 320-323
80 - Gifts 324-327
81 - The riddle 328-331
82 - The four elements 332-335
83 - The bluff game 336-339
84 - Calling names 340-343
85 - Thinking outside the box 344-347
86 - Like, like, like 348-351
87 - The newspaper 352-355
88 - The right answer 356-359
89 - The shoe tower 360-363
90 - Admiring 364-367
91 - Simon says 368-371
92 - Classifying 372-375
93 - Imagination 376-379
94 - The perfect team member 380-383
95 - The moment I knew 384-387
96 - Making a team logo 388-391
97 - The lunch game 392-395
98 - Music 396-399
99 - Projecting 400-403
100 - Self evaluation 404-407
101 - Create your own workshop 408-410

Introduction

Welcome to my 101 Team Building Exercises book. My name is Herman Otten. I graduated as an actor from the University of Acting in the Netherlands. After my graduation, I worked as an actor for television, film, and theater and as an acting teacher. In 2010, I started working as a communication and team building coach.
I strongly believe that the best way to help individuals bond into a highly functioning team is to do structured communication exercises in a lighthearted atmosphere.
Many times colleagues and friends have asked me if I know some good communication exercises. To help them, I decided to start my own YouTube channel. On this channel, I created animated videos of the exercises I do during my training and coaching. This book contains the first 101 team building exercises from my channel.
Whether you are a communication trainer, manager, teacher, conductor, or football coach, the exercises are suitable for everyone working with groups.
Each exercise contains step-by-step instructions. They are explained as precisely as possible so they are clear and easy to execute.
For each exercise you will find an explanation of why it would be beneficial to perform. By telling this to the group you work with, they will have a clear understanding of why they should do the exercise.
I included several variations for each exercise so you can adjust the exercise to the needs of the group you work with.
Each exercise comes with a QR code. You can scan this code with your smartphone or tablet. This will direct you to the corresponding YouTube video that shows an animated instruction of the exercise. These belonging videos will make it even more clear how the exercise can be performed. Just point the camera of your smartphone or tablet on the QR-code and it will link you to the belonging video.
I hope you will benefit from all of the exercises and you will use them to help individuals become a strong team!

Team Exercise 1 - Counting

"I believe in intuitions. I sometimes FEEL that I am right. I do not KNOW that I am."
- Albert Einstein

Necessities: A tennis ball is optional.

To start the exercise, tell the participants to stand in a circle. Tell them they are going to count together up to the highest number possible. Tell them that a random person from the circle will start by calling out the number "one". A second random person will say "two", a third random person will say 'three", and so on. Before they start counting they will set a goal. For example, the number ten could be their goal. Tell them that even though this seems simple, there are stricts rules to this exercise. The first key rule of the exercise is that a number can't be said by two or more people at the same time. If two or more people call out a number at the same moment, they have to start over from the beginning at the number one. The second rule is that one person is not allowed to say two or more numbers in a row. Otherwise, one person can just count to ten and that would be too easy. The third rule is that they can't arrange a certain order to say the numbers. So no one can, for example, point to someone whom he thinks should say a number next. They have to decide who is going to say the next number based only on their intuition and senses. The fourth rule is that next to numbers no one is allowed to say anything.

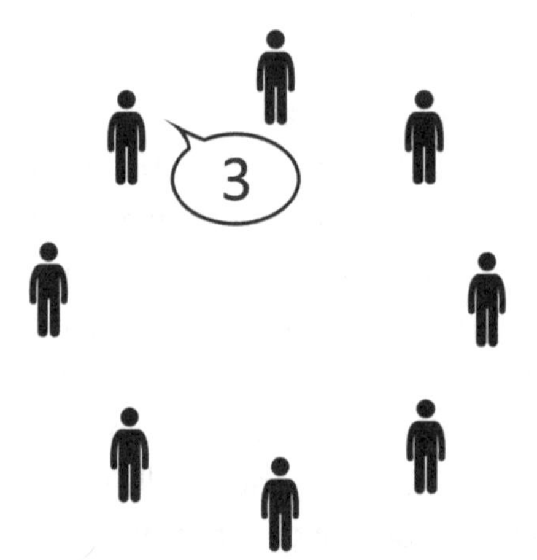

After you explain the rules, tell them to start the counting.
A random first person now calls

out the number one. This is followed by another person calling out the number two, etc. By doing this, they are trying to count towards their preset number. The moment two people call out a number at the same time they will have to start over at the number one. They keep on trying until they reach their preset number. You will see that it will not be easy for them to count without two or more people calling out a number at the same time. Between the attempts to reach the preset number, you can give them advice that will help them to not talk at the same time. You can tell them to close their eyes, so they are more focussed on their senses. You can suggest taking longer pauses between the sentences. This way it is easier to feel who's turn it is to call out the next number. It might be the case that someone calls out a lot of numbers during the exercise. This will increase their chance that people will say a number at the same time. Encourage people who normally talk a lot to stay a bit more quiet and feel when it is their turn to call out a number. Also give them the advice to lean a bit forward on their feet; this way you will see they will be more engaged in the exercise and feel who's turn it will be to call out a number next.

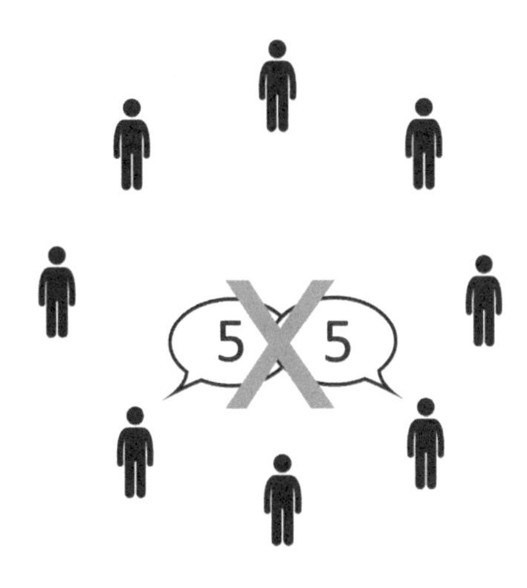

If they finally reach their end goal number, you will applaud them and tell them they can now try to break their own record. For example, if they reached number ten, which was their preset goal, now their new goal will be number eleven. If they broke their own record, you increase the end goal number with ten.

Go on until they can count to the number one hundred without talking at the same time. If they did that, they completed the exercise.

Variations

1. You can let the team walk around the room while counting. This especially helps when they are over focused during the exercise. It will loosen them up and make them more energetic.

2. If you are working with a big group, you can divide the group into smaller groups. The group that reaches the highest number without talking at the same time wins.

3. You can play some music during the exercise. This can create a similar vibe for the whole group. This will help them feel who is going to say a number next.

4. You can tell the group there is a minimum number of times that each person must say a number. By doing this, you will make sure that no one remains silent during an attempt to reach the end number. Of course, make sure the end goal number is high enough so that each person calls out a number the minimum times you told them to do so.

5. You can also give them numbers yourself rather than letting them choose the preset number. You can start with the number ten; if they reach it, you tell them to reach number fifteen, twenty-five, fifty, and then one hundred.

6. You can join the circle and count as well. You will still keep giving them advice between the attempts.

Why you should use this exercise

During the exercise, the team will have one common goal. This will make the group be all on the same page.
Because people are not allowed to talk at the same time, the exercise teaches talkative people that being quiet can sometimes be more effective to achieve the common goal. By doing this, the quiet people of the group will have room to show more initiative by calling out a number.
The exercise teaches the team members to listen to each other, be sensitive about who will say a number next, and feel when it is their turn to open their mouths. This will be good for group atmosphere and group communication.
When the group members reach their common goal, they will feel a relief and excitement that will cause a positive vibe in the group.

Scan this QR code to see an animated example video of this exercise:

You can also type: **Team exercise 1 Counting** into YouTube's search bar to find the video.

Team Exercise 2 - The Ball Game

"The way a team plays as a whole determines its success. You may have the greatest bunch of individual stars in the world, but if they don't play together, the club won't be worth a dime."
- Babe Ruth

Necessities: Three tennis balls.

To start this exercise, you will tell the team to stand in a circle at equal distances from each other. You give a random person from the group a tennis ball. You tell the person with the tennis ball to throw the ball towards another random person in the circle with an underhand throw while calling out the name of the person he is throwing the ball to. For example, if he throws the ball to Mike he says: "Mike". Now Mike will catch the ball and will do the same. He throws the ball to the next person while calling out the name of the person he throws the ball to. If someone doesn't know a name or forgot it, he can throw the ball and ask for the name of that person afterwards. Let them continue passing around the ball until everyone knows each other's names and they can practice the exercise smoothly. If they already know each other's names, you let them throw the ball around for two minutes. After two minutes, you tell them to throw the ball back to you and you start the second part of the exercise. In the second part of the exercise, you tell them that the one throwing the ball won't say the name of the one he is throwing the ball to anymore. Instead, he will now say the name of the person he wants the receiver to throw the

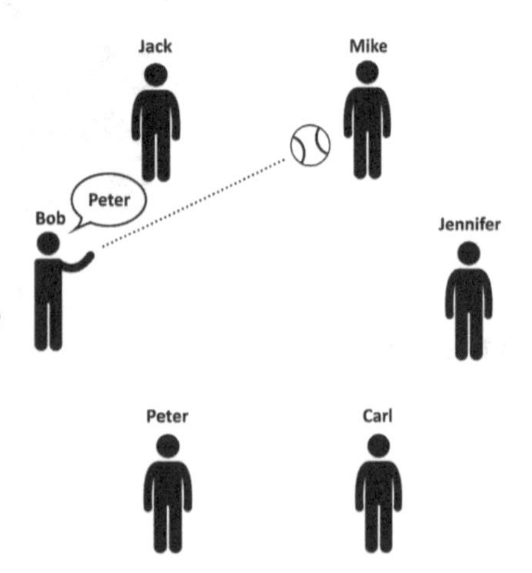

ball to. If for example, Mike throws the ball to Jennifer, he won't say her name, but he will say, for example, Bob. In this case, Jennifer will catch the ball and throw it to Bob while saying the name of the person she wants Bob to throw the ball to.

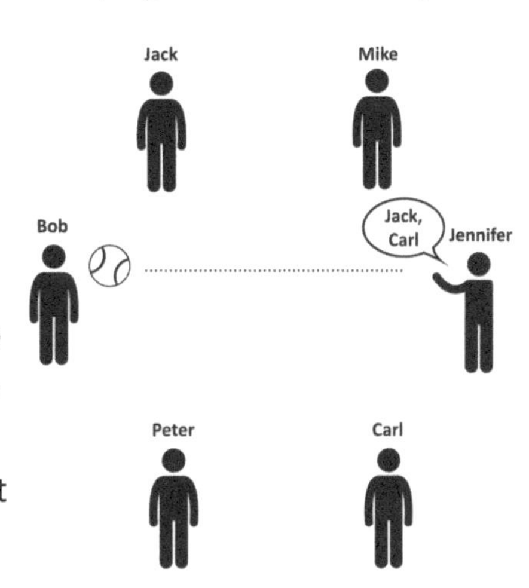

Let them play until they are able to pass around the ball smoothly for around two minutes.

Now, you start a third round by adding another layer of complexity. Tell them that the tennis ball will be thrown around while being not one but two names behind. So the first person who throws the ball calls out two names while throwing the ball to another person. For example, he calls out "Bob and Mike" while throwing the ball to Jennifer. Jennifer will now throw the ball to the first name the first person called out. In this case, it was Bob. She then calls out a new name, for example "Lois". Bob will catch the ball and throws it to the second name the first person called, in this case Mike and calls out a new name, for example: "Peter". Mike catches the ball and will throw it to Lois and calls out a new name to whom Peter will throw the ball. Let them play until they can pass around the ball smoothly for two minutes. You now tell the person who has the ball to hold it and you will now give a random person in the circle a second tennis ball.

Tell them that they will start playing the game as in the first round. However, now two persons will start by throwing the tennis ball to someone while saying the name of the person the ball is being thrown to. So, now the group plays the game with two tennis balls together at the same time.

If they master playing the exercise with two tennis balls at the same time, you can instruct them to play the second round and third round with the two tennis balls at the same time.

Variations

1. After playing the game with two tennis balls, you can also add a third tennis ball. If you give them the third tennis ball, let them begin in the first phase again.

2. For most groups, it will be the easiest to stand in a circle while passing the ball around. An alternative would be to make the team walk criss cross around the room while throwing the ball. They will still play the game as in the original exercise, but they are not bound to the circle formation anymore. This may be an option for groups that are very energetic or if you want a group to get energetic.

3. When you start the exercise, the tempo of passing the ball can be quite low. Especially when there is more than one tennis ball in the game. When the team gets good in passing the tennis ball(s), you can tell them to increase the pace every time you clap your hands. The faster the ball goes around the more it requires focus not to make mistakes. This variation can also be combined with the walking variation.

4. If the group is able to throw around the ball with the names being two steps behind, you can now let them try to pass the ball around while the names are three steps behind. In this case, the first person throwing the ball will have to call out three names while throwing it to another person.

5. Tell them that if the tennis ball drops on the ground or if someone doesn't know to which person to throw the ball, they will go on as if nothing went wrong. Together they will have to try to get back on track without showing their failure.

Why you should use this exercise

This is a great exercise to help people learn each other's names. It is also fine to play with a group of people who already know each other for a long time.
During the exercise, the team will have to combine multiple skills to be able to pass the ball around. Because they have to remember who to throw the ball to, the memory muscle is being trained. They have to keep their eyes on the ball at all times to catch it which will stimulate their focus. Losing focus means that someone will not know who to throw the ball to.
Because they all have the same goal - throwing the ball around without making mistakes - the group vibe will be stimulated in a fun and light-hearted way.

Scan this QR code to see an animated example video of this exercise:

You can also type: **Team exercise 2 the ball game** into YouTube's search bar to find the video.

Team Exercise 3 - Make-believe story

"No story lives unless someone wants to listen. The stories we love best do live in us forever."
- J.K. Rowling

Necessities: None.

To start the exercise, you tell the team to stand in a half circle at equal distances from each other. You stand in front of the group and tell the team you will start a fantasy story. You tell them that in the middle of the story you will suddenly say "and then..." while you will point to a random person in the group who will continue the story. Tell them that the person you will point to keeps on talking until you say "and then..." again and point to another person in the half circle. Tell them they have to listen carefully to the story and visualize what will be told, so the one you chose will be able to continue the story at the point where you left off. Tell them they can come up with anything. They can be as imaginative as they want and let their fantasies run wild.
You will now start the story. "Once upon a time there was a prince. He lived in a big castle in a forest and had everything he ever dreamed of - two lovely parents and more money than he could spend in a lifetime. All the girls living in the country were in love with him. There was only one problem. The prince couldn't fall asleep at night no matter how hard he tried. So he called in his ten servants and said, "The one who can give me the means to fall asleep at night will be rewarded with ten thousand golden coins."
One servant stepped forward.
At this point, you interject "and then..." and point to a random

person who will continue the story. If this person listened well, he should be able to know where to continue. For example, he tells that in the forest lived a witch who had invented a sleeping potion. Let this participant continue the story for about one minute. At a random moment, you interrupt him by saying: “and then...”. You now point to another participant who will continue the story where the previous storyteller has stopped. You keep pointing to people in a random order. It is important that the participants don’t know whom you are going to pick next. In this way, they can’t fabricate ahead of time what they are going to say. The moment they get their turn, they will improvise genuine new storylines on the spot.

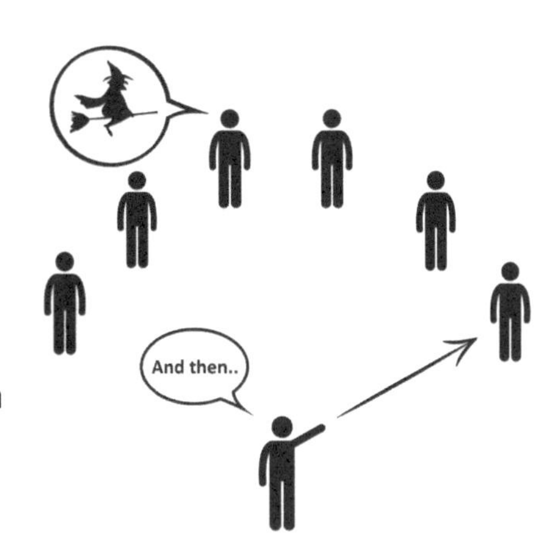

It can be the case that someone can’t think of anything to say. If this happens, you tell him that for now, you will point to someone else in the group to continue the story, and you will come back to him later. You also tell him that the more he visualizes the story someone else is telling, the easier it will be for him to continue the story. You now continue the exercise by pointing to another participant who will continue the story. After pointing at a few participants who continued the story, you come back to the person who went blank. You will see that now it will be easier for him to continue the story.

Go on pointing to people until you pointed to each person and everyone contributed to the story. When you point to the last person, you can instruct him to create an ending.

If he finishes the story, you applaud everyone and tell them that they did a great job.

Variations

1. Instead of your being the one deciding when it is someone else's turn, you can also allow the person who is telling the story to say "and then.." and point to another person. In this way, everyone can decide for themselves how long they want to speak.

2. You can tell the participants to let the characters in the story **do** things instead of telling what the characters are **thinking**. Explain that when they talk about the thoughts of the characters nothing in the story is really progressing, and people will have a harder time generating new input. Give them an example. Instead of saying that the prince **thought** about his father, they could use sentences with verbs such as "goes" or "walks". For example: "The prince **went** to his father and..."

3. You can tell them that concrete images stimulate the imagination more than abstract images. For example, "They saw a beautiful environment" is abstract. "They saw a lawn with green grass and an orange sun in the background" is concrete. The more they describe the story the easier it will be for them to keep on telling the story.

4. When a story is being told, you can instruct the team to continue the story from another character's perspective. For example, they can relate the story from the perspective of the prince's father. The more characters the story contains, the more perspectives they can choose.

5. You can let the participants play a second round. In this case, you ask someone from the group to start a new fantasy story and you will play the exercise in the same way.

Why you should use this exercise

This exercise will stimulate the team's creativity and fantasy. It will also give the team more insight into listening and visualizing what other people are saying.
During the exercise, the team members will be forced to listen very carefully to one another. If they don't listen closely enough, they won't be able to add to the story when it is their turn. Therefore, this exercise reinforces listening skills in a positive way. This exercise will also create team synergy. It is the whole team that must contribute to the very same story. This teaches the team to think and act collaboratively.
Because the team is telling one story, each person will have to relinquish some of his individual ideas to make it a success. Individual egos and ideas must temporarily be put aside to make the story process smoothly.

Scan this QR code to see an animated example video of this exercise:

You can also type: **Team exercise 3 make believe story** into YouTube's search bar to find the video.

Team Exercise 4 - Line up

"Everything will line up perfectly when knowing and living the truth becomes more important than looking good."
- Alan Cohen

Necessities: None.

To start the exercise, you tell the team to stand in a straight line. You go stand in front of the line and tell them that you are going to call out a characteristic. Tell them they will stand in line in a certain order based on the characteristic you are going to call out. Tell them that they will do this in complete silence. You now call out a first characteristic. Begin with a simple physical characteristic that is clearly visible. An example of an easy and specific characteristic could be height. After you call out the characteristic "height", you tell them to line up from short to tall. This should be easy to do and the group should be capable of quickly standing in line in the right order. When they correctly stand in line from shortest to tallest, you give them a few more characteristics based on appearance on which they will stand in a certain order. Some examples of these are hair color (from dark to light), shoe size (from small to big), or the amount of freckles they have (from no freckles to many freckles). Between calling out the characteristics, you tell them that where they stand in line is completely based on group intuition. Remind them that they are not allowed to discuss anything verbally. Make sure you don't pause too long between sentences. Make sure the team is constantly moving so they don't have time to think too much about the order. This will help them put themselves in the correct order faster.

After you have played the exercise with a few characteristics based on appearance, you will now call out a characteristic that is based on personality. An example of this would be the ability to be funny. Instruct them that the person who fits this characteristic the most will stand to the far left and the one who fits it the least will stand on the far right of the line. Without talking, the team should figure out how to stand in the correct order. Give them a few more characteristics based on personality on which they will stand in a certain order. Switch serious characteristics with lighthearted ones so there will be enough variation in the exercise. Examples of more serious characteristics are: who can handle feedback the best, who is the most giving, and who has the best ideas. Examples of lighthearted characteristics are: who has the funniest laugh, who loves butterflies the most, who is the biggest smartass, and who is the most musical.
With these more informal traits in the mix, they will feel more comfortable when they move in order based on more serious characteristics.
After playing multiple rounds with characteristics based on personality, you tell them that in the second part of the exercise they will line up based on a certain statement. Tell them they will now lineup in order from who agrees the most to who agrees the least with the statement. You now call out a first statement. For example: “Having fun is more important than working hard.” The person who agrees the most will start the line followed by the others in descending order. The last person in line is the one who agrees the least with the statement.

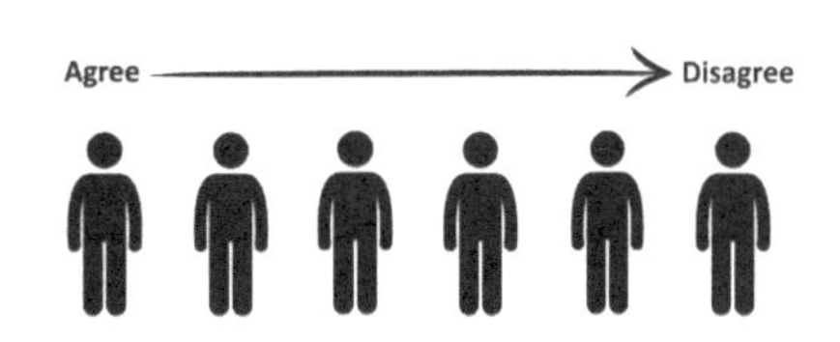

You also play this round with multiple statements.

Variations

1. You can write the characteristics and statements on a notecard prior to the exercise and bring them with you. This way, you don't have to be afraid of forgetting or not being able to create ideas on the spot.

2. While the exercise is being played, you can encourage the team to increase the tempo. This will motivate them to form a line based on intuition rather than conscious thinking. To assist the team in this process, you can start to count down from ten to one. In this case you can tell them for example: "Form a line based on the statement 'I need coffee in the morning' in 10, 9, 8, 7, ..."

3. You can let the participants suggest characteristics or statements themselves. Call out the name of a participant to suggest a trait or statement. After someone calls out the characteristic or statement, the team will perform the exercise in the same way as before. Continue until everyone comes up with a characteristic or statement.

4. Let the team walk around the room between each characteristic or statement. Because they keep on walking, it will keep the flow in the exercise.

5. Between rounds, you can explain that the spot someone is standing on doesn't necessarily mean something negative or positive. For example, if people are standing on the least "friendly" side in the line, that doesn't mean that they aren't friendly. It only means that in this group setting the characteristic "friendly" applies the least to them.

Why you should use this exercise

In a lighthearted way, the team members will gain insight into how they are being perceived within the team. Because it happens in a playful and casual manner, the exercise creates a natural vibe in which everyone gains insight into where everyone stands in the group regarding certain characteristics.
Because the team moves constantly and many characteristics and statements circulate, they won't think too much about it. They will just stand in a certain order based on what they feel is right. During the second part in which they stand in order regarding a certain statement, people can express their opinions without talking and getting into a discussion. Each person will discover literally and figuratively where he stands regarding a certain topic.

Scan this QR code to see an animated example video of this exercise:

You can also type: **Team exercise 4 line up** into YouTube's search bar to find the video.

Team Exercise 5 - The characteristic game

"Feedback is the breakfast of champions."
- Ken Blanchard

Necessities: Small papers, pencils and a hat or container large enough for notecards.

To start the exercise, you tell the team to sit in a circle. You put the hat in the center of the circle. You give everyone five pieces of paper and a pen. Tell them to write positive characteristics on three of the cards, and negative characteristics on two of the notecards. Tell everyone to fold the cards and put them into the hat. The total number of characteristics in the hat is now five times the number of people performing the exercise. You now point to a first random person from the circle and instruct him to take a card out of the hat, open it, and read the characteristic out loud. After he reads the characteristic, you tell him to choose the person who he thinks best exemplifies that characteristic. He then explains why he chose that particular person. When he gives his explanation, the chosen person listens to the feedback in silence. All the other participants also listen in silence. When the one giving feedback is finished talking, he gives the card to the person he just gave feedback to. That person lays the card in front of him on the ground.

Now, the person who just received the card takes a card out of the hat and does the same thing. He reads the characteristic out loud, says whom he thinks fits it most, tells this person why, gives him the card, and the person who received the feedback puts it in front of him.

You let the group continue this process until all cards are taken from the hat and are laying on the ground in front of different persons. Each person now has cards in front of him that were given to him by the other team members. Each person can now literally see what characteristics the group thinks fits him the most. Tell them to look for a moment at the cards in front of them and think about the characteristics.

You now start the second part of the exercise by telling the participants to trade a card with another participant. Tell them that the card someone trades will have a characteristic of which he wants less. He will give this card to someone whom he thinks needs more of this characteristic. After he gives his card to this person, he will take a card lying in front of that person. He will pick a card that has a characteristic of which he wants more. Give them an example to make it clear. Tell them that if someone has a card that says "insecure" laying in front of him and he wishes to be less insecure, he can choose someone from the team whom he feels could use a bit more insecurity. He trades the "insecure" card to that person for a card that has a characteristic of which he wants more. For example, he could trade the "insecure" card for the "arrogant" card. You now point to a first random person who starts to do this. After he trades his card and goes back to his seat, the person sitting on his left side does the same. Let them go clockwise around the circle until everyone trades a card with a characteristic of which he wants less with a card with a characteristic of which he wants to have more.

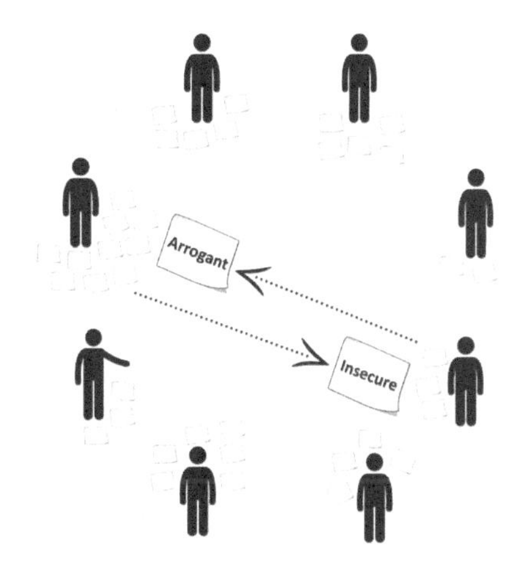

Tell them to look for a moment at the cards in front of them which now also contain the new card.

Variations

1. Tell them that the number of cards lying in front of someone also tells something about each person. Some people may have more opinions given to them than others.

2. Make sure the exercise is practiced playfully and everyone feels safe. You can do this by occasionally making a joke during the exercise. When the team feels comfortable and safe, they are more likely to see it as a game rather than something very serious. A lighthearted atmosphere will encourage more honesty from the people who give the feedback and more openness of the people receiving the feedback.

3. When you play only with positive traits, you can do a second round in which everyone puts the traits back in the hat. Each person then takes a card and gives it to someone he thinks can use a bit more of that characteristic. So when someone takes the "funny" card, he can give it to someone he thinks can use a bit more humor.

4. You can also let everyone write just positive characteristics on the papers that they put in the hat. This way the team creates a positive atmosphere.

5. If someone didn't get a card during the game, you can give a random person a blank card. Tell him to write a characteristic he thinks best suits one of the people who didn't get a card. He gives the card to that person and explains why he wrote that characteristic. Do this until everyone has a card with a characteristic.

Why you should use this exercise

During this exercise the participants will give each other feedback. Because everyone needs to give a card to someone, everyone will have the chance to clear their minds. This can be a big relief, because most of the time people keep their opinions to themselves. The result is that the atmosphere is more open after this exercise, and the team members are more capable of communicating with each other in an open atmosphere.
Because the person who is receiving the feedback isn't allowed to talk back, the feedback will be really pure without having a discussion. This will help everyone absorb the feedback without judgement.
Because of the trading part, the team learns that a characteristic can be wanted and unwanted at the same time. They will learn that each characteristic has its own positives and negatives.

Scan this QR code to see an animated example video of this exercise:

You can also type: **team exercise 5 the characteristic game** into YouTube's search bar to find the video.

Team Exercise 6 - The human typewriter

"Individually, we are one drop. Together, we are an ocean."
- Ryunosuke Satoro

Necessities: None

To start this exercise, you tell the team to stand at equal distances from each other in a straight line. You will stand in front of the line and will divide all the letters of the alphabet among all the people in the line. Tell them they have to remember the letter or letters they will get very well. From left to right, you assign the letters by pointing at each person while saying a letter aloud. The person standing at the farthest left side of the line gets the letter A, and the person standing next to him the letter B, etc. When you get to the end of the line, you go back to the left side of the line and continue where you left off assigning letters until you reach the letter Z. At this point, you should have given each person one or more letters from the alphabet. When there are less than twenty-six people in the group, one or more people will have multiple letters. Now you tell the team a sentence, which contains every letter of the alphabet. For example, "The quick brown fox jumps over the lazy dog." Tell them that it is now the team's job to use the letters to type the sentence. They do this by calling out the letters of the sentence in the correct order. One by one, they call out a letter. When someone calls out his letter, he also jumps. Each person is responsible for calling out the letters he was assigned. In this case, the first person who will jump and say his letter will be the person to whom you gave the letter T. The second person who will jump will be the

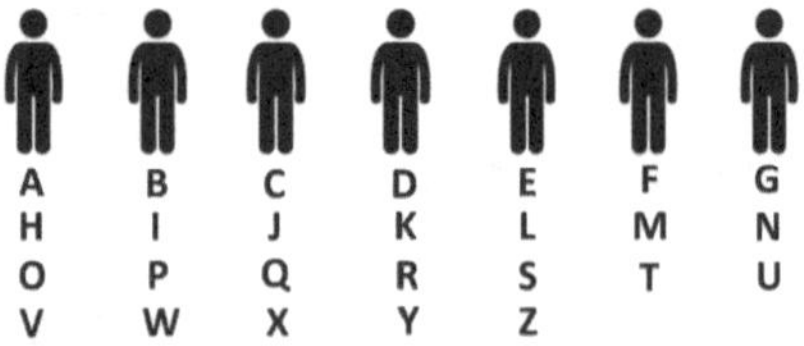

A	B	C	D	E	F	G
H	I	J	K	L	M	N
O	P	Q	R	S	T	U
V	W	X	Y	Z		

person to whom you gave the letter H. If a person has multiple letters, he might have to say more than one letter in a row. It is important that everyone knows exactly where their letters are in the sentence. They must pay close attention to the other people who are saying the letters so each person knows exactly when to call out his letter. Tell the group that during the exercise, the participants do not talk except for saying the letters. If the team gets lost, confused, or no one says a letter, you can tell them to start over. The participants starts over as many times as needed until the whole sentence has finally been typed.

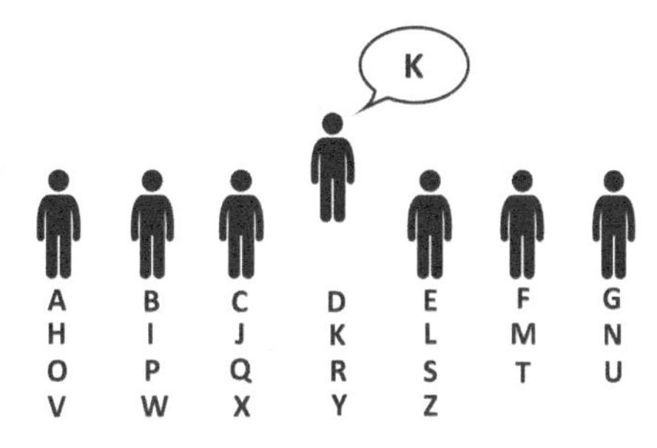

Now you start the second round. You tell the team to create its own sentences. Ask for a volunteer to call out a sentence which the group will type in the same way as they did in the first round. Now the sentence doesn't have to contain every letter of the alphabet. For example, "We are the best team in the company." Make sure everyone knows exactly what the sentence is before they start to type the sentence. The more the team listens to each other, the easier it will be for them to construct the sentence. If they are paying attention, each person will know when to speak.

After they generate a few sentences, you can start the third round. You tell them to begin a sentence through improvisation without knowing what the sentence is going to be. A first person starts by jumping while calling out his letter. Then a second person jumps and calls out the next letter. One letter at a time together they will try to form a sentence. This is difficult because they don't know where the sentence is going. However, it is possible if they are really focused and each person is able to relinquish his own idea. In this case, the sentence they create doesn't need to have interesting content. Often, it will be an absurd sentence. If the sentence is going nowhere, you can tell them to start over until they form a legitimate sentence.

Variations

1. Next to the sentence mentioned in the exercise, you can also use a few other sentences to play with that contain all letters of the alphabet:
"Pack my box with five dozen liquor jugs."
"How quickly daft jumping zebras vex."
"The five boxing wizards jump quickly."
"Turgid saxophones blew over Mick's jazzy quaff."

2. When they are comfortable with the exercise, you can let the team walk around the room while performing the exercise. This way they have to be extra focussed to know who has to say which letter when. Tell everyone to talk loudly so everyone can clearly hear the letters.

3. In addition to random sentences they come up with in round two, you can also tell the team to come up with sentences that say something about the group. For example, "Together we have excellent communication when we listen to each other."

4. When the exercise is too difficult for them, you can make it easier by writing the sentence they are typing on a whiteboard. This way, it is easier for the team to follow where they are in the sentence. You can also write each person's name with the assigned letters on the whiteboard. This makes it easier for each person to know which letters are his responsibilities.

5. You can make the third round easier by telling them to spontaneously type a word together instead of typing a whole sentence.

Why you should use this exercise

During this exercise, the team will realize that listening well and taking responsibility are very important. If they don't listen to each other, they won't know where they are in the sentence. They will get confused and need to start over again.
Each person in the line will focus on their individual responsibility to call out a letter at the correct moment. This will contribute to the common goal of the group: finishing the sentence. Because they all have to be focused at the same time and have the same goal, it is a very good exercise to improve team spirit.
The last round in which they have to improvise a sentence on the spot will cause hilarity in the group; no one knows beforehand what the sentence is going to be.

Scan this QR code to see an animated example video of this exercise:

You can also type: **team exercise 6 the human typewriter** into YouTube's search bar to find the video.

Team Exercise 7 - A step forward

"Apparently there is nothing that cannot happen today."
- Mark Twain

Necessities: None.

This team exercise is designed to do before and/or after a team building day, a brainstorm session, or another kind of group meeting. To start the exercise, you tell the team to stand in a circle at arm's length from each other. Tell the participants that the purpose of the first part of this exercise is to find out everyone's expectations for the day. You point to a first random participant who will tell the rest of the group what he or she expects from the team day. Tell them that the expectation can be anything. It can be something serious such as: "I expect that we are going to get to know each other on a deeper level today." However, it can also be something more lighthearted such as: "I expect that we will laugh a lot together." As long as it is an honest expectation, he can say anything he wants. After this first person calls out his expectation, you tell him to take one step forward into the circle. You now tell the other people that anyone who shares this expectation also takes one step forward into the circle. Tell them that they are allowed to think for a few seconds as to whether or not they agree with the expectation. It is important that everybody on the team understands what the expectation is. By understanding the expectation, they will be able to decide if they agree or not and if they want to take a step forward. Tell them that if someone doesn't

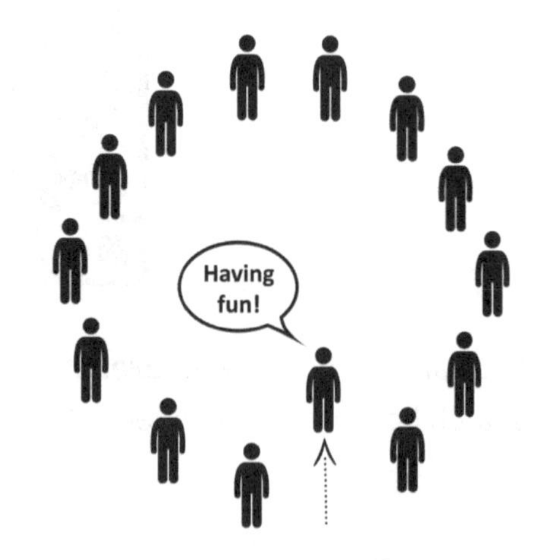

fully understand what the expectation means, he is allowed to ask a question. When everyone made their choices to step forward or not, tell them to stand still for a few seconds and look around to see who else shares the expectation. Then instruct them to step back into the circle again. Now, the person standing on the left side of the person who first shared his expectation will do the same. He shares his expectation, takes a step forward, and the people who have the same expectation take a step forward too. Everyone looks around and then takes a step back into the circle again. Go clockwise around the circle until each person shares his expectation and has a chance to see if the other people from the group agreed or disagreed.

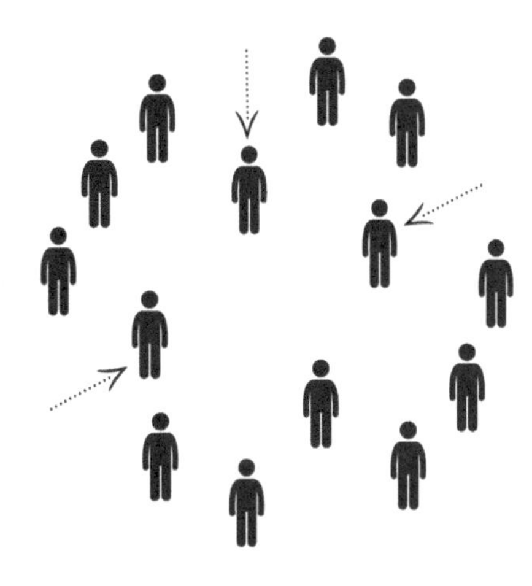

Now, you will start the team day. You now know what the expectations are. Therefore, you can adjust the day to their expectations. At the end of the day, you tell everyone to stand in the circle again. You tell them that now each person will say what he thinks was achieved during the day. Tell them it might be something serious such as: "We sorted out our differences and now have a better group chemistry." Or something lighthearted such as: "We found out we have the same sense of humor." As in the first round, you point to a first random person who tells what he thinks was achieved during the day and takes a step forward into the circle. Again, anyone who shares this achievement takes a step forward too. Everyone who just stepped forward looks around for a moment before stepping back into the circle again.
Go clockwise around the group so that everyone gets a turn to share what he thinks was achieved and see whether the others agree or not.

Variations

1. You can also take part in this exercise yourself. By participating, you can share what you expect from the day. After the day you can share how you experienced the group and the training. You can now see how the team agrees or disagrees with your opinions.

2. In addition to stepping forward you can let them step backwards if they disagree. In this case, someone steps forward if he agrees, stays where he is if he doesn't have an opinion, and takes a step backwards if he disagrees.

3. In addition to sharing expectations and achievements, you can also ask the team to share other things. At the beginning of the day they can share for example what they want to improve regarding their communication. At the end of the team day they can share for example what they would like to have seen differently during the day. In the same way as in the original exercise each person shares his opinion and the others show whether they agree or not.

4. If the person sharing his expectation or achievement thinks the expectation or achievement is very important to him, he can take two steps forward instead of one. The others can do the same. If they agree, they take one step forward. If they agree and also think it is important, they take two steps forward.

5. After everyone who agreed with the expectation or achievement stepped forward, you can ask who wants to explain why he agrees or not. One by one, these people now share why they stepped forward or not.

Why you should use this exercise

During the exercise everyone will literally see how strong an expectation or achievement is being felt within the group.
If everyone gets a chance to share their expectations at the beginning of the day, it becomes clear what the team expects. You will be able to adjust the day to fit these expectations. If the team expects to have a laugh, you can implement some humor during the exercises. If they expect to have a more serious vibe you can implement some more serious exercises.
By sharing their achievements at the end of the day, the group will remember these achievements better.
Because everyone will just step forward without commenting, there won't be a discussion. People will just see how the group thinks about a certain expectation or achievement.

Scan this QR code to see an animated example video of this exercise:

You can also type: **team exercise 7 a step forward** into YouTube's search bar to find the video.

Team Exercise 8 - Getting to know each other

"Without knowing the world of others, your own world will never get rich!"
- Mehmet Murat ildan

Necessities: None.

During this exercise, the team stands in a circle at equal distances from each other. You point to a random person in the circle. This person will choose a person to pair up with of whom he thinks he knows the least. You tell this duo to sit or stand together somewhere in the room. Now you point to the next person in the circle who will do the same. Continue doing this until the group has been divided into duos. Tell the duos to decide who will be person A and who will be person B. Instruct person A to tell person B the biggest blunder he has ever made in his life. Person A listens carefully to the story and remembers as many details as possible. When person A finishes the story, the roles reverse. Now person B tells his biggest blunder to person A and person A listens carefully and tries to remember as many details as possible. When all duos have finished their stories, they come back and stand in the circle again.

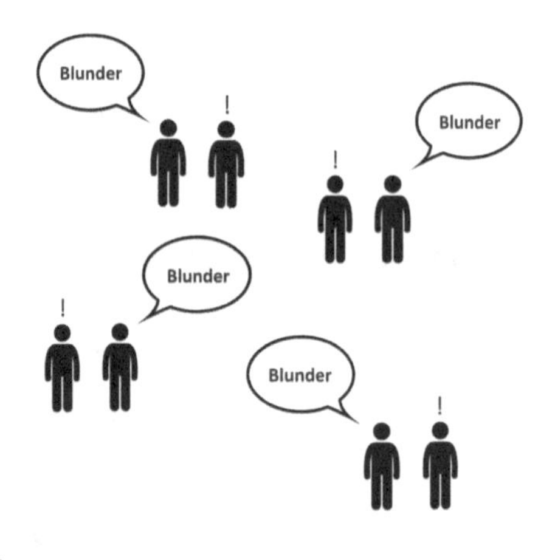

Now tell them that one by one, each participant will tell the story he just heard from his partner as if it is his own blunder. It is important that he will relate from a first person perspective; it needs to sound like his own blunder. Tell them it is important that everyone will try to remember as much as possible of all the blunders they will hear. Now, you point to a random person in the group who will start telling about the blunder. All the other participants in the circle listen carefully and try to remember as much as possible. Let them go clockwise around the circle until each person has told the story about the blunder as if it were his own.

Now you start the second round. You point to a random person who will choose a different partner than he had in the first round. Tell him it should be someone whom he thinks has a different vision about the future of the place they are all connected with. This can for example be their place of employment, school, or sport club. Give them an example to make it clear. If they all work at a school, tell them a personal vision can be that in the future they need smaller classes. In this case someone partners up with someone whom he thinks doesn't want smaller classes. After all the pairs have been formed, person A tells person B what his vision for the future is. Person B listens carefully and remembers as much as he can. Now person B tells person A about his vision and person A remembers as much as possible. After everyone tells his vision to his partner, they all go back to the circle. As in the first round, one by one each person now shares the vision he just heard as if it were his own. Tell them everyone should remember as much as possible of all the visions they hear. After everyone shared the vision, you start the third round. You point to two random people who didn't pair up before. The first person you choose will tell the blunder story of the second person as if it is his own. If he listened carefully before, he will be able to do so. Go on pointing to people until each person told a blunder story that was previously told by someone else. You now do the same thing with the vision story until each person told a vision story that was previously told by another person.

Variations

1. In the first round, people form duos with someone they know the least about. You can also let them form duos based on other aspects. For example, you can let them form duos with someone they have had the most differences with or with someone they wish to know more about.

2. In the second round, people form duos with someone whom they think has a different vision for the organization. You can also let them form duos based on other aspects. For example, you can let them form duos with someone of whom they think his vision might spark curiosity.

3. In addition to a blunder, you can let the couples tell each other stories. For example what in life has impacted them most, what they are strongly against, or what they heavily support. Just as in the original exercise, each person tells the story he just heard to the rest of the group as if it were his own.

4. When a person tells the blunder of his partner as if it is his own, he can also tell his own blunder. He doesn't say which blunder is his own and which blunder is from his partner. Let the others guess and unanimously decide which of one is his own blunder and which one is from his partner. You can also apply this variation to the vision round.

5. You can tell them at the beginning of the exercise that in round three they will have to tell a blunder or vision from a random person of the group. If they know this in advance they will listen even better during the exercise.

Why you should use this exercise

This is a great introduction game in which the team gets to know each other better. Therefore this exercise is appropriate for groups of people that don't know each other.
It is also appropriate for people who know each other but want to know each other on a deeper level. Sharing stories will generate better relationships, create respect, and form a better, more productive work environment. Telling someone else's story as if it were their own, will promote an understanding of another's vision. This will create a mutual understanding between the participants.
It is also a good listening exercise because they need to reproduce what they heard before. In the third round, the team will be amazed how many things people can remember if they pay attention.

Scan this QR code to see an animated example video of this exercise:

You can also type: **team exercise 8 getting to know each other better** into YouTube's search bar to find the video.

Team Exercise 9 - Read each other

"Until you realize how easy it is for your mind to be manipulated, you remain the puppet of someone else's game."
- Evita Ochel

Necessities: Little pieces of paper and pencils.

During this exercise, you tell the team to form pairs. Each pair decides who will be person A and who will be person B. Each duo will sit together at a table facing each other. You give all the A's five small pieces of paper, which they lay on the table in front of them. Tell all B's to turn around so they won't see the papers. Person A draws a cross on one of the pieces of paper. He folds each one up and places them on the table. Person A remembers carefully which paper has the cross on it. Person B now turns back to the table so he sees the folded papers lying on the table. Person B should not be able to see which paper has the cross on it.

Next, person B points to each paper, one at a time, and asks if it is the one with the cross. Person A always answers "yes" to the question. This means that person A lies four times and tells the truth once. Person B must try to intuitively figure out when person A is lying and when he is telling the truth. Based on what he has observed when person A answered his five questions, person B now has to eliminate one piece of paper of which he thinks has no cross on it. Person B now points to the paper he thinks is blank and opens it up. If he isn't correct and picked the one with the cross, the game is over and they switch roles. If he is right and there is no cross on the paper, he earns one point.

He then points to each of the four remaining papers and asks if there is a cross on it. Again, person A always answers "yes". Again, person B points to a paper, which he thinks is blank and opens it up. If he is correct, he earns another point for a total of two. For the remaining three papers, the same principle applies. Person A answers "yes" each time person B asks if it is the paper with the cross. Person B assesses whether or not there is a cross on the paper. Once again, person B points to a paper which he thinks is blank. If he is correct, he gets another point for a total of three points. For the last two papers, it is the same principle. Person B points one by one to the last two papers asking if it is the one with the cross and both times person A answers "yes". Now person B makes his final choice. He points to the paper he thinks is blank, and if he is correct, he earns a point for a total of four points. He can now open the last remaining paper with the cross on it. In this case, person B has completed the game and earned the most possible points - four.

The object of the exercise is for person B to pick the paper with the cross on it last. The object for person A is to get person B to choose the paper with the cross as quickly as possible to prevent him from earning points. Person A can do this by for example acting inattentive when person B asks if a particular paper is the one with the cross. Person B may think that it can't be the one with the cross, so he chooses it and the game is over. After the game, the guesser remembers his points and they switch roles. Now person B writes a cross on one of the papers and person A tries to eliminate the blank papers until the one with the cross is the only one left.

The one who earns the most points wins the game.

Variations

1. You can also tell the guesser he can talk during the game. Tell him to elaborate on his choice of why he thinks a paper does or doesn't have the cross on it. For example, he can say the following: "You were purposely tensed when I pointed at this particular paper. I think you did this because you wanted to manipulate me into thinking that's the one with the cross. That's why I think it's a bluff. I will pick that piece of paper because I think it is blank." This explanation can be interesting to share.

2. You can tell the one who wrote the cross that he can talk during the game. This way he can manipulate the guesser. The one who wrote the cross can for example manipulate the guesser by immediately saying where the one with the cross is. This way he can confuse the guesser. He could be lying, or he can be telling the truth but wants the guesser to think he is lying.

3. If all the pairs have finished the exercise, they can come together in a circle and talk about what they experienced. To encourage conversation, ask them the following: "How could they tell if someone lied? How could they tell if someone wanted them to think that they lied? Can you spot a lie in someone's eyes or voice?" Let them share their experiences so everyone can learn from each other.

4. You can turn this game into a tournament. The winners of the first round can pair up for a second round and play against each other. The winners of this round can play a third round. Go on until there is one final winner. The people who lost the game can watch the other people play and try to guess in silence where the paper with the cross is.

Why you should use this exercise

This exercise makes the participants pay close attention to each other. Everyone will have to look closely at how the person in front of them is behaving to see when he is speaking the truth and when he is not. Therefore their human knowledge will be trained. They will discover who can read people really well, who is a good bluffer, and who is just too honest to win this game.
Since this is a fun exercise, it will help the participants learn about communication in a light-hearted way. Therefore this exercise is a good introductory lesson or training about communication.
The game element makes the exercise competitive. This will stimulate the participants to be extra motivated. Each person will be excited when he discovers where the paper with the cross is.

Scan this QR code to see an animated example video of this exercise:

You can also type: **team exercise 9 read each other better** into YouTube's search bar to find the video.

Team Exercise 10 - Stereotypical thinking

"What were we spending so much time doing if not getting to know each other?"
- Jonathan Safran Foer

Necessities: You can use tape, but it is not necessary.

To start the exercise, you tell the team to stand in a circle at equal distances from each other. You point to one person in the circle and tell him to come up with a lighthearted topic that can be used to sort people into categories. For example, he might come up with the topic: places people like to go for dinner. Now tell him to point to a second person in the circle who will come up with three categories regarding this topic. Tell this second peron he will place all individuals from the team into these categories. The first category this person chooses could be a snack bar. After he calls out the category, he chooses people from the team whom he thinks like to go to a snack bar. He puts all of the snack bar people together in one group. Now he comes up with a second category, for example people who prefer to go to a pizzeria. He puts all the people whom he thinks prefer to eat at pizzerias into a group. Now he comes up with the third and last category that could be: people who prefer to go to a stylish restaurant. Again, he puts the people whom he thinks prefer to go to a stylish restaurant together into a group. You tell the divider that if he doesn't know in which category to put a certain person in, he will just guess in which category that person fits most and puts that person into that category.

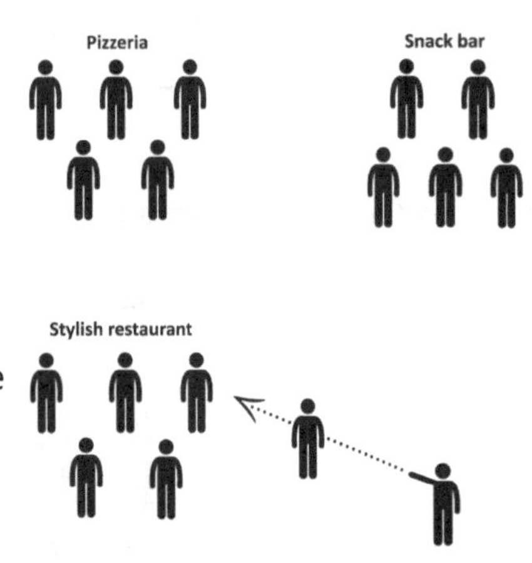

In the second part of the exercise, the divider will discover whether he was wrong or right. You now tell the participants that if they feel they are in the wrong category, they should move to the group in which think they belong. Let people change groups until everyone feels that they are standing in the correct category. Now the person who sorted everyone into the categories can see if his assumptions were correct or incorrect. Everyone goes back to the circle and you tell the person who just did the sorting to create a new topic. Tell him this time the topic must have something to do with communication. For example, he might come up with the topic: ways to give feedback. He now points to someone else in the circle who will sort the team into three categories regarding this topic. The first category can be for example: people who give feedback in a direct way. He now puts the people whom he thinks prefer to give feedback in a direct way together in a group. The second category could be: people who give feedback in an indirect way. An example of the third category could be: people who give feedback with humor. When all the people are divided, instruct anyone who feels that they are in the wrong group to switch. The person who sorted everyone into the categories gets to see whether he was correct or not. Everyone goes back to the circle and you tell the person who just did the sorting to come up with a lighthearted topic.

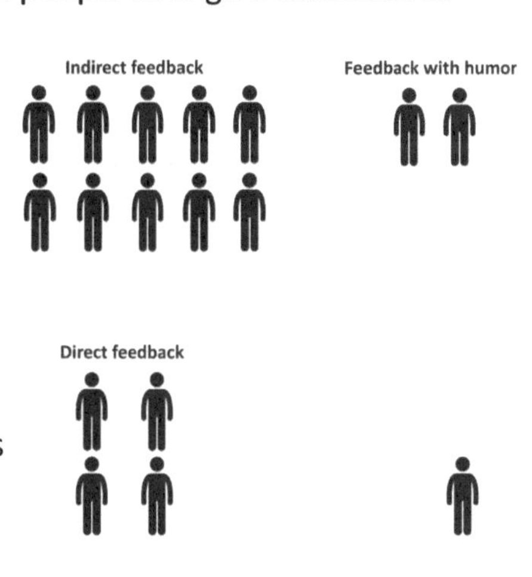

Next, he will point to someone who will create three related categories and divide the people into these categories. Let them play this round in the same way as before. Continue the exercise until everyone had the chance to divide the group into three categories. To keep the variety, let them alternate light hearted topics with more serious topics about communication.

Variations

1. You can also suggest topics and categories yourself. Tell them the topic and the three categories and point to someone who will divide the group into these three categories. A few topics and categories you can suggest are the following: What is your favorite animal? The categories could be cat, dog, or dinosaur. What kind of communicator are you? The categories could be introvert, extravert, or both. What is your favorite movie? The categories could be “Legally Blonde”, “The Godfather”, or “Mission Impossible”.

2. You can switch the first and the second part of the exercise. Before someone divides the team into categories, the participants can stand where they think this person will put them. Then, the one dividing will put them where he thinks they should be instead. However, if he agrees, he can leave them standing where they are.

3. You can bring tape to the exercise so you can divide the room into three spaces. The divider tells the group which space belongs to which category. He then instructs each person to stand in the space he thinks that person belongs.

4. Instead of just three categories, you can let someone create more than three categories. This especially helps when it is a big group.

5. You can give the divider time to elaborate on his choices. In a few sentences, he can explain why he put certain people into certain categories.

Why you should use this exercise

In a lighthearted manner, this exercise gives the team members more insight into how they are perceived by others and how they perceive themselves. It is fun to do this exercise when no one knows each other. All the choices will be made based on prejudices and stereotypical thinking. Stereotypical thinking is generally perceived as negative, but in this exercise, it is meant to be funny. Some choices will be perfectly correct while other choices couldn't be more wrong. This makes the exercise fun and makes will make the participants laugh. Laughing together will help them form a bond.
It is also a great exercise to do with people who work together often; in-depth topics such as communication can provide insight into how people are being seen by others and whether they agree or not.

Scan this QR code to see an animated example video of this exercise:

You can also type: **team exercise 10 stereotypical thinking** into YouTube's search bar to find the video.

Team Exercise 11 - Forming shapes

"Alone we can do so little, together we can do so much."
- Helen Keller

Necessities: A room big enough to walk around with a group.

To start the exercise, you tell the team to walk crisscross through the room. Tell the team that when you clap your hands, they will have to form a straight line. This needs to be done without talking. They are also not allowed to physically direct each other to a location. It is forbidden to point to others to instruct them where to stand. Now you clap your hands at a random moment and all the participants will form a straight line. When the line is formed, the team stands still until you clap your hands again. That is the signal to walk through the room again. Now you do the same with another form, for example, a square. You clap your hands and the team tries to intuitively feel who will take what spot while forming the square. Tell them that everyone's place in the shape is essential and giving each other space is of great importance. Sometimes it can take a while before the team establishes a connection with each other before the shape is formed. If they formed the square they stand still for a bit, and when you clap your hands again, they will continue to walk through the room. You now do the same with a third shape, for example, a circle. You clap your hands and they will stand in a circle as quickly as possible. Now, you tell the group the next shape they will form will be one of the three previous ones - a line, square or circle. Now you will not tell them which form it is going to be, they will have to find that

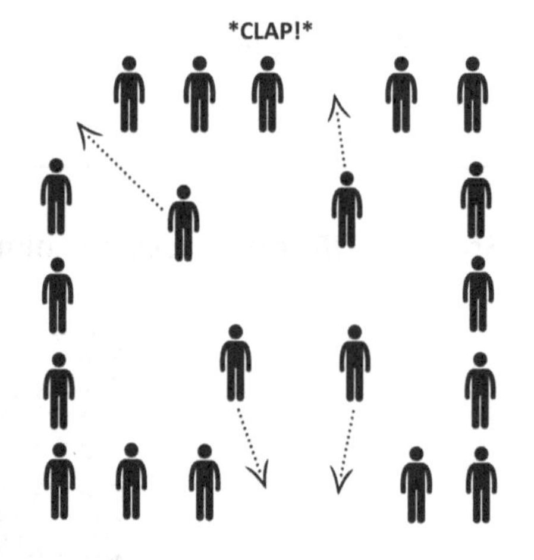

out together. Clap your hands and the team will form one of the three shapes. There can be some confusion because people might have different shapes in mind and are not talking. When they concentrate really well and focus on each other's movements, they will be able to instantly feel which of the three shapes they are going to make. After they form the shape, let them stand still for a few seconds. When you clap your hands they walk around again. Tell them to do the same when you clap your hands again. Continue with this "one out of three forms" round for a few minutes. Each time their intuition will improve and they will get better and faster at sensing what the form will be. The less they think, and the more they can relinquish their preconceived ideas the better the group will perform. In the next round, you tell the team that when you clap your hands, they will form a random, new original shape. It can be anything, a star, heart, triangle, etc. As long as it can be clearly identified when they are done. Without discussing verbally or nonverbally, they have to sense what the form is going to be. After they all recognize the form, have them stand still for a few seconds. You clap your hands and they walk around again. Continue with this for a few rounds until the team masters it.

Now tell the team to continue forming random shapes without waiting for your clap signal and without walking between the different shapes. When the group decides a shape is ready, they spontaneously merge their current shape directly into a new one. They will stand still for a while so it becomes clear to everyone what shape they have made before they will form a new shape.

Let them do this for a few minutes until they perform this round smoothly.

Variations

1. In addition to the line, square, and circle you can also add other creative shapes during the first part of the exercise. For example, you could add the shape of a heart, a star, a table, a chair, or a cloud.

2. You can change the pace of the exercise. For example, you can instruct the team to form a shape slowly or quickly. You can also change the walking tempo. For example, you can tell them to walk quickly but form a shape in slow motion.

3. You can assign a number to a shape and call out the number instead of the shape itself. For example, number one is a square, number two is a triangle and number three is a star. This will require the team to pay closer attention and adds extra difficulty to the exercise.

4. When the team finds it difficult to form a shape without talking, you can allow the team to discuss verbally who will stand where. After a while, you can add the no talking rule again. This way they will become accustomed to the exercise, and forming shapes without talking will be easier for them to do.

5. When in the last round the team can spontaneously create original shapes without talking, give them permission to verbally communicate and do the same thing. They will notice that it won't necessarily be easier to form shapes while talking than it was in silence. When they were quiet, they had to rely only on their senses which might be easier than to talk.

Why you should use this exercise

This exercise is an entertaining and educational group energizer. An active energizer like this gets the energy flowing and the oxygen going while the cooperation in the team will be stimulated.
Because they are not allowed to talk, they will have to sense the energy and dynamics of the group. This will help provide a greater instinct into the group dynamic.
Everyone needs to relinquish their individual ideas in order to work together as a group. This is an important concept when people want to work constructively together as a team.
They will feel a flowing group vibe while together transforming from one shape to another. If they will be able to easily transform from one shape into another they will feel a victorious feeling.

Scan this QR code to see an animated example video of this exercise:

You can also type: **team exercise 11 forming shapes** into YouTube's search bar to find the video.

Team Exercise 12 - Describe each other

"Feedback often tells you more about the person who is giving it than about you."
- Stephen R. Covey

Necessities: Piece of paper for all participants. Pens for all participants. A container or hat for the pieces of paper.

During this exercise, the team sits in a circle at equal distances from each other. You tell the team they are going to describe each other in one sentence. You choose someone from the group who you instruct to leave the room. When the person leaves the room, you give everyone a pen and a piece of paper and tell them to write a sentence on the paper that characterizes the person who has just left the room. Give them a few examples of descriptive sentences or phrases. For example, "a ray of sunshine" or "an inspiring person who sometimes forgets that other people also want to say something". Tell them they can be as creative as they want. A sentence can be very concrete, but it is also fine to write a very abstract, symbolic sentence. Maybe some people will even write a sentence that is a bit poetic. If someone doesn't know the absent person very well, he can come up with a sentence that describes the impression he made on him thus far. Tell the team that the description can contain only one sentence, not more. You give the team a few minutes to think about the sentence.

After all the sentences are written, put the container in the center of the circle. Each person now puts the paper into the container. You now

tell the absent person to return the room. Tell him to draw a random piece of paper from the container. He reads the sentence aloud.
He now chooses the person in the circle whom he thinks wrote the sentence and explains why he thinks this person wrote the sentence. Make sure he gets enough time to explain why he thinks this particular person wrote the sentence. While he talks, everyone else is silently listening without interrupting him.
Now the person who wrote the sentence reveals himself and explains why he wrote that sentence.

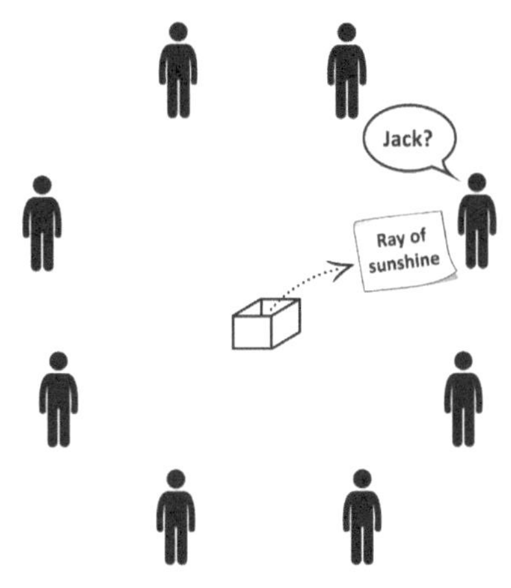

If it was correct, the guesser earns one point. If he guessed incorrectly, he earned no points. Now he draws a second card from the box and reads it aloud. Again, he points at the person whom he thinks wrote the sentence and explains why he thinks that person wrote it. Again, the person who wrote it reveals himself and explains the sentence. This process will be repeated until all the cards are drawn. The guesser gets one point for each correct guess. At the end of the round, he adds up the points and remembers how many points he has earned.
Tell him he can keep the papers as a nice memory. This way he can always read back how the others were describing him the moment this exercise was played.
The guesser now points to another person who will leave the room and the same game will be played.
The game will be played until everyone has had a chance to leave the room, read the sentences, and guess who wrote them.
The one who gained the most points at the end of the exercise is the winner.

Variations

1. If there are tied scores at the end of the exercise, you can give the participants with an even amount of points another turn to determine a final winner. Everyone will now characterize the final participants, one by one, in another way. For example, what if a person were an animal? What kind of animal would he be? The game will be played with the winners in the same way as before. The one who finally earns the most points wins the game.

2. You can also use this exercise as a problem solving game. In this case, they come up with a problem they want solved and each person writes down a solution for a problem. They then put the pieces of paper in the container. Now everyone will draw a card from the hat one by one, read the solution aloud, try to guess who he thinks wrote it down, and explain why he thinks so. If someone draws his own card, he puts it back in the hat and draws a new one. At the end, everyone finds out, in a playful way, who wants to solve the problem and in what way.

3. In addition to characterizing someone with a sentence, you also can instruct the team to write down a positive personality trait and/or something the person who left the room could improve upon. Continue to play the exercise in the same manner. This will add a deeper layer to the exercise.

4. You can tell the people writing the sentences beforehand that the one they write a sentence about will guess who wrote it when he comes back into the room. However, you can also choose not to tell them beforehand that he will find out who wrote which sentence. If you don't tell them, the people writing the sentences won't anticipate this information while they are writing.

Why you should use this exercise

During this exercise, everyone shows, in a playful and creative way, what they think of each other. You can view this exercise as a lighthearted way of giving feedback.
Because they are only allowed to write one sentence, they need to think precisely about what they write. The writers will also get some feedback because the guesser will guess the writer and tells why he thinks that person wrote the description.
Because of the game element, giving feedback will feel like a fun game. It can be very amusing when the guesser is really convinced that he knows who the writer is, and it turns out to be the wrong one. The laughter that ensues is good for team spirit.
At the end of this exercise, each person has a note with a personal description from every other person. In the future they can always read it back to remember how they were seen by the others during the time of the exercise.

Scan this QR code to see an animated example video of this exercise:

You can also type: **team exercise 12 Describe each other** into YouTube's search bar to find the video.

Team Exercise 13 - Eye contact

“Eye contact beats any conversation.” - **Christina Strigas**

Necessities: None.

During this exercise, the team will form a circle. You tell the team this whole exercise will be played in silence. You point to one person from the circle who will start the exercise. Tell him to make eye contact with another random person in the circle. They look at each other for one second. When the one who started the eye contact thinks the other has received the eye contact, he nods his head to the person with whom he made eye contact. The person who receives the eye contact nods back to confirm he received the eye contact. Now the person who just received the eye contact has a turn. In the same way as the first person did, he makes eye contact with another random person in the circle. When he thinks the other person received the eye contact, he nods his head and the other person nods his head to confirm. He will now be the one that picks a new person with whom to make eye contact. Let them do this until everyone has given and has gotten a nod.

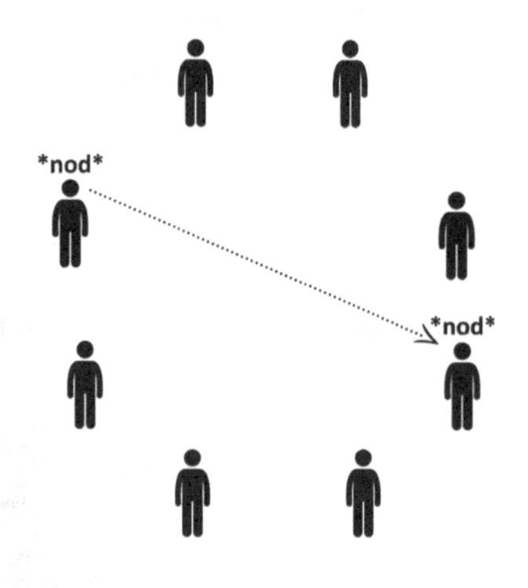

In the second part of the exercise, a game element will be added. The participants are going to “toss over” the eye contact. To start the game, you select a random person to leave the room. When this person has left the room, you point to a person from the circle who will have the first turn to start the eye contact. After you selected this person, the person who just left the room can now return. The person who has left the room will have no idea who will start the eye contact. Tell the person who just returned to go stand in the center of the circle. The person you selected will now start the eye contact by looking and nodding at someone from the circle who will nod back if he received the eye contact. The person who just received the eye contact will pass it onto someone else from the circle by looking and nodding at him, and so on. Just as in the first round, they pass the eye contact around the circle. The person in the center of the circle will try to find where the eye contact is as quickly as possible. If he caught the eye contact, he points to the person whom he thinks has the turn. The group tries to pass the eye contact around as long as possible without being caught by the catcher in the center. They try to pass the eye contact when the person in the center is looking elsewhere, so he won't spot where it is. You will keep track of the score by counting how many times the eye contact has been passed on around the group until the person in the center has caught the eye contact. Keeping track of the number of times the eye contact has been passed on is easy because you know where it started. For you, it will be easy to follow. The faster the person in the center has spotted the eye contact the fewer points he receives and the better he has done. When the person in the center has spotted the eye contact, the round is over. He joins the circle and selects a new person who will leave the room. Again, you point to someone who will begin passing the eye contact. The person who just left the room returns to spot the eye contact. The game will be played in the same way. Continue until everyone has been the catcher once. The one who spotted the eye contact the soonest has the least points and wins the game. When multiple people have the same score, you can do a second round with the winners until there is one final winner.

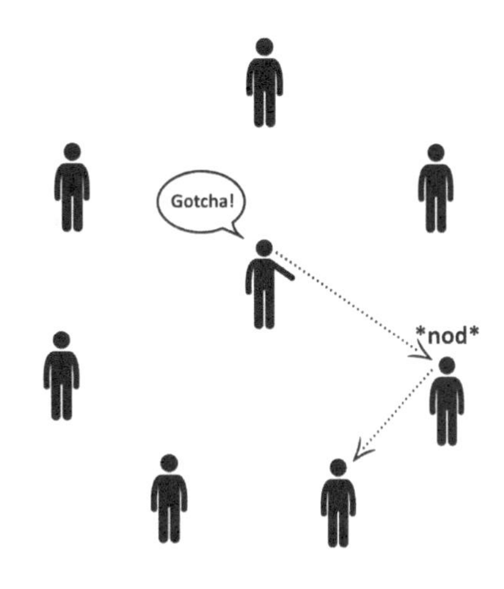

Variations

1. In the first phase of the exercise, you can make the team walk criss cross through the room while passing on the eye contact. This will loosen up the group. Only let them walk around during the first phase and not when someone has to catch the eye contact. If people are moving, it will be too difficult to spot the eye contact.

2. To prevent people from randomly pointing at someone and guessing they have seen the eye contact, you can give them an extra point every time they guess it wrong. This way they will only point to someone if they really think they spot the eye contact.

3. At the end of the exercise, you can stand in the middle of the circle and try to spot the eye contact. Now the team can work all together cohesively not be caught by you.

4. If the catcher is not able to find the eye contact, you can give him advice on how to catch it. Tell him to turn his head very quickly at an unexpected moment. The chance of catching the eye contact will be greater because there is a big chance the group will try to pass on the eye contact behind his back.

5. There is a possibility that the team will lose track of where the eye contact is. Multiple people might think that they are the ones whose turn it is to pass on the eye contact. This makes it impossible for you during the game round to count the times the team passes the eye contact. In this case, you can just follow the original track of eye contact until the catcher catches someone who nods. The times the eye contact in the original track was passed around are the points the catcher gets when he catches someone nodding.

Why you should use this exercise

During the exercise, the team works together by passing around the eye contact in silence. By being silent, they have to pay close attention to each other. If they don't focus precisely, they will lose track of where the eye contact is. This will enhance the group focus of the team.

Eye contact is a form of nonverbal communication; it can have a big impact on how we are perceived by others. When having a conversation, people make eye contact to let the other person know they are listening. For some participants, it might be difficult to directly make eye contact with someone. This exercise is a good way to practice making eye contact.

At the end of the exercise, each person has made eye contact with everyone in the group. This will contribute to the affinity of the group.

The game element also makes the exercise a great energizer that is fun to play.

Scan this QR code to see an animated example video of this exercise:

You can also type: **team exercise 13 eye contact** into YouTube's search bar to find the video.

Team Exercise 14 - Back writing

"We all need people who give us feedback. That's how we improve."
- Christina Strigas

Necessities: A piece of paper, tape or a safety pin, and pen for each participant.

To begin the exercise, you give everyone a piece of paper, a piece of tape and a pen. You tell the group that everyone draws a horizontal line in the middle of the paper on the front and back side. Instruct each person to attach the paper to his back by using the piece of tape or a safety pin. They can help each other to make sure the paper is attached properly. With the papers attached to their backs and a pen in their hands, the participants now walk crisscross through the room. Tell them that when you clap your hands everyone will form random pairs and stand still. One person of each duo writes on the paper attached to the other person's back, a celebrity that resembles that person. He writes it down on a random spot above the line. It can be anyone as long as it is a famous person. Now the roles switch and the other person writes on the paper of the first person the name of a celebrity above the line. After they both write a celebrity on each other's paper, you tell them that everyone continues to walk through the room again. You clap your hands again and the group stands still and forms pairs with someone they didn't pair up with earlier. Again, all pairs write the name of a celebrity of whom their partner reminds them of above the line on the paper on the other person's back. Everyone walks around again and forms new duos. Continue this part

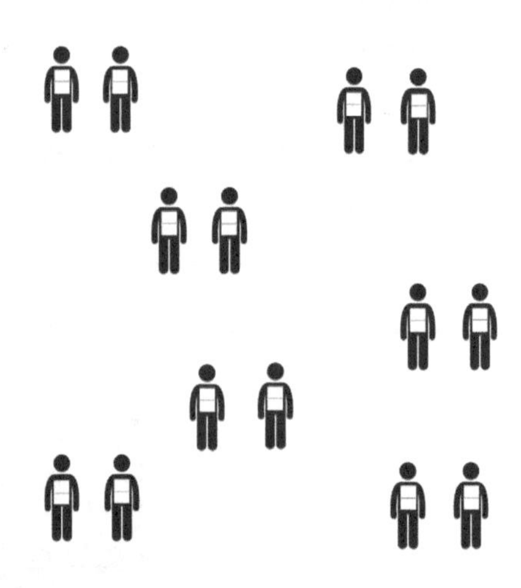

of the exercise until everyone has paired up with each other and each person wrote down the name of a celebrity on the back of every other person.
The second round will now be played with another theme: holiday destinations. Everyone walks through the room again and when you clap your hands everyone forms pairs. Now you tell them that everyone writes below the line on the paper on their partner's back a holiday destination they think fits that person most for a vacation. Even if they don't know each other, they write down a destination based on how they perceive that person. In the same way as in the first round, this process continues until everyone has paired up with each other and written a holiday destination on the other person's back.
Now you tell everyone to flip over the piece of paper and reattach it to their backs with the blank side facing outwards. The third round will be played. Everyone walks around and when you clap your hands, they form pairs. Now you tell them that everyone writes above the line on the paper on their partner's back a positive characteristic that they think most fits that person. In the same way as before, this process continues until everyone has paired up with each other and has written down a positive characteristic on the other person's back.

In the last round, everyone will write a characteristic below the line that he thinks the other person can improve upon. They go on forming pairs until they all have traits to improve upon written by everyone.
Now, at the end of the exercise, everyone's papers are filled with traits they could improve upon, positive characteristics, holiday destinations and celebrities. Tell them that each person can now detach the paper from his back and look at what all the other people wrote. Tell them they can keep the paper and take it home.

Variations

1. After the exercise, the group can form a circle. Each person circles on the paper, per category, what he thinks suits him the best. He now has four circled sentences or words. With these four aspects, each person creates one sentence in which he describes himself. You point to the first person who reads the sentence aloud in front of the group. For example: "I am a Good-humored (positive characteristic), Tom Hanks (celebrity), who arrives late (something to improve upon), on his holiday in Austria (favorite holiday destination)". Go clockwise around the group until each person reads his sentence aloud.

2. Instead of making the final sentence with the words someone thinks fits him the most, you can also let them make sentences based on the words written on their papers to which they agree the least.

3. You can vary the things you let them write down on the paper. For some groups, it is better to keep the subjects lighthearted and playful. For example, what do you think this person's favorite sport is? Or if this person were an animal, which animal would that be? When you feel the group is up for it, you can also vary with more serious topics such as: which emotion do you think can show this person more often? Or from whom can this person learn something?

4. At the end, you can tell the participants to guess who wrote what on their backs. After a guess, the right person reveals himself. The one with the most correct guesses wins. This way the anonymity is gone, but it adds a fun game element.

Why you should use this exercise

In the exercise, each person gains insight into how the rest of the group sees him. Because they all write down the sentences on a random spot in a certain area of the paper, in the end no one knows who wrote which sentence. Because of this anonymity, it will be easier for people to write things down.
If you do this exercise with people who don't know each other, it will be fun to see how people see someone based on their first impression.
The exercise is also fun to do in groups where there are disparities in status. The anonymity makes free speech to "higher ranks" more accessible.
Because of the playful and lighthearted way the exercise is being performed, everyone will learn in an entertaining manner how other people perceive them.

Scan this QR code to see an animated example video of this exercise:

You can also type: **team exercise 14 back writing** into YouTube's search bar to find the video.

Team Exercise 15 - Positive gossip

"Be kind whenever possible. It is always possible."
- Dalai Lama

Necessities: None.

To start this exercise you tell the team to form groups of three people. Each trio will sit or stand together somewhere in the room. Tell them each trio will decide who will be person A, person B, and person C. Tell them that each trio will start to gossip about each other in a positive way. Person A and person B will start gossiping in a positive way about person C. They can talk about what they generally like about person C. When you play this exercise at the end of a team day, they can talk about what person C did well during the day. Tell them they can gossip about anything as long it is positive; from character traits, like 'inspiring', to physical traits like 'very well dressed'. Tell them that while person A and B are gossiping about person C, person C remains silent and will try to remember as much as he can from the things he will hear. When the group members don't know each other very well, person A and person B can just gossip positively about their first impressions of person C. Tell them that during the gossip process person A and B will compliment each other by saying "yes and..". For example, person A says about person C that he was such a great listener. Person B continues the positive gossiping with a sentence that starts with "Yes, and..". For example: "Yes, and.. he was also really motivated today." They keep on gossiping for a few minutes. It depends on the person how many sentences he will say during the gossip. It can be a

few sentences before the other one says "Yes, and..", but it can also be just a short sentence. They will notice that if someone doesn't know what to say anymore, he can be inspired by the things the other gossiper says. This will help them to keep the flow going in the gossip conversation so there will be no long pauses. Tell them that it is important that the gossipers are sincere about what they are saying. The positive things they say about person C have to be something they really believe. They might also think negative things about person C, but in this exercise, they won't say that. Tell them to just focus on the positive things they can devise. After all of the A and B people have gossiped for a few minutes about person C of their trio, you tell them that the roles switch.

Now person B and C will gossip positively about what they like about person A. Person A tries to remember as much as possible. After a few minutes of gossiping, the roles switch again, and person A and C will gossip about person B. Person B remembers as much as he can from the things he hears from person A and C. When all the trios are done gossiping, the whole group will come together again and form a circle. You point to a first person who will share with the rest of the group what the other two of his trio said about him. He will say this in the first person so it sounds as if he is saying it about himself. For example, if the other two have said that he is such a great listener, he will tell the group, "I am such a great listener." He will produce as much as he can remember. When he has told everything he could remember, it is the next person's turn. Go clockwise around the group until everyone had a turn to share the positive things that were said about him.

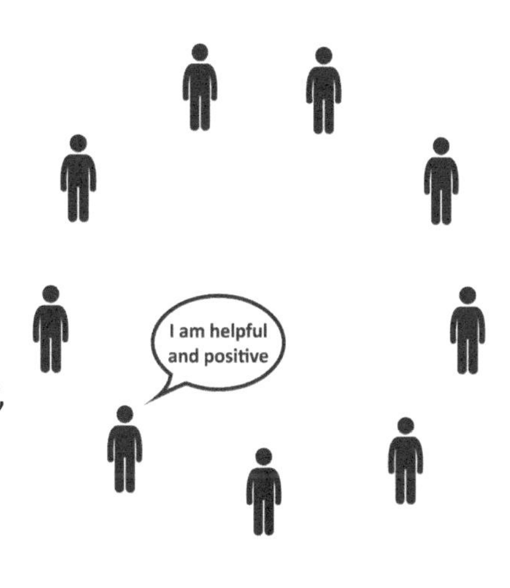

Variations

1. When the group is big enough, instead of forming trios, you can also let them make subgroups of four or five people. In the same way as in the original exercise, the people in a subgroup positively gossip about one other person in that subgroup. They continue to change roles until there has been gossip about each person in the group.

2. Instead of forming groups of three, they can also do this exercise with the whole group at the same time. They all sit in a circle, and you point to someone who will be the person all the others will gossip about. Someone from the group begins to gossip about this person. At a random moment, a different random person takes over the gossiping beginning his sentence with "Yes and...". Let them continue for a few minutes.
Next every one will positively gossip about the person sitting on the left side of the first person. Go on until there has been gossip about each person.

3. You can mention at the start of the day that you will do this exercise at the end of the day. This will make the participants more aware of the positive traits of other people, which will make the group atmosphere throughout the day more positive. The exercise will be easier to perform because they are already in a positive mindset.

4. You can encourage the group to form trios with people with whom they often disagree. In this way, they will be motivated to think and talk positively about each other.

5. After the exercise, you can encourage the group to keep on gossiping about each other in this positive way. This way an uplifting, positive group feeling will be kept intact.

Why you should use this exercise

During the exercise, all of the nice things being said will create a positive climate. This will have a great impact on the group's ambience.
This exercise is especially effective for groups that tend to negatively gossip a lot. During the exercise, they can still gossip, but the content will now be positive instead of negative. In this way, their behavior will be channeled in a positive direction.
The gossipers have to complement each other's sentences with more information. This will make them listen carefully to what the other person says to make it a natural conversation. Therefore their listening skills will be expanded.
In the last part of the exercise, everyone shares positive traits about himself without having the feeling of sounding arrogant; he knows that all the others know he is just repeating what he just heard. Each person will hear himself say positive things about himself, which will give everyone a positive confidence boost.

Scan this QR code to see an animated example video of this exercise:

You can also type: **team exercise 15 positive gossip** into YouTube's search bar to find the video.

Team Exercise 16 - How do people see you

"The mind's first step to self awareness must be through the body."
- George Sheehan

Necessities: None.

To start the exercise, you tell the team to sit or stand in a half circle. You will stand in front of the group. Tell them that in this exercise, each person will find out how other people see him when he introduces himself to others. Tell them that they will discover things of which they might be not aware of doing it. These can be things with their body or face, voice, etc. You point to the first person who will introduce himself to the group. Instruct him that he will try to do this in the most neutral way he can without any additional movements in his face or body. Tell him to go to one side of the room, walk in front of the half circle, and introduce himself by saying, "My name is..." and then say his name. For example, "My name is Rob". Tell him that neutral doesn't mean lifeless or in slow motion; it means just as his neutral self.

Tell the others who are sitting in the half circle to pay close attention to what the person who will introduce himself does in his face or body that adds other expressions or movements that are not neutral. Tell them they can focus on facial expressions; for example, someone raises his eyebrow when he says his name. They can also focus on body language; for example, someone slaps his arms onto his upper legs before he introduces himself. After the first person walked up, introduced himself, and walked to the other side of the room, the people in the half circle who just watched will now react to what they observed. The people who spotted a face or body expression that was more than neutral will tell the person who just introduced himself what they saw. Tell them to make only concrete, technical observations without any interpretations. So if someone says, “He looked shy”, that is an abstract comment. The one who introduced himself now doesn’t know what he did that made him look shy. So in this example, you can ask the commenter what it was he saw that made him look shy. For example, “He scratched his leg after he said his name”. This way the one who introduced himself knows what he did that made him look shy and is able to change it. Tell them that subconscious behavior doesn’t have to be a negative thing. Smiling is positive, but it can be helpful to be aware when smiling, so someone can also not smile if he doesn’t want to. After the feedback, the person who just introduced himself comes up and introduces himself again in the most neutral way he can. This time, he won’t do the things he just heard from the other participants he did in addition to being neutral. So in this case, he tries not to scratch his leg; he will keep his arms at the side of his body. After this second introduction, the group gives feedback again about what they have seen that was more than neutral. It can be something new, or something they see for the second time. After they give the feedback, the participant introduces himself for the last time while being as neutral as possible. He now rejoins the rest of the group and selects a new candidate to do the exercise.

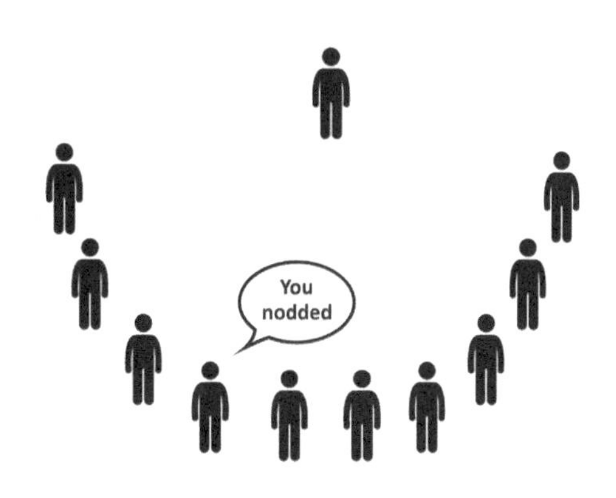

This process will be repeated until each person has had a turn to introduce himself and find out what tics he has that he wasn’t aware of before.

Variations

1. If the observers find it difficult to spot the unaware behavior of the person who introduced himself, you can start by giving him feedback yourself. In this way, the participants get a feeling of what to look for. When you lead by example, the rest of the group will become more comfortable with naming and stating observations themselves.

2. Sometimes, someone has difficulty undoing the tics. In this case, you can let him introduce himself again, and instead of trying to undo the tics, tell him to perform the tics he heard from the audience in an exaggerated way. This will help him to become extra aware of his tics and habits. When he introduces himself again, it will be easier to undo the ticks; it will look more neutral.

3. After someone introduces himself in as neutral a way as possible, you can first ask the participant himself what he thinks he did in a more than neutral way while introducing himself. By doing this, you can see if it matches with what the group saw.

4. After everyone has had a turn, you can point to someone who is going to imitate a random person from the group. He will come up to the stage with the same tics and habits as the one he is imitating; however, he will introduce himself using his own name. Now, everyone will try to guess whom he imitated. The ones who guessed correctly earn a point. The one who did the impression now selects the next person to do an impression. Continue until everyone has had a turn to do an impression of someone. The one with the most correct guesses is the winner.

Why you should use this exercise

This exercise makes the participants conscious of their subconscious, nonverbal communication. It brings awareness to tics in the body or face that they weren't aware of before. For example, someone might find out that he always presses down his eyebrows without being aware of it. It can explain why other people might think he always looks a bit angry. Someone who always laughs a little can find out why people might not always take him as seriously as he would like.
By making the participants aware of this subconscious behavior, they have the option to continue or discontinue the behavior. Because the feedback will be nonjudgmental, no one will feel offended by the feedback they get.
They will learn that by giving technical, concrete feedback, the one who receives the feedback knows literally what to do to easily change his subconscious behaviour.

Scan this QR code to see an animated example video of this exercise:

You can also type: **team exercise 16 how do people see you** into YouTube's search bar to find the video.

Team Exercise 17 - Blind guiding

"A leader is one who knows the way, goes the way, and shows the way."
- John C. Maxwell

Necessities: Blindfolds for all participants.

To start the exercise, you instruct the team to pair up with someone they don't know well. When everyone has paired up, one person from each pair will be blindfolded. Tell them to make sure this person can't see anything. This blindfolded person will be the walker. The other person will be the guide. Tell them that the guide now puts his right hand on the walker's left shoulder and his left hand on the walker's left upper arm. On your mark, all the pairs will walk slowly through the room at the same time. Each blindfolded person will be guided by his leader. Tell them that the guides may also give spoken instructions. For example, "walk a bit to the left" or "take a sharp turn to the right". The guides make sure that the walkers won't bump into anyone or anything in the room. When you notice all the duos move smoothly through the room, you can tell them they may increase their walking speed a bit. The duos will walk around for a couple of minutes. You tell them they can stand still again. The guide releases the walker's arm and the blindfolded person will now guess his position in the room. He says aloud where he thinks he is in the room at that moment. He now removes his blindfold and checks if his guess was correct. Now, the roles switch. The person that was blindfolded will now put his blindfold onto the other person's head. He puts his right hand on the other person's left shoulder and his left hand on his left upper arm. Again, all the pairs will walk slowly through the room.

When you notice they walk around easily, you can tell them they may increase their walking speed. On your signal, the pairs will stand still again and the blindfolded person will guess his position in the room, remove his blindfold, and check whether he is correct or not. Now you tell the team to make new pairs. Again, one person will be blindfolded and the other will guide him around the room in the same way. Only now, you tell them that the blindfolded walker will be guided in silence without any spoken instructions. Make sure no one speaks during this part of the exercise. When this goes well, you can challenge them to increase their speed a bit. After a few minutes, they stand still again. Each blindfolded person will guess his position in the room, remove his blindfold, check if his guess is correct, and then switch roles. Now all the duos do the same again. They start slowly walking around the room. Now, you tell them that the guides can increase or decrease the walking pace whenever they want to. Tell them to alternate between a slower pace and a faster pace. After a couple of minutes, the pairs stand still again. The blindfolded people guess their positions in the room again and check if they are correct.

In the last part of the exercise, you tell them that everyone will walk blindfolded individually through the room at the same time without any spoken instructions or physical guidance. They use their ears and intuition very carefully so they won't bump into each other. They start the exercise very slowly with their arms stretched forward. When you feel the team can do this this in a relaxed way, you challenge the team to slightly increase their speed. After a few minutes, they stands still again. They guess their position in the room, take off their blindfolds, and check if they are correct.

Variations

1. You can turn this exercise into a game. Every time someone guesses his position in the room correctly, he earns a point. The one who has the most points in the end is the winner.

2. When the duos walk around the room, you can tell them that when you clap your hands, everyone stands still and the guiders will switch places. Now, all the walkers have a new guide without knowing who that is. Do this in the round where spoken instructions are not allowed. In this way, the blindfolded people won't have any idea who is guiding them. You continue by clapping your hands every two minutes until every guide has led every blindfolded person.

3. When you start variation two, you can tell them that the blindfolded people will memorize the number of the guide with whom they felt safest while being guided. Tell the guiders they have to memorize the order of when they guided each walker. If it is difficult for them to remember, they can write it down between switches. For example: "1. Patrick, 2. Sarah, etc.". When each guider has guided each walker, the blindfolded people remove their blindfolds and tell at which number they felt the safest. The one that was the guider at that moment reveals himself.

4. To disorientate the walkers, you can spin them around at the start of the exercise before they start walking through the room. In this way, it is even harder to guess where they are after being guided around. They will make a guess purely based on their senses regarding how they have been guided through the room.

Why you should use this exercise

This is a playful exercise in which the participants will have to trust the guidance of another person. By building trust, the team will feel safer while being together. This will cause the group to become more open towards each other and will have a positive effect on the group's chemistry.
The guessing part is a fun element in the exercise. You will see that after walking around blindfolded, almost no one will guess correctly their location in the room. This will create a fun atmosphere in the group.
During the last part when they all individually walk around at the same time, their sensibilities are being tested as to not bumb into each other. Because they are all blindfolded, they are all in the same situation. This will create a common group feeling.

Scan this QR code to see an animated example video of this exercise:

You can also type: **team exercise 17 blind guiding** into YouTube's search bar to find the video.

Team Exercise 18 - The first thought

"Intuition is a very powerful thing, more powerful than intellect, in my opinion."
- Steve Jobs

Necessities: Blindfolds for all participants.

To start the exercise, you tell the group to form two straight lines facing each other. Tell them that between the two lines, there should be an arm's length distance. Between the people in a line there should also be one arm's length distance. You now point to one row that will be row A. The other row will be row B. Tell them that the people facing each other will now make eye contact for approximately five seconds without talking. Tell them to just look into each other's eyes and nothing more. If people have to laugh, you can reassure them that that is okay as long as they maintain eye contact without talking. After each person has made eye contact for five seconds with the person in front of him, you now tell row A that all the people in that row can move one spot to the right. The far right person in row A will move to the far left spot of the line. Row B stays in place. Each person now silently makes five seconds of eye contact with the new person in front of him. After five seconds, row A moves another spot to the right and the people in row B remain in place. Again, each person makes eye contact for five seconds with the person he is facing before the people from row A move one spot to the right. Repeat this until everyone from line A has made eye contact with everyone from line B. You now start the second round. In the second round, the participants will say the first positive characteristic that comes to mind after making eye contact. In the same way as in the first round, the two rows are facing each other again. After a brief moment of making eye contact,

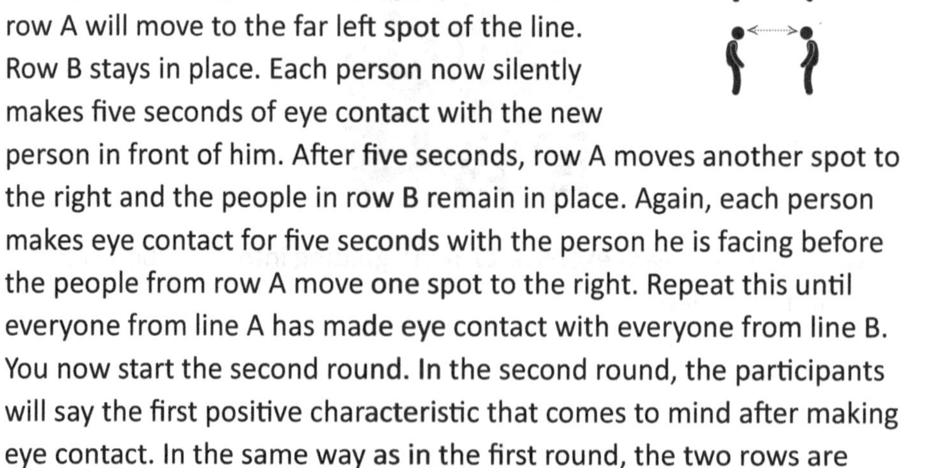

each person from row A now calls out a positive trait that first occurs to him while looking at the person B in front of him. Tell the team that they may say the first thing that occurs to them while looking at the other person; tell them to be spontaneous. They can just say a word, for example, sensitive or humoristic. They can also say a short sentence, for example, "I see a strong woman who knows what she wants in life". Now the roles switch. The people from row B now call out the first positive characteristic that occurs to them while looking at the person in front of them. You tell row A to move one spot to the right again and they repeat the exercise. They go on until everyone has told each person from the other row which positive characteristic occurs while looking at him.

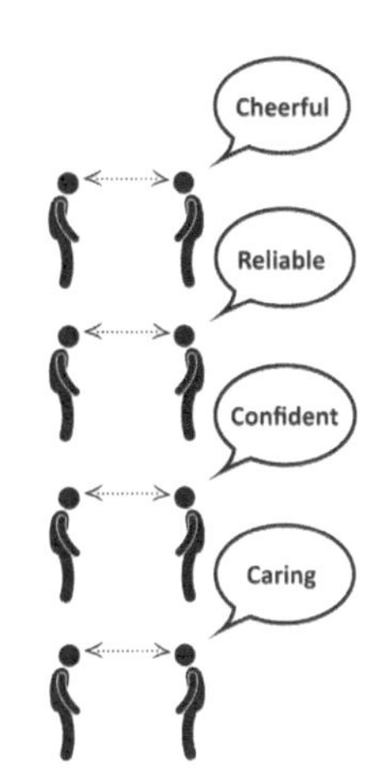

Now, you start the third part of the exercise. You tell them that now each person will say the first animal that occurs to him while looking at the person in front of him. This animal theme will be played out exactly the same way as the positive trait round. So in the end, everyone has called out an animal that occurred to him while looking at each person from the other row.

Now, the last round will be played. Each person will look at the person in front of him for a few seconds and calls out the thirst thing that occurs to him regarding what the person in front of him can improve upon. This round will be played out the same way as the previous rounds.

After the last round, they form a circle to evaluate. Encourage the discussion by asking what they expected to hear, and what they didn't expect to hear during the exercise. Go clockwise around the circle until everyone has shared his experience.

Variations

1. You can give them more themes to play the exercise. You can tell them, for example, to look at each other and sing the first song that comes to their minds while looking at the person in front of them. You can also tell them to call out the first emotion they feel while looking at the other person.

2. You can ask the participants to create themes as well. They can pick a theme they think will fit the team. Playful themes are fun to experiment with, but also encourage them to create more in-depth themes.

3. After a few rounds you can let one-half of a row switch spots with the people they are facing. In this way, the lines are mixed. After one line moved a spot to the right each person will face new people in the next round.

4. Tell them that before someone expresses his thoughts, the person in front of him can first guess what he thinks will be said about him. For example, "I think the person in front of me will say I am very funny." After the other participant says what came to his mind, they can now immediately check how accurate the prediction was.

5. If you have a big group you can let them make subgroups and to the same thing. Between each round round you can tell them that each line A switches with another line A. This way they will face different people each round.

Why you should use this exercise

During this exercise, everyone gets a lot of spontaneous feedback, which gives them a clear view of how the others see them. Because they will say the first thing that occurs to them while looking at the person in front of them, they won't think too much about what they say. Consequently, people will dare to be more open and honest. Some people might say things to others they wouldn't expect to say about a particular person. Also, people might hear things told to them that they didn't expect. This can be really surprising and will give them new insight into how they see others and how others see them.
In the beginning, looking into each other's eyes can feel a bit awkward. However, you will see that each time they do this they will feel more comfortable looking at each other in silence.

Scan this QR code to see an animated example video of this exercise:

You can also type: **team exercise 18 the first thought** into YouTube's search bar to find the video.

Team Exercise 19 - Truth and fantasy

"Inside each of us is a natural-born storyteller, waiting to be released."
- Robin Moore

Necessities: None.

To start the exercise, you tell the team to stand or sit in a circle. You tell the group to think of two extraordinary stories that really happened in their lives. Tell them they can be any kind of story - a fun story, a weird story, an exciting story or a sad story. The stories must be extraordinary and true. Tell them that these stories should be stories they haven't told to anyone in this group before. You give them a minute to think about it.

After everyone has found two stories, you now tell them to create a third exciting story that didn't happen at all. Encourage them to fabricate a credible story that the other participants can believe is true. Give them all a minute to think of the fake story. Now everyone has three stories in his mind - two real ones and one fake one. You now point to a first random person in the group. He will start by telling his three stories in a random order to the rest of the group. The listeners don't know which stories are real and which one has been invented. The goal of the listeners is to find out which one of the three stories is a fake. Each participant will try to determine which story has been fabricated. The storyteller tries not to give any signs that give the listeners clues as to which story is true and which story is false. Encourage the storyteller to try to fool the listeners by giving them certain lying signs when he is telling a true story. For example, looking at the ground could cause the listeners to think the real story is the fake story. Because the real stories are

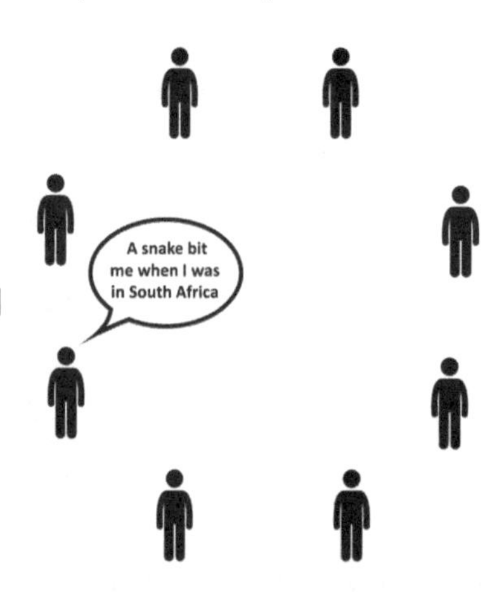

extraordinary, it will be difficult for the listeners to guess which one is not real. Since the storyteller tells stories he hasn't told anyone in the team before, every listener will have to try equally as hard to spot the fake story.
After the storyteller has told his three stories, the listeners will now guess which story is the fake one. You will sum up the stories individually by briefly describing them in a few words. For example, when you call out "the holiday story", they will know which story you mean. After each time you name a story, the people who think the story you called out is the fake one will now raise their hands. After you have called out the three stories, and after each story people raised their hands, you now point to one random participant who will explain his choice. He will tell the rest of the group why he thinks the story he raised his hand for is the fake one. After his explanation, the one who told the three stories now reveals which two stories were the real ones and which story never happened. All the people who guessed correctly earn one point. Now, the participant sitting on the left side from the one who just told his stories does the same. He tells his two real stories and one fake story. After he is done telling his stories, you sum up the three stories in the same way as before. The participants who think a story is fake raise their hands. You point to a new random person to explain his choice, and the storyteller reveals which story was fake. The participants who guessed correctly earn a point. Repeat the exercise in the same way until everyone has had a turn to tell three stories and everyone has explained once why they thought a certain story was a fake. At the end, everyone shares how many points they earned. The one with the most points is the winner.

Variations

1. Instead of letting people tell two real stories and one fictional story, you can instruct them to tell two fictional stories and one real story. The team has to guess which story is the real one. Again, the people who guessed correctly earn a point. The one with the most points in the end is the winner.

2. You can also let the participants tell one long story instead of three short ones. In this case, the story starts as a true story, but slowly develops into a story that is not true. Each person tells a story. When a story has finished, one by one, the other participants guess at what point the story became fictional. The people who guessed correctly earn a point. The person with in the end the most points is the winner.

3. You can also tell one person to leave the room. When he leaves the room, you point to one person from the circle who will fabricate a story. The others will tell a true story. You call the person back into the room and everyone from the circle will tell their story. The one who left the room tries to guess who is the liar. After he has guessed, the real liar reveals himself. Continue until each person has left the room and has guessed which person told a fake story.

4. In case you want to use this exercise as an energizer, or you don't have much time, you can let them tell personality traits instead of stories. Someone will call out three personality traits he thinks belong to him. He is lying about one personality trait; he doesn't really think that trait belongs to him. The listeners try to guess which trait is the one the speaker doesn't seem to identify with.

Why you should use this exercise

This is a great exercise to do with people who don't know each other yet. They get to know stories about each other's lives, which will help them form bonds.
If a group already knows each other really well, it is still a great exercise to do. They will get to know each other in a different way and will hear stories from each other they didn't know before.
Because everyone has to create a fantasy story, the creativity of the group is being stimulated.
Since they all try to identify the fake story, you will see that all the participants pay close attention to the stories that are being told.
The game element makes it a fun exercise. When they find out which story was the lie, the group will be very amused. This will bring positive energy to the group.

Scan this QR code to see an animated example video of this exercise:

You can also type: **team exercise 19 truth and fantasy** into YouTube's search bar to find the video.

Team Exercise 20 - Zip zap boing

"Life is more fun if you play games."
- Roald Dahl

Necessities: None.

To start the exercise, you tell the team to form a circle at equal distances from each other. Tell them to make sure there is enough space between each participant, so that if everyone stretches their arms sideways no one touches each other. You tell them they are going to send a "ZIP" to each other. Explain to the team that the ZIP will be sent by looking at someone in the circle, and energetically stretching their arms in the direction of that person while loudly calling out "Zip!". The one who received the ZIP will then send the ZIP to another random person in the circle by stretching his arms directly towards that person while calling out "Zip!". Again, the person who received the ZIP now passes it on to another person in the circle in the same way. Tell them that it is important that everyone pay close attention to the location of the ZIP, so that each person knows exactly when someone passes a ZIP to him. Let the group pass on the ZIP until they can play the game smoothly.

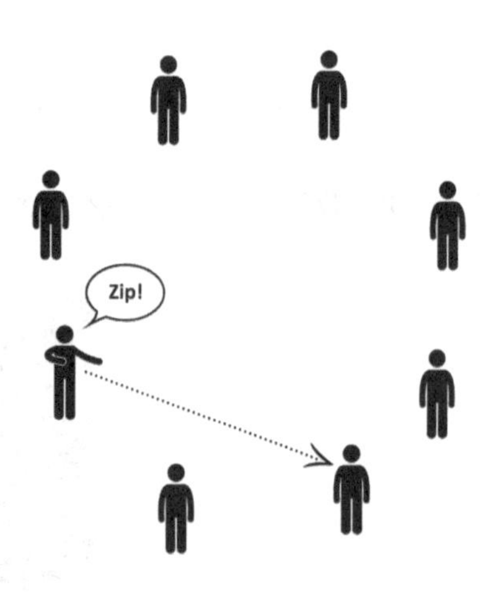

Now you will introduce a second rule of the game. You tell the group that if someone wants to pass the turn onto the person who is standing directly on his left or right side, he isn't allowed to say ZIP anymore. Instead, he has to say "ZAP". The arm movements will stay the same. Now you let the team play the game in the same way as before, but now also with the new ZAP rule. They keep on saying ZIP if they give the turn to someone who is not standing directly next to them.

When everyone in the circle has passed around the ZIP and ZAP for a couple of minutes, you bring a third rule into the exercise. Tell the group that after someone gets a ZIP or ZAP, he isn't allowed to return it to the same person by saying ZIP or ZAP. He can now only return it to the same person from whom he got it by crossing his arms in front of his body while saying "BOING!". Tell them that it is not allowed to BOING back someone else's BOING. Therefore, when someone gets a ZIP and he BOINGS it back, the person who got the turn back has to pass the turn onto someone else by saying ZIP or ZAP. Let the team get used to the new BOING rule, and let them play until they can pass on the ZIP, ZAP and BOING smoothly.

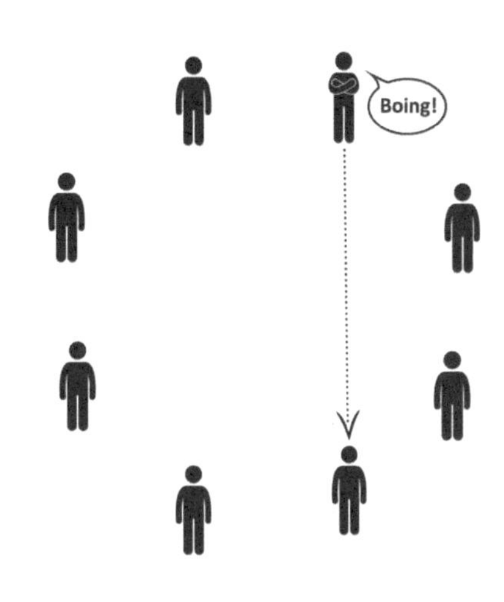

Now you tell the group that a match will be played. Tell them that each participant has two lives. When a participant makes a mistake, he will lose one life. Tell them a mistake is made when someone calls out something wrong. For example, someone calls out ZIP when he passes the turn onto a person standing next to him. It is also a mistake if someone gets the turn and takes too long to think about what to do. Saying something no one can understand, for example, "ZIOP" will also count as a mistake. When someone has made two mistakes, he will sit down on the same spot as he was standing and the remaining participants will continue to play. For the duration of the game, the people sitting down will be skipped. For some people, this means that the ZAP will be passed onto the person standing next to the one that's sitting next to them.

Tell them to play the game at a fast pace; this will make it harder for them not to make a mistake. The match will be played until there are only three people left. These are the three winners of the game.

Variations

1. When the team has mastered passing around the ZIP, ZAP, or BOING, you can make the exercise more difficult by using new names to send on the turn. For example, instead of ZIP, ZAP, and BOING, they can now use "BIF, BAF, and BOF". In this way, the participants have to shift their concentration to the new words and keep paying close attention.

2. Tell the group that someone will lose a point if he says ZIP, ZAP, or BOING at an energy level that is too low. In this way, everyone will send the ZIP, ZAP, or BOING like energetic explosions. This will keep the energy flowing within the group.

3. After you have explained and practiced the BOING rule, you can tell the group that a fourth rule will enter the game. When they pass the turn unto the person next to the person next to them, they will have to call out "WHOOP". While doing this, they will simulate throwing a ball over their neighbor's head. Let them practice this a few times before playing the game with the extra WHOOP rule.

4. Let the participants switch places in the circle every minute. In this way, they won't get used to their place in the group and to whom stands where. This helps to make the exercise more challenging.

5. When they practise before they play the game, you can also tell them to send the ZIP, ZAP, or BOING at a fast pace. This will basically force everyone to concentrate. With a fast tempo instead of a slow tempo, the team's cooperation will be tested.

Why you should use this exercise

In this exercise, everyone in the group has the same goal - passing around the ZIP, ZAP, or BOING to each other without making mistakes. Because everyone in the team has to remain focused and keep an eye on each other, the group will form a common group focus.
Everyone will be physically involved during the exercise. Therefore it is a great energizer with which to start the day and to get the group into an energetic mode.
The game rounds will make the exercise exciting. The participants must focus extra carefully not to lose their points. This will motivate them being engaged.
You will see that people will often make mistakes. This will cause hilarity in the group and a lot of laughter.

Scan this QR code to see an animated example video of this exercise:

You can also type: **team exercise 20 zip zap boing** into YouTube's search bar to find the video.

Team Exercise 21 - Whispering

"There is only one rule for being a good talker – learn to listen."
- Christopher Morley

Necessities: None.

To start the exercise you tell the participants to stand or sit in a circle. Tell the participants to think of a story they want to share with the group. The story can be true or fictional and can last around thirty seconds. Let them think about it for a minute.
Tell them that they are going to whisper a story around the circle from one person to another. Their goal is to keep the story as intact as possible.
You point to a first random participant who will tell his story to the person sitting to his left by whispering the story into his ear. He will whisper it very quietly to make sure the other people in the circle can't hear a word he is whispering. The listener tries to listen as carefully as possible and tries to remember as much of the story as he can. When the first person is done telling the story, the person who just heard the story now tells the same story to the person who is sitting to his left. Again, he makes sure that the other participants can't hear what he whispers into his neighbor's ear. Again, the person who just heard the story now whispers the story to the person sitting to his left. Let them continue until the story is passed around the circle, and the last person, (the person sitting on the right side of the person who started the story), has heard the story.

After this last person in the circle has heard the story, he now tells the story aloud to the other participants. You will see that usually some details of the story will be forgotten or distorted, and that in some cases, the story has completely changed. The one who originally began whispering his story now tells the original story to the group. If there are differences with the story that the last person in the circle eventually told, the participants will now try to figure out where the differences occurred. They will also try to find out how the differences occurred. For example, a word could have been misheard that completely changed the story. It is also possible that someone forgot to tell a part of the story. Let them discuss and investigate together until they have reconstructed what happened to the story from the first person until the last person. Now, tell them they can also devise a plan to keep the story more intact next time. You can give them advice by telling them that if they talk slower, it will be easier for the listener to remember the story and pass it on in an accurate way.

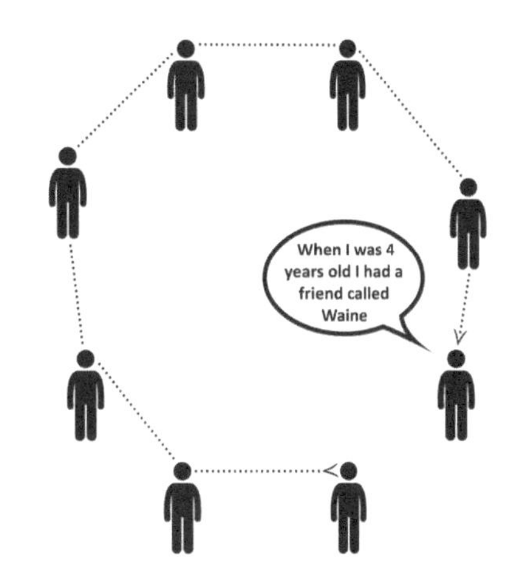

Now, the person who began the story in the first round may select a new random person in the circle who will start whispering his story into the ear of the person sitting to his left. The exercise will be played in the same way. They whisper the story around the circle until it reaches the last participant in the circle. He will relay the story he just heard to the group. Again, the person who told the original story now tells the story to the rest of the group. The group then tries to determine together where and how the errors occurred. The person who originally told the story now selects a new person who will whisper his story into the ear of the person sitting to his left. In the same way, the story will proceed around the circle. Continue doing this until each person's story has gone around the circle. Next, you evaluate the exercise by asking them how they think the stories get changed so quickly and what techniques worked to keep the stories intact.

Variations

1. When the team masters the exercise, you can challenge them to whisper the story at a faster speed. This will speed up the exercise and put their listening skills to the test. With a faster whispering speed, the story will often be completely different at the end.

2. Instead of increasing the speed of the exercise, you can also make the exercise more challenging by telling the team to tell longer stories. Instead of thirty-second stories, they can tell two-minute stories. The longer the story is, the more challenging it is to completely remember and correctly retell all the details.

3. If you work with a team that is big enough to be split into two groups, you can turn the exercise into a competition. This time, you can create a story yourself and whisper the same story to one participant in one group and one participant in the other group. Now, both groups let the story go around the circle in the same way as in the original exercise. The last person to hear the story in each group will retell the story. You can now compare which group did a better job keeping the story intact. This group is the winner.

4. After the exercise, you can encourage the team members to discuss their own communication and misunderstandings in real life. Ask them if they recognize aspects of the exercise that have similarities with their daily communication. In this way, the link between the exercise and real life situations will be established.

5. If people can't come up with a story you can tell them they can come up with a fantasy story.

Why you should use this exercise

When the participants whisper the story around the circle, they will try to keep the story completely intact. Because they all have the same goal, they will experience a common group spirit, which will contribute to the cohesiveness of the group as a whole. Keeping the story intact will prove to be very difficult. It is nearly impossible for a group to retell a story exactly the same way repeatedly. The team will learn how easy it is to misunderstand things and how careful they must be when they positively believe that they know exactly what was said to them. Therefore it is a great exercise to start a conversation about communication.
It is also a fun exercise, because the participants will laugh about all the things people will subconsciously add to a original story. Because they will all hear each other's stories, the group will get to know each other better in a fun and educational way.

Scan this QR code to see an animated example video of this exercise:

You can also type: **team exercise 21 whispering** into YouTube's search bar to find the video.

Team Exercise 22 - Drawing

"Every act of communication is a miracle of translation."
- Ken Liu

Necessities: A pen for each participant and papers around ten times the number of participants.

To start the exercise, you tell the group to form pairs. Tell them that everyone should pick someone they don't know well to form a duo with. Each pair now takes two chairs, goes somewhere in the room together, puts the backs of the chairs against each other, and sits down. In this way, each duo sits with their backs to each other so they can't see each other. Tell them that each duo will now decide who is person A and who is person B.
You give each person a paper and a pen and tell the duos that person B will now draw an abstract drawing on his paper that shows simple shapes. He can draw for two minutes. After they finish their drawings, you tell them that person A will try to recreate person B's drawing. Person A will have to recreate the drawing without seeing it. Person A's copy will be based only on verbal instructions from person B. Person B tries to describe his drawing as accurately as possible so person A can make the most accurate copy of his drawing. When person B is done describing, and person A thinks he has drawn the most accurate copy possible of person B's drawing, they both turn around and compare their drawings. They will now evaluate the differences in the drawings. Tell them to discuss what went right, and what went wrong during the communication. Next, they switch roles. They resume sitting with their backs against each other and now person A creates a drawing. Tell them that in addition

to abstract things, person A may now also draw concrete objects or things. In order to not give the object away, person A may still only use figurative instructions. He can describe the image by using all kinds of shapes. However, he can't name the object. For example, if he drew a light bulb, he can't say it's a light bulb. That would be too easy. Using the light bulb example, he could say: "Draw a circle in the center of your paper. Under the circle, draw a few horizontal cylinders on top of each other. Lastly, draw short stripes around it." Person B will copy the drawing of person A as accurately as possible. After person B thinks he drew an accurate copy of person A's drawing, they turn around. They compare the original drawing with the copy and see how well they match. They will discuss again what went well and where the communication could have been better.

Now, you instruct the participants to form new pairs. You give each person a new paper and each duo will repeat the exercise in the same way. They now can draw abstract shapes or specific objects and may only use figurative instruction to tell their partners what to draw. They compare their drawings, discuss how their communication went, and switch roles. After they have both instructed and copied a drawing, you tell the participants to form new duos again.
After having changed duos a few times, the group will form a circle and evaluate what they've experienced during the exercise. Encourage the discussion by asking them the following questions: "What style of communication works most efficiently to copy the drawing? What style didn't work at all? Is an abstract drawing more difficult to draw than a specific drawing?" Ask the participants what they think, and let them share their experiences.
Tell them they can keep their drawings as a memory.

Variations

1. If the participants get really good at the exercise, you can play another round and make it more difficult for them. Instead of doing the exercise in pairs of two, you can also add a third person: person C. Person A makes a drawing and whispers the description into person C's ear without person B hearing it. Now, person C describes to person B the instructions he just heard; person B tries to draw the most accurate copy as possible. Let them change roles until each person of the trio has been role A, B and C once.

2. You can do the exercise with the whole group. One person describes his drawing, without showing it, to the rest of the group. Everyone tries to copy the drawing as precisely as possible. The person who makes the best copy wins.

3. You can bring prepared drawings for the exercise. Make sure you have a copy of each image for half of the group. You give copies of the same image to all A's and copies of another image to all B's. They perform the same exercise in the same way as before. After performing this variation, it is easy to measure which duo made the best copies and communicated the best. This is also a good variation to play in case they are not inspired to create drawings themselves. You can also use this variation when you play this exercise with children.

4. During the round in which the instructor draws a concrete image, the one who is copying the drawing can guess what the object is before comparing the drawings. When the instructor shows the original drawing, they can see if the guess was correct.

Why you should use this exercise

During this exercise, the participants will train their communication skills. Communication is all about visualizing what someone else is telling you. The more someone visualizes what the other person is describing the easier it will be for him to copy the drawing.
Based on the result of the copied drawing, they will evaluate the way they communicated. This will motivate them to talk about communication. They will get insight in how to improve their communication and facilitate better, more efficient interactions.
The participants will learn that when something is described, the person listening will never have the exact same view of it as the speaker; there will always be some differences.
Because everyone will draw multiple times, each person's creativity will be stimulated in a fun and challenging way.

Scan this QR code to see an animated example video of this exercise:

You can also type: **team exercise 22 drawing** into YouTube's search bar to find the video.

Team Exercise 23 - Similarities and differences

"Our similarities bring us to a common ground; Our differences allow us to be fascinated by each other." - **Tom Robins**

Necessities: None.

To start the exercise, you tell the team to split up into two groups. Tell them that the two groups will stand far enough apart to not hear each other. The purpose of each group is to find similarities that apply to all of the people in that group. Encourage the group to not only look for similarities based on appearance such as hair color or height, but also for more meaningful similarities based on personality characteristics. One person from each group will be the writer. He takes a pen and a paper and will write all the similarities the group will find. Each group will find the similarities in the following way: one by one, each person from a group comes up with a characteristic he identifies with and of which he thinks the rest of the group identifies with also. He tells the others this characteristic and the people who identify with the characteristic raise their hands. If some people don't raise their hands, the characteristic is not similar. If so, the same person will come up with another characteristic with which he identifies and with which he believes the rest of the group identifies too. He continues announcing characteristics until he discovers a characteristic with which everyone in his group identifies. This characteristic will now be written on the paper, and it is the next person's turn to find a similar characteristic. Everyone in the group gets a turn to find a characteristic with which everyone identifies. At the end, the number of similarities written on the paper will be equal to the number of people in the

group. Now, both groups come together and present the similarities they just found. It will be interesting to see how the groups both found different similar characteristics and to see which group has the most unusual similarities.
Next, the second part of the exercise starts. The participants form two new groups, and each group stands or sits on different sides of the room again. However, instead of similarities, the groups will now look for differences. Again, you will give one person in the group the paper and pen, and he will write the characteristics that will be revealed. One by one, each person from the group will come up with a characteristic with which he identifies. This time it should be a characteristic with which he thinks all the other people in his group don't identify. After he mentions a characteristic, the other people reveal if they also identify with this trait by raising their hands. If someone raised his hand, the characteristic wasn't unique and another characteristic will be suggested. It will be continued until he finds a unique characteristic for which no one raises his hand. The writer then writes the name of this characteristic on the paper. After the first person has uncovered a unique characteristic, another person from the group will do the same. Continue until everyone from each group has gotten a turn to find a unique characteristic with which no one else in his group identifies. Next, both groups come together and present the unique traits that they just discovered.

The participants now evaluate the exercise. You encourage the discussion by asking them if it was easier to find similarities or to find differences.

Variations

1. You can add a third round to the exercise: a game element. After the two groups join and discover all the unique characteristics within their group, one group will guess which person from the other group has which unique characteristic. One group names one by one the unique traits they found without mentioning to whom the trait belongs. The other group will now discuss until they unanimously make a decision as to whom they think the trait belongs. If their guess is correct, they receive one point. Proceed until all unique characteristics have been named. Now, it is the other group's turn to guess which trait belongs to whom. The group with the most points wins the guessing game.

2. In addition to personality traits, you can also identify other similarities and differences within the team. Some examples of these are music tastes, things they want to improve upon, visions for the company, etc. Adjust the theme according to the group's preferences and interests.

3. If you are working with a smaller group, you can perform this exercise with just one group. Even if you have a big group, you can perform the exercise without splitting the group into two. If you keep one big group, finding similarities and differences will become even more of a challenge. The moment they eventually find a common characteristic in the first round or a unique characteristic in the second round, the joy will be even greater. If you decide to do this variation and keep one group, variation number one cannot be played.

Why you should use this exercise

This is a great exercise to do with a group of people who don't know each other yet. They will find things they will have in common, so after the exercise they have things to talk about.
If the members of the group already know each other, it is still a perfect exercise to do. It will help the participants get to know each other in a new way.
Because the participants will first find similarities, a group connection will be formed. A homogeneous group energy will occur because they all recognize themselves in a certain characteristic.
In the second round, when each person finds his unique characteristic, they will all learn new things about each other.
When both groups share their newly discovered unique traits, you will see that the participants will be surprised and excited to hear what unique characteristics the people in the other group found.

Scan this QR code to see an animated example video of this exercise:

You can also type: **team exercise 23 similarities and differences** into YouTube's search bar to find the video.

Team Exercise 24 - Crossing the line

"It's better to cross the line than to just stare at that line for the rest of your life." - **Paulo Coelho**

Necessities: Duct tape and prepared statements.

Before this exercise, you need some information from the group. Ask the group which themes they would like to use to get to know each other better. After they tell you the themes, you will prepare statements based on those themes. For each theme, you prepare a few lighthearted statements and a few serious statements. The participants can identify with these statements or not identify with these statements. For example, if one of the themes is childhood, a lighthearted statement could be "When I was a kid, I liked school". An example of a more serious statement could be "I was bullied when I was young". You write each statement on a notecard. Pile up the notecards by organizing all the statements from lighthearted to serious. To start the exercise, you tell the whole group to move to the right side of the room. You will now make a line with tape in the center of the room. You tell the team you will read statements aloud and that the people who identify with the statements will cross the line by walking to the left side of the room. Tell them that the people who don't identify with the statement should stay on the right side of the room. You now start by reading the first most lighthearted statement. All the people who identify with this statement cross the line to the other side of the room. When everyone who identifies with the statement has crossed the line, you ask the participants to raise their hands if they are willing to answer a question about their feelings regarding

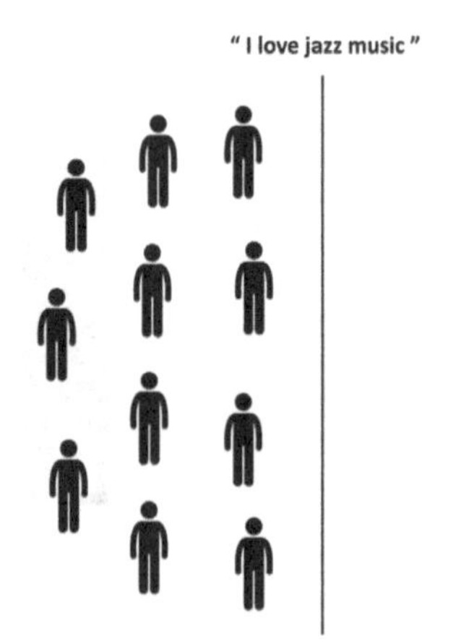

the statement. People from the other side of the room will ask the questions. Emphasize the fact that no one is obliged to answer any questions if they don't want to. The participants who did not cross the line may now ask the people with raised hands questions. Tell them that anyone who has a question will now raise his hand. You select one participant to ask a question. He will say for whom the question is meant and ask the question. The person on the other side of the line answers the question. Tell them that when someone is answering a question, the rest of the group remains silent. When the question has been answered, you point to the next person who would like to ask a question. Continue until all the questions has been asked.
After having exchanged the questions and answers, the participants on the left side of the line now go back to the right side of the room again. Next, you will read the second statement. The procedure is the same as it was for the first statement.
Each person who identifies with the statement crosses the line, stands on the left side of the room, and answers questions. In each round, the statements you read will get more personal and in-depth. It is very likely that people won't cross the line immediately if the statement is more personal. In this case, people may need to think a bit more about whether they identify with the statement. Therefore, before starting the question round, it is important to wait a while until everyone who identifies with the statement has crossed the line. Follow the same procedure as above. Continue reading the statements until all the prepared statements have been played and all the questions have been asked and answered. You now proceed to the second theme and do the same thing with the prepared statements belonging to that theme. Continue until all themes and statements have been played.

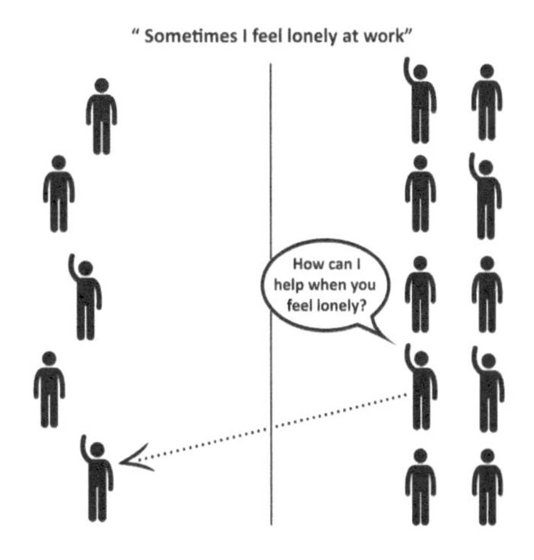

Variations

1. During the processing of the more personal, in-depth statements, an emotionally charged atmosphere might develop. If that happens, you can end each theme with a lighthearted statement to make people feel more cheerful after each theme.

2. You can also use this exercise as a fun energizer. You can do this by using only lighthearted themes or funny statements. This will keep the emotions at bay and will warm the group up for the rest of the day. This will make the exercise great as an introduction game in which everyone gets to know each other in a playful way.

3. If people are emotional when they cross the line, you and the rest of the group can show your support by making a heart shape with your two hands. Point the heart at the people who are walking. In this way, the people struggling will feel supported.

4. The exercise is also an excellent way to work out conflicts or disagreements that are prevalent on the work floor. You can read a statement regarding the conflict. For example, "I think I work too many hours". People who agree with the statement will now cross the line. During question rounds, people will feel heard without getting into discussions.

5. Tell them that if people identify slightly with the statement, they can walk to the line and stand on the line. By doing this, they let the others know that they recognize themselves in the statement, but they don't totally identify with it.

Why you should use this exercise

During this exercise, the team will get to know each other at a deeper level. Some people might also get to know themselves better, because they won't know ahead of time how they feel regarding a certain statement.
Most people will find it easier to open up this way because they just have to walk to the other side of the room. They don't have to say anything to let the rest of the group know that they identify with the statement. Therefore you will see that most people will be honest; their bodies just start walking when they identify with a statement. By letting them question each other, this level of honesty will facilitate conversation.
This exercise has an impact at many levels. It builds trust and improves communication through the questions being asked. This combination is a great key to team building.

Scan this QR code to see an animated example video of this exercise:

You can also type: **team exercise 24 crossing the line** into YouTube's search bar to find the video.

Team Exercise 25 - Role play game

"To change a habit, make a conscious decision, then act out the new behavior." - **Maxwell Maltz**

Necessities: None.

You begin the exercise by telling the team to form an audience on one side of the room. Tell them that in this exercise, the participants will perform scenes. The scenes will be about topics that are important to the group, and of which the group thinks could use some improvement. You select a first random person who may suggest the first topic for performance. This person chooses a topic of which he thinks the team can improve upon, for example, "giving feedback on social behavior". You now ask him how the situation is being handled currently and how he would like to see the situation unfold in the future. For example, his answer might be, "Right now, I think we are too direct and insulting when we give feedback to each other. I'd like us to be more subtle when we give feedback to each other in the future." You now ask the people who would like to perform the scene to raise their hands. From everyone who has raised their hands, you pick a number of people who you think would be suitable to perform the scene. The scene will be performed in accordance with how the one who suggested the topic told the situation is at this moment. In this case, "giving feedback in an insulting and direct manner". Let the people you choose improvise the scene for about two minutes in front of the audience. Tell them that the scene can be both serious and funny. The actors must adhere to the original topic of giving feedback in a rude and insulting manner.

When they are done performing the scene, they will stay in front of the audience. You ask the audience to objectively describe what kind of behavior they have seen and how they think that has affected the scene. After a few people in the audience have given comments, you ask them for ideas. Ask them what they think can be done differently, to achieve the situation the one who suggested the topic told he would like to see it in the future. In this case "change the delivery of feedback from rude to subtle". Let the audience provide some suggestions as to how they can give feedback in a more subtle way. Tell the actors to listen very carefully to what the audience members say and to memorize as much as possible. Next, ask the actors to perform the scene again. This time they should incorporate the audience's suggestions for making the feedback more subtle. After the scene has been performed, the actors will stay in front of the audience again. Volunteers from the audience now describe what they have seen go differently and how this has affected the situation. Now, the actors describe how they experienced the two different ways of interacting with each other. You ask them if they felt any changes in the scene after they incorporated the suggestions from the audience. Ask them if they felt emotionally different now that they have acted out the scene in a different way.

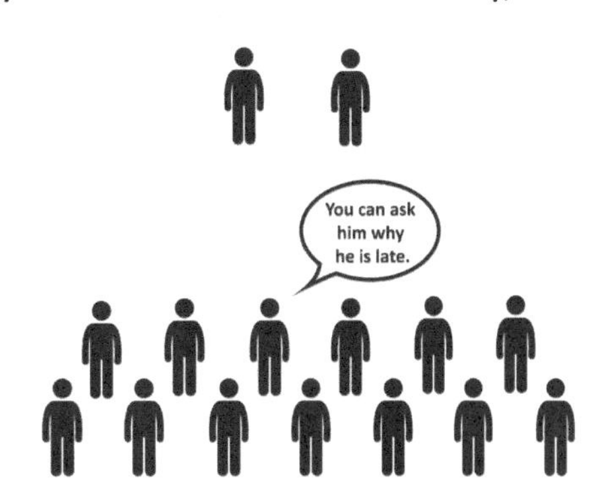

When the actors from this first scene are done sharing their experiences, you will point to another person who will suggest a topic he would like the team to improve upon. Again, he tells how the team deals with this topic currently and how he would like to see it in the future. You pick people to act out the scene. After the audience gives comments and suggestions, the actors perform the scene again.
Let them perform scenes based on given topics until each person has acted in a role at least once.

Variations

1. Instead of letting the actors from the first scene perform the scene again after the audience's comments, you can let new people perform the scene regarding the comments. In this way, more people act concerning one topic. Therefore you need less time and topics in order to let everyone act at least once.

2. You can instruct the audience to interrupt during the second time a scene is being performed. They can interrupt if they see old behaviour again, that was already corrected by the audience's feedback after the first time the scene was acted out. In this way, the actors are immediately alerted if they return to their old behaviors.

3. After the first time the scene has been performed, next to the audience, you can also ask the actors what behaviors they think would be beneficial to demonstrate the desired outcome. Next to the behaviours suggested by the audience, they can now also implement their own suggestions the second time they act out the scene.

4. A week before the exercise, you can ask the team if they feel comfortable with acting. If they really don't want to act, you can also ask professional actors, or other people who like to act, to act out the scenes. The exercise will be performed in the same way. Except now, other people will act out the scenes instead of people from the team itself.

5. If you think the actors are having trouble improvising, you can join the scenes yourself. In this way, you can provide input so it will be easier for the participants to perform the scenes.

Why you should use this exercise

During this exercise, tensions and conflicts can be solved within a group in a lighthearted way. Because the actors will act out practical solutions brought forward by the team itself, the team will work together in a constructive way.
Through the performances of the actors, the participants will see what they can change in their behaviour to change certain situations. They can use these insights in their daily lives.
It is also a really fun exercise. Because most people aren't accustomed to acting, some situations can become hilarious. Because all the participants in the group will perform a scene once, the group spirit will be stimulated.

Scan this QR code to see an animated example video of this exercise:

You can also type: **team exercise 25 role play game** into YouTube's search bar to find the video.

Team Exercise 26 - Form a group with..

"We construct worldviews that give us a sense of meaning. It is about belonging to a group and having a sense of identity and purpose."
- Carmen Lawrence

Necessities: None.

This exercise is best suited for big groups consisting of ten or more participants. To begin the exercise, you tell all the participants to spread out through the room. Tell the participants that they will divide themselves into different groups based on various topics. You give the team a lighthearted topic to start with, for example, musical preferences. Tell the participants to walk around the room, mingle and discuss what musical preferences they have, and sort themselves into specific categories. Tell them to do this by forming different groups based on similar musical tastes. Tell them they can form as many groups as they think is necessary, but that they should try to avoid letting people stand alone. Each group will now stand together somewhere in the room. After the participants have sorted themselves into different groups based on their taste of music, you now point to one group who will tell to the other groups which musical preference they represent. Go on pointing to groups until each group has told the others which music they like.

Next, you tell everyone to spread out through the room again and you give them another lighthearted topic. Based on the topic, they divide themselves into separate groups again. You will see that for some topics, the participants can divide themselves into just two groups. Other topics might require five or more different groups for specific categorization. This, of course, also depends on how big the group is. After you have played a few rounds with lighthearted topics, you now present a more serious topic. You tell the team to categorize themselves into different groups based on communication styles. Give them a few examples of categories belonging to that topic. Tell them that some people may prefer to communicate in a direct way. Other people may communicate in a way that makes people feel comfortable. Others may like to communicate while using humor. After you have given a few examples of communication styles, you tell the participants to walk around the room and talk to each other to discover what kind communication style preferences there are in the group. They will form groups based on the different communication styles. Each specific group will then stand somewhere in the room separated from the other groups. Again, each group will then share with the other groups the communication style they represent.

You now start the second part of the exercise. The team will form groups as they did before. However, they will now do this in complete silence. You state the next topic: receiving feedback. The participants will form groups with others who they believe deal with feedback in the same manner. The participants will do this without talking to each other. Purely based on intuition, they will feel who belongs in each group. After the groups are positioned, you tell them the people in each group can talk to each other and check to see if they really deal with feedback in the same way. If not, people can change groups. This time, they can talk to make sure everyone is in the correct group. When everyone feels that they are standing in a group with people who deal with feedback in the same way, each group can share with the other groups what kind of feedback they prefer.

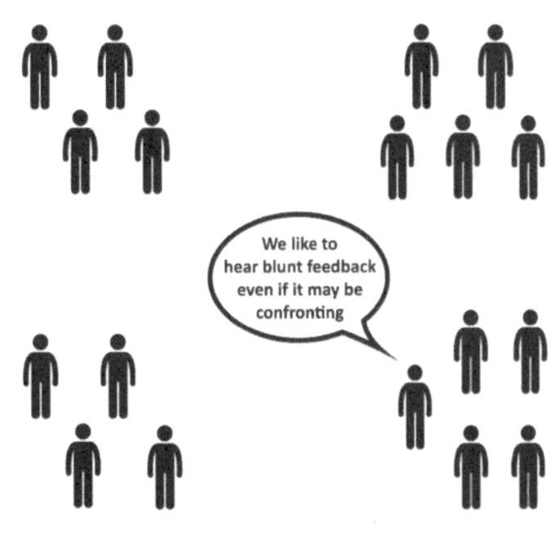

Variations

1. This exercise can also be done as a quick warm up. You announce a topic and tell them that in ten seconds they will have to form groups. A few seconds later, you announce another theme and the participants have to regroup themselves again. The more practice the group gets, the faster they will be able to form specific groups. In this way, the exercise can be played as an energizer.

2. After all the subgroups have been formed based on specific topics and before each group shares their topic, you can let each group guess the topics of the other groups. After each group shares their guesses, all groups can now share what their preferences are. This adds a fun game element to the exercise to keep it lighthearted.

3. Instead of the topics previously mentioned, you can also create your own topics that apply directly to the team. For example, food, humor, or ways to argue - preferences.

4. You can let the group generate topics they would like to play. Tell them to create two lighthearted topics and two serious topics.

5. After a subgroup has told the other groups what their group represents, you can tell people from the other groups that they can now ask questions. For example, "Why do you prefer to receive only positive feedback?" Ask for a volunteer in the group to answer the question.

Why you should use this exercise

This is a great exercise for the participants to get to know each other in a playful and active way. The participants will find out what things they have in common. They will also see how much variety can exist within a group.
Because they have to divide themselves into different groups based on their preferences, this is a good exercise to train their communication and cooperation skills.
After each group has told the other groups what their preference is, it will be obvious what everyone thinks regarding a certain topic. Therefore, this exercise provides a great foundation for people to get to know each other on a deeper level. Because everyone learns how the others think about communication and feedback, they can take that into account while working together. This will help them perform better as a group.

Scan this QR code to see an animated example video of this exercise:

You can also type: **team exercise 26 form a group with..** into YouTube's search bar to find the video.

Team Exercise 27 - Stop, start, continue

"The tipping point is that magic moment when an idea, trend, or social behavior crosses a threshold, tips, and spreads like wildfire."
- Malcolm Gladwell

Necessities: A flip chart or whiteboard, a marker, paper, and pens.

This exercise is suitable for people who already know each other. To start the exercise, you tell the participants to sit in a circle. You give each participant a piece of paper and a pen and tell them that they are going to write what they want the team to stop, to start, and to continue doing. Tell them to form their opinions based on their experiences with the team. They can write anything that occurs to them. First each person writes down on the paper what he thinks the team should stop doing. An example can be "gossiping". Give them a minute to think about it. Next, you tell them to write down what they think the team should start doing from now on. For example, "It would be good to start inspiring each other more often".
Lastly, they will write down what they think the team should continue to do. For example, "we should continue laughing together". While everyone is writing, you write the three categories on the whiteboard: stop, start, and continue. Leave enough space below each category to write two sentences. When each person has written their answers on his paper, you will collect all the papers and examine what the participants have written. For each category, you determine which answer is the most common. You write on the whiteboard below each category, a word or phrase that captures the group feeling concerning that category. After you

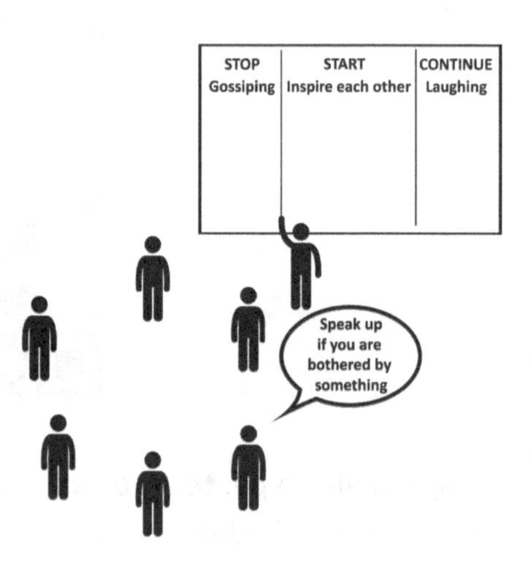

have written a word or phrase below each category, you will discuss the topics with the group. Begin with discussing the category "stop". You ask the participants, one by one, to come up with a solution to stop doing what's written on the whiteboard below the word "stop". When someone is talking, the rest of the team remains silent. Let each participant create a solution until everyone has given a suggestion. Below the thing they would like to stop, you now write the most common solution which you think best represents the group's input. Next, the second category "start" will be discussed. You ask the team how they would like to begin what's written below the word "start". Everyone comes up with a solution and shares it with the rest of the group. Again, you write the most common solution on the whiteboard below thing they would like to start.
For the third category, you ask each person to share a memory regarding the thing they would like to continue. For example, if they want to continue laughing together, they can share a memory of a moment in which they all laughed together. After everyone has shared a memory, you write the most representative memory on the whiteboard below what they would like to continue. Now, tell the team to silently look at the whiteboard for a minute. They now have a clear picture of what they would like to stop, start and continue. They also have suggestions on how to achieve their goals.

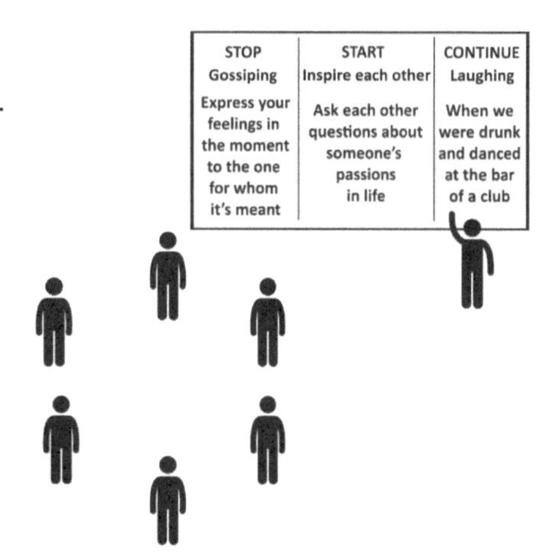

Next, you summarize aloud the three topics and their solutions. In addition to seeing it on the whiteboard, the team will now also hear what they can stop, start, and continue and what solutions are available to achieve this. In this way, they will remember it even better and it will be easier to implement it into their daily behavior.

Variations

1. Instead of using stop, start and continue, other words or phrases can be used. If you think other sentences work better to achieve a goal for the group, you can generate different sentences. For example, "I would like to change…", "I would like to see more of…" and "What I love about this group…"
By phrasing differently, different outcomes will occur as a result.

2. Instead of collecting all the pieces of paper and selecting the most common topics, everyone in the team can read their own papers aloud to the group. By doing this, not only the common topics will come to light, but also topics that the majority did not think about. Even a topic only one participant might have written can be very valuable. For example, all participants agree that they would like to continue laughing with each other. However, there is one participant who would rather continue having serious conversations. It can be valuable to have heard this as well.

3. After everyone wrote down a topic for each category, you can let them guess who wrote which topic. After you have collected all the papers, you pick a random paper and read it aloud. You now point to a random participant who will guess who wrote the topics. Make sure that they write their names on the papers; you don't want to choose the person who wrote the paper himself.

4. Tell everyone that they can take a picture of the whiteboard, so they can review it later.

Why you should use this exercise

In the exercise, the team will discover what kind of behavior they would like to stop, start, and continue. This will give the team insight into their own behavior and goals.
Because you will write down the thoughts they have most in common, a group feeling will be created.
There is a great possibility that they will actually stop, start and continue the things they suggested because it is right in front of them on the whiteboard. Since they created the solutions themselves, they will be motivated to put them into practice.
After the exercise, they literally know what to do to achieve their goal to stop, start and continue certain behavior.

Scan this QR code to see an animated example video of this exercise:

You can also type: **team exercise 27 stop start continue** into YouTube's search bar to find the video.

Team Exercise 28 - Catch the pillow

"There is little success where there is little laughter."
- Andrew Carnegie

Necessities: A soft pillow and three prepared questions.

To begin the exercise, you will stand on one side of the room and the participants will sit or stand on the opposite side of the room. Tell the group that you will throw a pillow to them and that the one who catches the pillow will stand up. You throw the pillow underhand with a bow to the audience. One of the participants catches the pillow and stands up. You now ask the participant who caught the pillow three questions. Make sure you prepare these questions before the exercise. You start with fun, lighthearted questions. For example, "What's your name? What's your hobby? What is your guilty pleasure?" The participant who caught the pillow now answers the three questions. Tell them that when someone is answering the questions, the rest of the group listens carefully in silence. After answering the questions, that participant throws the pillow to someone else in the group. The person who caught the pillow answers the same three questions. If someone caught the pillow who has already answered the questions, he just throws it to someone who did not answer the questions yet. If a participant gives a very short answer, you can ask him an additional question or ask him to tell a bit more. For example, when someone says that his hobby is listening to music, it might be interesting to ask what kind of music he likes to listen to. Each person who has caught the pillow and answered the three questions throws the pillow to someone else in the audience.

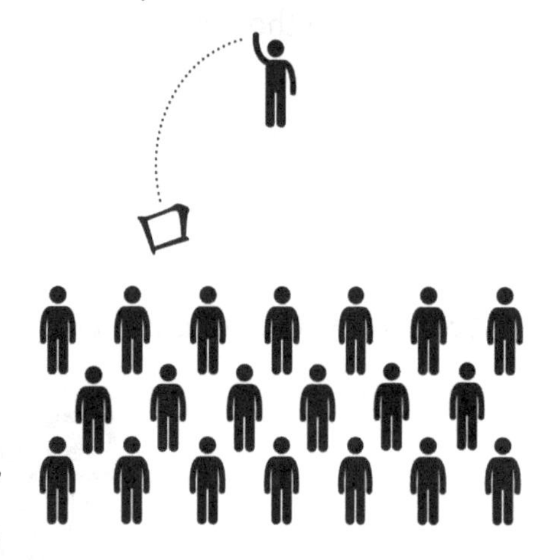

Let the group continue doing this until everyone has caught the pillow once and answered the three questions.
Now you start the second part of the exercise. Ask the one who has the pillow to throw it back to you. You tell the participants that they will now create questions themselves. You start by throwing the pillow into the group and asking a random question. The participant who caught the pillow and answered the question now throws the pillow to a new random person. The moment he throws the pillow, he must spontaneously create a new question to ask. The participant who caught the pillow answers the question and throws the pillow to someone else in the group and asks a new question. Let them throw the pillow around until everyone has asked and answered at least one question. Ask them to throw the pillow back to you so that you can start the last part of the exercise.

You throw the pillow into the group again, and ask the question: "What would you like to improve within this group?" The one who caught the pillow now answers the question by creating a suggestion, for example, "I like the group to have a better focus". Now this person throws the pillow to another participant. Tell the participant who caught the pillow that he now may respond to the suggestion previously given and add something new to that suggestion, for example, "I like the idea of being more friendly towards each other. Maybe it helps if we go out together sometime". When he is done commenting and adding ideas to the suggestion, he will throw the pillow into the group again. The one catching the pillow will repeat the procedure. He comments on the things being said and adds something to the answer. Let them throw the pillow around until everyone has commented on the previous answers and added their ideas.

Variations

1. To ensure that the pillow will end up with a random participant, you can turn around and throw the pillow over your shoulder. The participants can do the same. They can also throw the pillow with their eyes closed.

2. In addition to the questions given as examples in the exercise, you can ask them other questions. For example, in the first round you can ask, "What's your favorite meal? What is your favorite animal?, etc." In the last round, examples of serious questions could be: "What do you love about this group?" or "How do you want this group to work together?"

3. If you have no pillow, you can also use other objects such as a tennis ball, a stuffed animal, or any other soft object that can be easily thrown around. You can also buy very soft wire free microphones that can be thrown around. With one of these, the exercise will be done more efficiently when you work with a big group in a big room. They can answer in the microphone so everyone can hear all answers clearly.

4. During the round where they have to create a question themselves while throwing, it is possible that someone won't be able to think of a question and remains silent. In this case, you can come up with a question on the spot. By doing this, the exercise can continue smoothly.

5. Tell the group that if someone doesn't want to answer a question, that person can throw the pillow into the air while asking himself a question that he would like to answer. He then catches the pillow and answers the question he just asked himself.

Why you should use this exercise

This exercise is a great energizer to start the day. By hearing everyone's answers they will learn more about each other.
Because you start the exercise with light and funny questions, the group will become accustomed to answering questions when they catch the pillow. This will help them answer more serious topics later on.
The second part, in which they have to generate questions themselves, is a good way to stimulate their creativity. They have to spontaneously create a question without thinking. By doing this, hilarious questions will be asked. That will provide a fun element to the exercise.
During the last part, it will be easier to answer questions that are more in-depth because the exercise is being performed in a lighthearted way. In this last round, the "adding element" will improve the team spirit; they all are answering and adding to the same question.

Scan this QR code to see an animated example video of this exercise:

You can also type: **team exercise 28 catch the pillow** into YouTube's search bar to find the video.

Team Exercise 29 - Trust fall

"Teamwork begins by building trust. And the only way to do that is to overcome our need for invulnerability."
- Patrick Lencioni

Necessities: None.

To start the exercise, you tell the team to form pairs and spread throughout the room. One person stands with one leg in front of the other, with his arms stretched forward, and with his hands open. The other person stands with his back towards his partner at half a half arm's length from the open hands of his partner. The one with his back towards his partner will now close his eyes and slowly lean backwards while purposely allowing himself to be out of balance. He will lean backwards until he falls into the hands of his partner. The other person catches him by letting him lean into his hands while ensuring that he won't fall onto the ground. The faller leans into the hands of the catcher for a few seconds before the catcher pushes him back up straight on his feet again. Tell them that if the falling participant have difficulties doing this with his eyes closed, he may let himself fall backwards with his eyes open. This will make the exercise a less scary. Let them repeat this a few times. When the faller feels comfortable falling into his partner's hands, the duos may increase the distance a little bit between the catcher and the faller. All catchers will now take a small step backwards to increase the distance. Of course, they should not step back too much; they need to make sure the exercise is safe at all times. Tell them that during the exercise, it is very important that all participants remain very focused. Again, each faller falls into the hands of his partner. When the faller feel comfortable with the longer distance, the roles switch. The faller

becomes the catcher and the catcher becomes the faller. The faller will lean back and let himself fall backwards into the catcher's hands. Again, the distance between the hands of the catcher and the back of the faller is just half an arm's length. When both participants are confident, just as in the first round, they can increase the falling distance a little bit. They must maintain a safe distance from which it is easy for the catchers to catch the fallers. Let the duos continue doing this until the faller feels comfortable with the longer distance.
Now, you tell the group to change partners. Each new duo will repeat the same routine.
Next, you start the last part of the exercise. You tell the participants to form a circle. Ask the group which participant wants to volunteer to let himself be caught by the whole group. This participant will now stand with his eyes closed in the center of the circle. If he wants he can cross his arms before his body. The rest of the group will form a tight circle around him. Everyone in the circle will stand in the same way as they did when they were catchers: one leg in front of the other with their arms stretched out in front of them. With his back straight, the volunteer now leans in a random direction in the circle until he loses balance and falls into the hands of someone in the circle. This catcher will now push the volunteer into a different direction in the circle. In this way, the volunteer will be pushed around from one direction to another by the participants in the circle. Now he might also fall sometimes with the front of his body into the hands of one of the catchers. In this case the catcher catches him by putting his hands onto the front of his shoulders.

When the volunteer has been pushed around for a minute, another participant can volunteer. Continue doing this until every person who feels like it has been caught pushed around by the rest of the group.

Variations

1. If during the first round someone is uncomfortable with falling backwards, this participant can let himself fall forward with his eyes open. If he want he can cross his arms. In this way, he sees what is happening. The catcher catches him with his open hands and pushes him back up straight on his feet. If the falling person feels comfortable after doing this a few times, he can try to fall backwards.

2. If someone doesn't feel safe being caught by one single person, instead of duos, you can let them form groups of three. One person will fall backwards, and the two other people will be the catchers. By doing this, there will be four hands to fall into. When people feel safe doing this, they can form duos again and do the regular exercise.

3. To make sure that everyone understands how the exercise should be implemented, you can ask for a volunteer to help you demonstrate the exercise before you start. You will instruct him how to stand and show the team how the exercise is performed correctly.

4. Between the falls, the partners can describe their experiences to each other. They can tell each other if the falling distance should be increased or decreased.

5. After the exercise, tell the group to form a circle to share their experiences. The group will discover how everyone experienced the exercise differently. Some have an easy time falling into someone's hands, while others think it is more difficult.

Why you should use this exercise

During this exercise, trust will be created among the participants. Because each person has to rely on the person who is catching him, he has to relinquish control and put his trust into another person's hands.
When they change partners, they will notice that feelings of trust can be different with different people. They will learn that the longer they perform the exercise with someone, the stronger the trust between them will grow.
At the end of the exercise in which each person lets himself fall into the whole group's hands, they will all work together to catch the faller the best they can. This will make them work together and feel responsible for the same thing.
It is also a great exercise to play as an energizer. The participants will be physically active during the exercise and an energetic atmosphere will be created.

Scan this QR code to see an animated example video of this exercise:

You can also type: **team exercise 29 trust fall** into YouTube's search bar to find the video.

Team Exercise 30 - Selling each other

"If you want to lift yourself up, lift up someone else."
- Booker T. Washington

Necessities: None.

To start the exercise, you tell the team to form pairs. All the pairs will spread throughout the room. The duos will decide who will be person A and who will be person B. Tell the duos that person A will ask person B questions in such a way person B will tell something positive about himself. Give them a few examples of positive questions to make it clear: "What is the best compliment someone ever gave you?" or "What do you think is your biggest talent?" Person A will remember as much as possible of the answers that person B gave him. After five minutes, the roles switch and person B will now ask person A positive questions and remember as much as possible. After all the duos have shared their positive traits, the whole group will form an audience at one side of the room. Tell the group that each participant is going to present his partner's positive traits. You ask the group which duo would like to present first. If no duo volunteers, you point to a random duo. You tell the duo to stand in front of the audience. Person A now starts to give a presentation as enthusiastically as he can about person B. The presentation should sound like a commercial about person B. During the presentation, person B stands next to person A, remains silent and only looks at the audience. Person A presents as accurately as he can based on the things he remembered of the answers person B gave him earlier. Of course, it is possible that person A didn't remember everything

correctly and says something inaccurate about person B. Tell the duo that if this happens, person B will still remain silent and just keep looking at the audience. After the presentation, the rest of the group may ask person A questions to learn more about person B's positive traits. Person A will answer the questions with the same enthusiasm as he had during the presentation. Let the participants ask questions for about two minutes. Now, the roles switch and person B will give an enthusiastic presentation about person A. After the presentation, the audience may ask questions about person A which person B will answer with the same positive energy. Next, a new duo will stand in front of the audience and will follow the same procedure. Continue doing this until each duo has presented themselves in a positive way and answered the questions from the audience.

In the second part of the exercise, each participant will present himself in front of the group. He uses the same text and displays as much enthusiasm as his partner just did. In this way, everyone will give a positive pitch about himself. You ask the participants who would like to start. This person will stand in front of the group and portray himself based on the positive things his partner told the audience earlier. Tell them that the more convincing and positive each person presents himself during the presentation, the better. Continue until each person has given a positive presentation about himself.

Lastly, the group will form a circle and each person will share how he experienced the exercise. To encourage the conversation, ask them if they would rather be quiet in front of the audience while others talk about their positive traits, or if they would rather present themselves while standing in the spotlight. Let everyone share their experiences.

Variations

1. You can turn the exercise into a competition. Instruct the audience to applaud after each presentation. The presentation that receives the loudest applause has won the competition.

2. If someone is presenting the other person's or his own traits with not enough enthusiasm, you can encourage him to talk really loudly. By doing this, his enthusiasm will be triggered. If that person normally talks really softly, he may now think that he is yelling. However, the audience will just hear an enthusiastic voice.

3. If you play the exercise with a big group you can also let them form trios. Each trio asks each other questions to let everyone come up with positive traits about himself. In this case two people present the other person's positive traits while he is standing next to them looking at the audience.

4. To make the exercise more amusing, you can let the one being described look at the audience while performing the things that are being said about him. For example, he can play air guitar while his partner is reporting that he is a great guitar player.

5. This exercise can also be done with new ideas or concepts for the team. People are sometimes more comfortable speaking enthusiastically about another person's ideas; they feel less vulnerable talking enthusiastic about it. After the participant's partner praises his idea, the original creator of the idea will then present it by himself with the same enthusiasm. Because he already heard his idea being presented by his partner it will be easier for him to present it with a lot of enthusiasm himself as well.

Why you should use this exercise

Because of all the positive questions, this exercise is great to add some positivity to the team. The participants will get to know each other in a worthwhile and constructive manner.
When people state their own positive traits, they will get a confident feeling about themselves. Since each person is repeating the positive things his partner just said about him, he doesn't have to be afraid that people will see him as arrogant. This will eliminate the barrier for each person to talk positively about himself.
It is a very good exercise for people who want to work on their job interview skills. Many people are too modest during job interviews when they talk about themselves. During this exercise, they will become more open about sharing their positive traits; that will help them to look more confident.
The fun part of the exercise is that the person who is being described will just look quietly into the audience. This will produce a comic effect and laughter which will make the exercise lighthearted.

Scan this QR code to see an animated example video of this exercise:

You can also type: **team exercise 30 selling each other** into YouTube's search bar to find the video.

Team Exercise 31 - Werewolves

"We do not stop playing because we grow old. We grow old because we stop playing." **- Benjamin Franklin**

Necessities: Cards with "villager" written on them, equal to the number of participants minus two. Two cards with "werewolf" written on them.

During the exercise, the team sits in a circle. You give each participant a card with werewolf or villager written on it. There are two werewolf cards. The rest of the cards are villager cards. Each participant makes sure no one else besides himself can see the card he got. Tell them the villagers have won when they have killed all the werewolves. The werewolves win when they have eaten all the villagers. The exercise has two phases that will be repeated during the game - a day phase and a night phase. During the night, everyone has to close their eyes; when you say it is day again everyone can open their eyes. You now start the game by announcing that it is night and they all have to close their eyes. When everyone's eyes are shut, you tell the group that only the werewolves may now open their eyes. You instruct the werewolves to silently pick out one villager to eat that night. They do that by pointing to a villager who has his eyes closed. They make their choice in complete silence so as not to reveal that they are the werewolves. After they choose a villager to kill, the two werewolves now close their eyes again. You now tell the group that the sun has come up and the day has begun, so everyone can open their eyes.

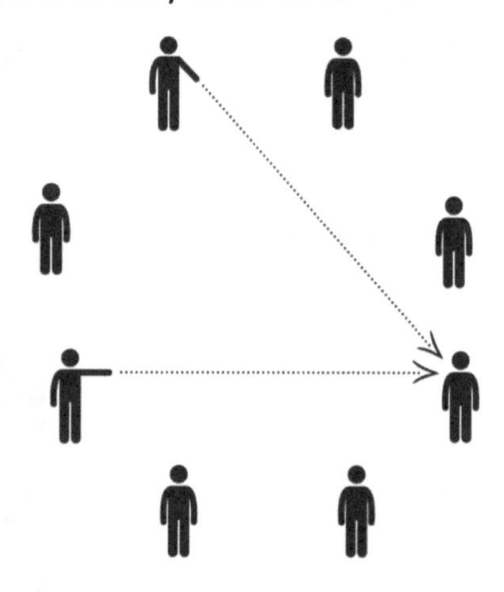

The day phase has started. You tell the group that you have witnessed which villager the werewolves have eaten during the night. You now point to that person. This person has now been eliminated from the game and has to relinquish his card. He leaves the circle and silently observes the remainder of the game. It is now up to the villagers to eliminate someone by popular vote whom they think is a werewolf. The villagers don't know who the werewolves are and will discuss who will be eliminated. The werewolves will participate in the discussion of who to eliminate as if they are villagers themselves. They all start discussing who the werewolves are by using arguments to convince the others. The people who are accused of being werewolves can defend themselves with arguments that support the fact that they aren't werewolves. After a short discussion, you announce that the voting can begin; you state the names of each person. Each time someone's name is mentioned, people raise their hands if they want to eliminate that person. Of course, the real werewolves know who is a villager and who is a werewolf. They will always plead and vote for the elimination of a villager. The person who receives the most votes is now eliminated and reveals his card. The card will prove if he was, in fact, a werewolf, or if they just eliminated a villager. The person who was killed leaves the circle and becomes a quiet spectator.

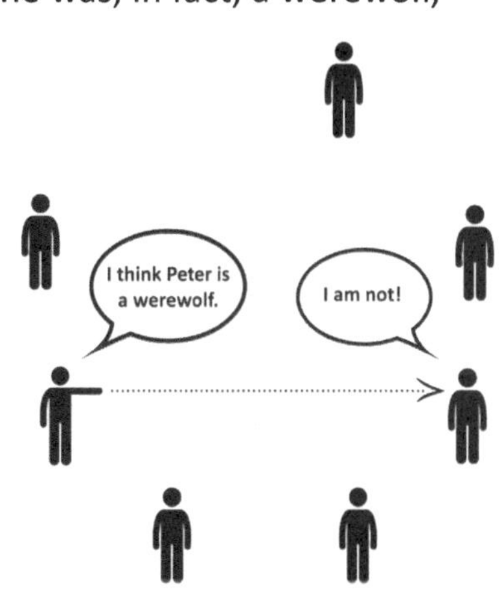

Now you tell them that night has fallen, and everyone must close their eyes. On your mark, the werewolves open their eyes again and pick their new victim. After they have made their choice, they close their eyes. The day phase starts, everyone opens their eyes and a new discussion about the elimination starts and will end in a vote. The person being eliminated shows his card and is out of the game. It becomes night again. Continue playing these rounds until either the two werewolves have been eliminated (the villagers have won) or all the villagers have been eliminated (the werewolves have won).

Variations

1. After the villagers or the werewolves have won the game, you can discuss the exercise with the group and let them evaluate the choices they made during the game. Ask them questions to encourage the discussion: Why were certain people so suspicious? What made someone believe one person and not the other? What can they do better next time to make sure their group wins?

2. You can also play the game with three werewolves. By doing this, you make it more difficult for the villagers to win.

3. You can also play the game with one werewolf. This makes it more difficult for the werewolf to eat all the villagers and not be killed.

4. If you know that two people in the group don't get along well, let them be the two werewolves. This will make them work together and have the same goal in a fun and playful environment.

5. You can also give someone a fortune teller card. Each night, when everyone has closed their eyes and after the werewolves have killed someone, you tell the fortune teller to open his eyes. He now points to someone. You reveal if it is a werewolf or villager When it is a werewolf you nod yes, when it is a villager you nod no. Each night, the fortune teller will learn who is a villager and who is a werewolf. However, can he convince the villagers during the discussion that he is the fortune teller and knows the truth? Because werewolves can also lie and say that they are the fortune teller, it can be difficult to convince the others that his nightly discoveries are true.

Why you should use this exercise

This is a great game to enable the participants to have discussions in a fun and playful way. They all need to generate creative ideas to accuse someone of being a werewolf or to defend themselves by convincing the others that they are a villager.
All the villagers have the same goal: kill the werewolves.
Both the werewolves have the same goal: eat the villagers.
Everyone in each group has to work together to eliminate the persons of the other group. These shared goals will stimulate the group's cooperation.
While trying to solve the mystery of who are the actual werewolves, there will be many surprises. Each round, when the eliminated person reveals what is on his card, everyone will feel excited to find out if that person was a werewolf or a villager.
The team will have a lot of fun together during the exercise which will contribute to good teamwork and team spirit.

Scan this QR code to see an animated example video of this exercise:

You can also type: **team exercise 31 werewolves** into YouTube's search bar to find the video.

Team Exercise 32 - Seeing, thinking, feeling

"Make feedback normal. Not a performance review."
- Ed Batista

Necessities: None.

To start the exercise, you tell the group to form random trios. Tell them that each trio will now stand or sit somewhere in the room and separate themselves from the other trios. Instruct each trio to decide who will be person A, person B, and person C. Tell them that in the first part of the exercise, person A will look at person B for a minute and say aloud what he sees in person B. It is important that he only objectively describes what he sees without interpretation. Tell them it can be anything as long it is nonjudgmental. "I see that you raise your eyebrows" is a perfect objective observation. "I see that you are curious" isn't an objective observation, but an interpretation of what someone sees. Tell them that each person A begins each sentence with "I see...". While person A is talking, person B remains silent. The moment person A says something that isn't purely objective, person C will intervene. Person C makes person A aware by telling him what wasn't objective about his observation. Let them play this first round for around one minute.

Now the second part of the exercise starts. In this part, person A will say what he thinks while looking at person B. He will now start every sentence with "I think...". Tell them that if person B, for example, raises his eyebrows person A's thoughts might be: "I think you are curious." Person C makes sure that person A only says what he is thinking while he looks at person B and not what he is seeing or feeling. If person A talks about what he sees, or how person B makes him feel, person C may intervene. Person C then tells person A why he intervened. This round will also continue for one minute.

In the third part, person A will say what he is feeling while looking at person B. He will only talk about how he feels himself while looking at person B, not how he thinks person B is feeling. He starts every sentence with "I feel...". Tell them that they can say everything they feel while looking at person B. For example, "I feel inspired by looking at you" is correct. However, "I feel inspired because I see you are curious" isn't correct in this round, because then someone also says what he sees. Again, person C pays close attention to person A. Person A must only express his feelings and is not supposed to say what he is seeing or thinking. If this happens, person C may intervene and tell person A why he intervened. Tell the participants that it is okay if there are long silences. Before he verbally expresses it, person A may need time to register what he feels when looking at person B.

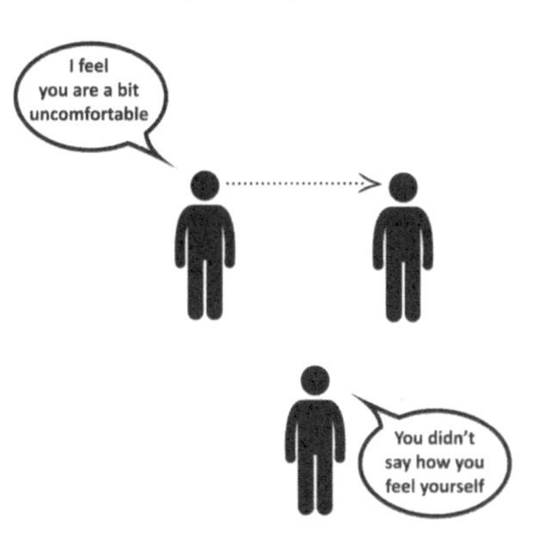

After the third round has been played, each trio switches roles. Person A becomes person B, person B becomes person C, and person C becomes person A. Each trio plays the exercise again in the same way as the first time. After they have finished playing the seeing, thinking and feeling part, the roles will rotate again in the same way as before and they perform the exercise again.

After everyone has had a turn, the group will form a circle and discuss the exercise. You encourage the discussion by asking the following questions: Is it easier to be the observer or the observed? Did you comprehend the differences among seeing, thinking and feeling? How did you feel about person C's intervention? Let everyone share with the rest of the group how he experienced the exercise.

Variations

1. Person A and B can switch roles every time they exchange a sentence. Person A says what he sees (or in later rounds what he thinks or feels) while looking at person B and immediately person B says what he sees (or in later rounds what he thinks or feels) while looking at person A. This way it becomes kind of a conversation. You will see that what person A said to person B will affect what person B will say while looking at person A. In the same way person C intervenes if necessary.

2. Tell person B to repeat aloud each sentence person A just said to him. So if person A, for example, says, "I feel comfortable with you", person B will respond, "You feel comfortable with me." This will help the person being observed to really listen to the things he has heard. Even if the observed disagrees with the observer, he still has to repeat what the observer is saying.

3. To speed up the exercise, you can tell person A to say the sentences starting with "I see, I think, and I feel" all mixed together. Person C now has to be extra focused because there now is a bigger chance that person A will, for example, talk about feelings while starting a sentence with "I think...".

4. At the end of the exercise, you can instruct the team to form a circle and perform the exercise with the whole group. You point to one participant who will look at another random person in the circle and say what he sees. This other person now proceeds to look at another participant in the group, and tells what he sees. Do this until everyone has had a turn to say what he sees while looking at another participant. Then they do the same thing for "I think.." and "I feel..".

Why you should use this exercise

During this exercise, everyone will get insight into how other people see them, think about them and what feelings people get from them. Because of this awareness they will all get to know themselves in a deeper way.
The participants learn how to clearly distinguish the things they see, think and feel. This comes in handy if they want to bring some structure into the way they give feedback. If they are able to separate what they see, think and feel, the person getting the feedback will clearly understand what someone objectively sees, what his interpretation is, and how that makes him feel. This will give the team a toolset to use when giving each other feedback in the future.

Scan this QR code to see an animated example video of this exercise:

You can also type: **team exercise 32 seeing, thinking, feeling** into YouTube's search bar to find the video.

Team Exercise 33 - Contact

"Keep in touch without touching."
- Amit Abraham

Necessities: None.

To start the exercise, you tell the participants to spread out through the room. You tell them to quietly walk crisscross through the room and make eye contact with someone who is wearing a piece of blue clothing. Next, you tell them to look at anyone who is wearing a piece of red clothing. Lastly, everyone looks at someone who is wearing glasses. You can instruct them to look at each other based on various other physical features such as hair color, earrings, or eye color. You continue this eye contact round for around three minutes. When the team is warmed up, you start the next part of the exercise.
Now, instead of looking at each other based on physical characteristics, the team will shake each other's hands based on the mood they think someone is in. Everyone continues to walk crisscross through the room again and you tell the participants that they may now shake someone's hand whom they think is in a great mood today. After everyone has shaken someone's hand, the participants continue to walk crisscross through the room.
Now, you tell them to shake hands with someone who they believe is in a bad mood. Continue telling them to shake hands based on various other moods such as cheerful, tired, or energetic. Choose moods that you think are appropriate for the group you are working with. It is possible that someone tries to shake another person's hand because he thinks that person is in a certain mood. However, the person whose hand he is trying to shake doesn't

agree that he is in that certain mood. It is also possible that this person doesn't think the person who is trying to shake his hand is in that certain mood himself. Either way, he has to return the handshake; it is a fact that the other person thinks he is in that certain mood.
After they have shaken hands for a few minutes based on various themes, you start the third round.
You now tell the participants that they are going to give a high five to each other based on things they think will be good for the other. After the high five, the one who initiated the high five will tell why he chose that person so the one who received it knows why. You begin this round by telling the team to high five someone whom they think should stand up for himself more often. After everyone has high fived someone and told why, you tell them to high five someone whom they think can be nicer to himself. Finally, you tell the team to high five someone whom they think should relax more often. Continue telling them to high five based on various topics you think are appropriate for the team.

In the last round, you tell the participants they will now hug each other based on things they are proud of. Again they will tell the person they hug why they choose him. You start by telling them to hug someone of whom they are proud because he is such a go-getter. After they have all hugged the go-getter, you tell them to hug someone of whom they are proud because he is always there for others. Finally, you tell them to hug someone of whom they are proud because he is so reliable. Continue telling them to hug based on various topics you think are appropriate for the team. For some people, hugging can be a bit awkward. You can speed up the pace for this part of the exercise by saying they should hug someone as quickly as possible. This will make it less awkward.

Variations

1. In addition to shaking hands, high fiving and hugging, you can also suggest other physical activities. Some examples are wave at someone who..., give a box to someone who..., or squeeze someone's nose who....

2. If the participants are uncomfortable with hugging, tell them that they are always free to just give each other a handshake or a high five instead. If they happen to be more comfortable later in the day, you can always perform the same exercise at the end of the day again. They might be more open to giving each other a hug then.

3. After they have played a round, you can ask the team if they can create topics themselves regarding handshakes, high fives, or hugs. For each round, you point to someone who will create a topic for that round.

4. After the exercise, you can tell the participants to form a circle and discuss the exercise. Ask each person what he learned about himself during the exercise.

5. If you play the exercise with people who don't know each other yet, and you think that they will be uncomfortable with the hugging part, you can play the first two parts of the exercise only. In this case tell them to shake hands with people they would like to get to know based on their first impression. After the handshake they can introduce themselves to each other.
Then instruct them to high five someone who they think could use a high five today. This can easily break the ice at the start of the day and shortens the exercise.

Why you should use this exercise

This exercise is great to do as a warm up, because the participants are physically moving around the room. Because the team has to make physical contacts such as handshakes, high fives and hugs to show whom they think fits the topic, they will think less and will automatically use their intuition.
It is a playful way of giving feedback because during the high five and hug rounds, they verbally share their motivation with the person they choose. This will provide insight into how others see them and in how they see others.
The last round in which they physically hug each other will provide a physical connection between people. Because it is done in a playful way, people will dare to hug each other more easily.
All the physical contact in this exercise will quickly produce a group bond.

Scan this QR code to see an animated example video of this exercise:

You can also type: **team exercise 33 contact** into YouTube's search bar to find the video.

Team Exercise 34 - Circles

"If it scares you, it might be a good thing to try." - **Seth Godin**

Necessities: Tape.

At the start of the exercise you create two circles with tape in the center of the room: one large circle and a smaller circle inside the larger circle. The participants stand around the big circle. You explain to them what each circle represents. Tell them that the area outside the big circle stands for "panic". The area between the big circle and the center circle stands for "challenge", and the area inside the center circle stands for "comfort". You now start the exercise by announcing a challenging activity, for example, rock climbing. Now each participant chooses where he stands in the circle in relation to the topic of rock climbing. The ones that feel comfortable and enjoy rock climbing walk to the center of the circle. Participants who find rock climbing challenging will stand in the challenge area. The participants who think they are really afraid of rock climbing will stay outside the circles in the panic zone.

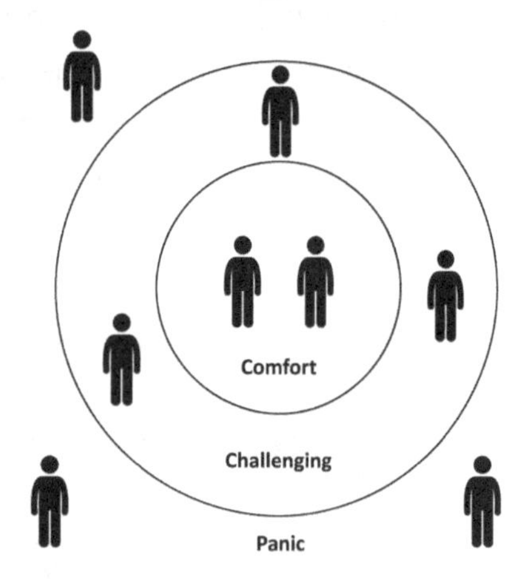

After they have stood in a zone for a few seconds, they move back to the outer zone again and a new activity will be played. Continue practicing the exercise with a variety of activities until you get the feeling the group has been warmed up. When the group is well warmed up, the next part of the exercise will be played. In this part, you play with more in-depth topics, for example, having bad news conversations. This time you will instruct the participants to elaborate on their choices. You announce the topic, and the participants will stand in the zone that best describes their feelings concerning this topic. You now ask each participant individually to explain his choice and share with the rest of the group why this topic causes panic, why he thinks this topic is challenging, or why he feels comfortable regarding this topic. Play this round in the same way with a variety of topics.

In the last part of the exercise, the team will gain insight into changing their feelings about a given subject by moving from one circle to another. You announce an in-depth topic again, for example, working overtime. The participants proceed to take their places in the circle considering their relationship with the topic. First, you ask each participant individually to explain his choice. Everyone will share with the rest of the group why they chose to stand in that particular zone. Next, you ask a participant who is standing in the panic zone what he would need to move from the panic zone into the challenge zone. Tell him that when he gives his answer, he will simultaneously walk into the challenge zone. One by one, all the people in the panic zone will do the same. You ask each participant who was originally standing in the challenge zone what circumstances would cause him to feel comfortable. When he gives the answer, he simultaneously walks to the comfort zone. Lastly, you ask each person who earlier moved from the panic zone into the challenge zone what they would need to go from the challenge zone into the comfort zone. While they answer this question, they move into the comfort zone. Finally, everyone from the group is standing in the comfort zone.

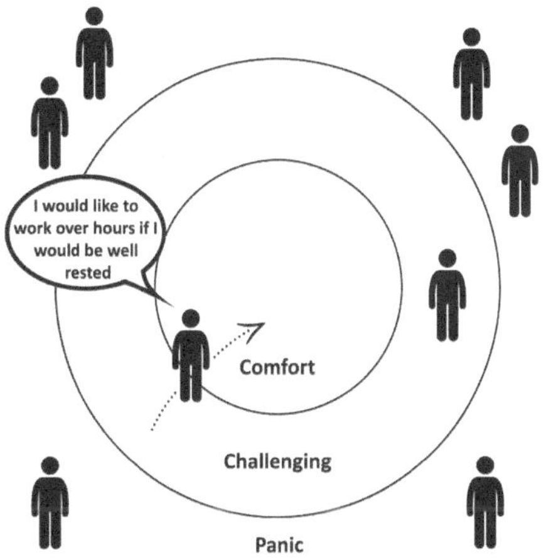

Let them stand there for a few seconds before you tell them to move to the outer circle again. Go on playing this round with a few other in-depth topics in the same way.

Variations

1. You can give new meanings to the areas, for example, drains energy, neutral, and gives energy. You call out an activity and the exercise will be played in the same way.

2. Instead of topics, you can also call out statements to see whether they agree or not. When you ask participants to respond to statements, the areas stand for disagree, neutral, or agree. The rest of the exercise remains the same.

3. After everyone has taken their positions in the areas, you can encourage the participants to start a dialogue by asking each other questions. Anyone who wants can now ask another participant a question. Tell them they only have to answer a question if they want to.

4. You can join this exercise as well. It might be helpful to break the ice with a topic that you don't enjoy doing at all. You tell them the topic, stay in the panic zone, and explain why.

5. You can let the participants create topics themselves as well. You point to someone who creates a topic he would like to play. Give each participant a chance to create a topic. Participants should choose topics that satisfy their curiosity as to where each person decides to stand.

6. During the last part in which everyone moves from circle to circle, you can ask people standing in the comfort circle what would cause them to go into the panic circle. Let them walk one by one to the panic circle while giving their explanation. This will give them insight into other people's fears.

Why you should use this exercise

This exercise is very suitable for helping people open up about their relationships with certain topics. They first only walk physically to the area that fits their feelings. This is easier than talking to other people about something of which they might be afraid. Once they stand in a certain area, it will be easier to open up and talk about their feelings.

The part in which they come up with a reason to go to a more comfortable area will provide solutions they can use for the rest of their lives.

Because the team will see that everyone has different relationships with different topics, they will learn how varied everyone in a group can be. Since everyone is playing the same exercise and is opening up, the group will form a bond.

After this exercise, everyone will know each other better and will consider each other's feelings more often.

Scan this QR code to see an animated example video of this exercise:

You can also type: **team exercise 34 circles** into YouTube's search bar to find the video.

Team Exercise 35 - Scene of thought

"For me really good acting is about subtext." - **Clive Owen**

Necessities: None.

To start the exercise, you tell the participants to form an audience in the shape of a half circle. You ask them for four volunteers: two people who are willing to be actors who act out a scene in front of the group and two people who are willing to communicate the thoughts of the actors acting out the scene. These four volunteers stand in front of the half circle. Each participant who will communicate the thoughts will stand behind the actor whose thoughts he is communicating.
You ask the audience to pick a topic for the scene that relates to the team. If, for example, showing up late for work is an issue, the topic can be "showing up late". You now tell the actors that they will improvise a scene in which someone is late for work and that each time you clap your hands, the actors will pause. You tell the actors to begin improvising the scene and at a random moment, you clap your hands and point to one of the two people standing behind the actors. Tell him to communicate the thoughts of his actor. When he is done, you tell the other person behind the other actor to do the same. Tell them they can come up with any thought they want. The thoughts can be serious, for example, "I hate it when he's late", or funny, "I think I'm in love with him". After both people standing behind the actors have communicated their thoughts, you clap your hands. The actors now continue acting out the scene in which someone is late for work. The actors will not repeat the thoughts they just heard aloud, but will just use it as a subtext to influence the scene. Each actor pretends

not to have heard the thoughts the other actor just received. They continue the scene, and at a random moment, you clap your hands. Again, each person behind the actors communicates the thoughts of his actor. You clap your hands again, and the scene continues inspired by the thoughts the actors just heard from the people standing behind them. Now, shorten the time between the claps. By shortening the moments before the actors pause and hear new thoughts, the scene will be more entertaining. Each time the thoughts are spoken, the scene will get new energy. You keep on clapping your hands until there is a convenient ending point to the scene. You now tell the four participants to rejoin the group.
You ask the group for a new, relevant topic and four new volunteers who will do the same. After you have played this first round a few times with different volunteers and the group understands how it works, you now start the second part.
In this second part, you ask them for a new, relevant theme and four volunteers. However, now the actors will repeat the thoughts aloud provided by the people behind them. The moment you clap your hands, each actor will hear the thoughts and repeat the thoughts to the other actor. Go on clapping your hands and letting the thoughts be repeated by the actors until the scene is finished. These four people now join the rest of the group. Ask for a new, relevant theme and four new people to act out the scene in the same way. Continue playing this last round until each participant has been an actor or a speaker of thoughts at least once in the first or second part of the exercise.

Variations

1. After the exercise, you can discuss preferences with the group. In daily life, do they prefer to express their thoughts or not? Ask them if it is easier to express thoughts or if it is easier to hold thoughts in. This will bridge the gap between the exercise and real life.

2. You can also put two actors on the stage with no one behind them. During the scene, you clap your hands and point at a random participant from the audience. Let him choose one of the actors and give a thought to this actor. This will help the participants stay alert during the scene, because they can be chosen to come up with a thought.

3. You can tell the people who communicate the thoughts to whisper the thoughts into the actors' ears. This way, each actor doesn't know what thought has been given to the other actor. The audience also doesn't know what the thoughts of the actors are. After the scene, you can let the audience guess what the thoughts were.

4. You can play this exercise without the people behind the actors. Instruct the actors to speak their own thoughts the moment you clap your hands. When you clap your hands, the actors will look at the audience and each actor will communicate his thoughts. When the scene continues, the actors pretend that they didn't hear the thoughts of the other actor.

5. Tell the people standing behind the actors they can give a thought to their actor whenever they think it can help propel the scene forward. In this case, you don't clap your hands.

Why you should use this exercise

This is a great, active exercise for going outside one's comfort zones and laughing at the same time.
Because the actors will improvise scenes based on topics that are relevant to the group, the audience will recognize situations from daily life. This will engage the audience in the scene.
Since the actors receive input from the people standing behind them, they will not go blank during a scene. This will help them continue the scene at all times.
After playing the first and second parts of the exercise, everyone will see and feel the difference between holding a thought or speaking a thought aloud. This exercise will inspire a conversation about which is more beneficial - speaking your thoughts aloud or keeping them to yourself.
There will be a lot of laughter during the exercise because the communicated thoughts will have a comical influence on the scenes. Having fun together will be good for group bonding.

Scan this QR code to see an animated example video of this exercise:

You can also type: **team exercise 35 scene of thought** into YouTube's search bar to find the video.

Team Exercise 36 - Moving in the group

"We cannot sense without acting and we cannot act without sensing."
- Thomas Hanna

Necessities: None.

To start the exercise, you tell the participants to spread out through the room and stand still. Tell them that when you clap your hands, they will slowly walk crisscross through the room without talking. When you clap your hands again, everyone will stand still and remain where he is at that moment. When you clap your hands, everyone walks around again. Repeat this process for a few minutes until the team has warmed up. Now, you instruct the group that the moment you clap your hands only one participant will walk through the room while the rest remains standing in place. When you clap your hands again, the one walking will now stand still and immediately a new participant will start walking. This way, there will always be one participant walking. They have to intuit each other's intentions to make sure that not more than one person starts walking at the same time. If two or more people accidentally start walking, they have to correct themselves as quickly as possible. Continue clapping at intervals until everyone has had a turn to walk through the room while the rest remain in place.

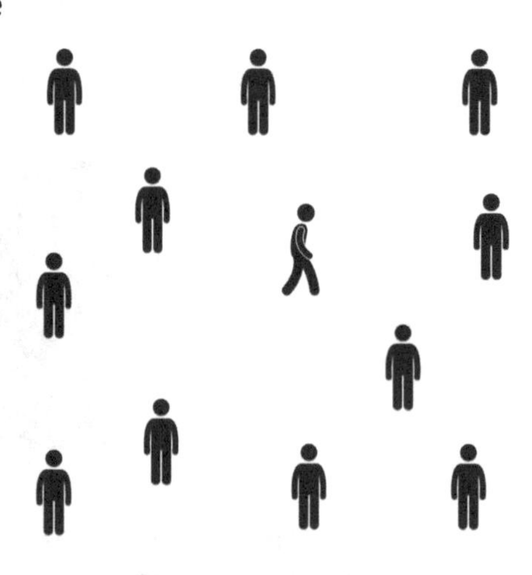

Next, you instruct the participants that when you clap your hands, one participant starts walking. However, instead of your clapping again, the walker will now stand still at a self chosen moment. At the moment the walker stands still a next participant must directly take over the

walking so that it connects seamless and there is no moment that no one is walking. If these instructions are followed, there will always be one person walking through the room. After each person has walked through the room while the rest of the team stands still, you instruct the team that the next time you clap your hands two people will walk through the room. Again, at a self-chosen moment, the two people walking stand still. The two people walking don't have to stand still at the same time. The moment one of the two stands still, another person has to take over the walking. If the two people stand still at the same time, two new people have to take over the walking. In this way, there will always be two people walking. It is imperative that the group is aware of each other so there is no time in which no one is walking. When everything is going smoothly, you can make the exercise more challenging.
Tell the team that when you clap your hands, there always has to be four people walking at the same time. Again, each of the four people can decide when to stand still at a self chosen moment. If the exercise is progressing smoothly, you can start the last round. You instruct the team that when you clap your hands, there always has to be one participant walking, one participant jogging, and one participant skipping. Each of these participants decides for himself when to stand still. Another participant will then take over this specific movement. Perform this part of the exercise by varying the number of participants who have to walk, jog or skip.

Continue until the team can perform the exercise flawlessly and everyone has gotten a chance to walk, skip or jog at least once.

Variations

1. It is possible that the team hasn't got the synergy yet to smoothly execute the exercise and keeps on making mistakes. If this is the case, you can clap your hands and point to someone to assume the walking. This will help them learn how to implement the exercise. If you feel that they understand the procedure, you can then clap your hands and let them sense who will be the next person to walk around the room.

2. After the first round in which you clap your hands, and before the round in which you don't clap your hands anymore, you can add an extra round in which the participants will give the clap signals themselves. At the moment the one who is walking stands still, he claps his hands. The one who will assume the walking will clap his hands the moment he starts walking. By doing this, it will be clearer who will walk next.

3. You can play a bonus round in which everyone except one person walks. The moment you clap your hands, another person should stand still while all the others walk. You can vary this with the number of people standing still. For example, everyone walks except for two people.

4. In addition to walking, jogging or skipping, more movements can be added. For example, you can tell them that someone has to walk backwards, take really big steps, or crawl. Use your imagination to create any type of movements.

Why you should use this exercise

This exercise will stimulate the group's intuition. Playing the exercise correctly demands cooperation based on sensitivity.
It is a great exercise to perform with groups that want to cooperate better. Because all the participants have the same goal and have the responsibility to meet the given task, a positive team spirit will develop.
They are not allowed to talk during the exercise and have to do everything based on their senses. After performing the exercise, they will be more sensitive towards each other while performing group tasks.
It is possible that they will make mistakes and more or less people will be moving than should be. If so, they will correct themselves as quickly as possible. This will train them to correct mistakes quickly without giving it too much attention.
Because the exercise requires physical movement, this exercise is a great energizer with which to start the day.

Scan this QR code to see an animated example video of this exercise:

You can also type: **team exercise 36 moving in the group** into YouTube's search bar to find the video.

Team Exercise 37 - 1, 2, 3

"Concentration is the secret of strength"
- Ralph Waldo Emerson

Necessities: None.

To start the exercise you tell the team to form pairs. Each duo decides who is person A and who is person B. Tell them that each duo will have to count to three. They do this by each saying one number at a time. First, person A says "one". Then, person B says "two". Lastly, person A says "three". Now, they continue counting to three again. Because person A ended the counting by saying "three", person B will now start the new sequence by saying "one". Person A says "two" and person B says "three". Tell them that they can't pause between the numbers, so between one and three, there can't be a pause. It is just one, long sequence of numbers. Tell them that in addition to saying the numbers, they have to remain silent. This might seems easy. However, in each sequence a different person will say one, two, or three. Therefore concentration is required, because the participants have to pay close attention to where they are in the sequence. Let them execute this sequence for a few minutes. After the pairs have gained proficiency in using this sequence, the numbers will now acquire new meanings. The participant whose turn it is to say "one", will now clap his hands instead. Now, the sequence looks like this: Person A will clap; person B will say "two"'; person A will say "three"; person B will clap, etc. Let them continue for a few minutes. Because the number one has been replaced with a clap, it is even more important to stay focused. When the pairs have mastered the above exercise, a new replacement will be added. The participant

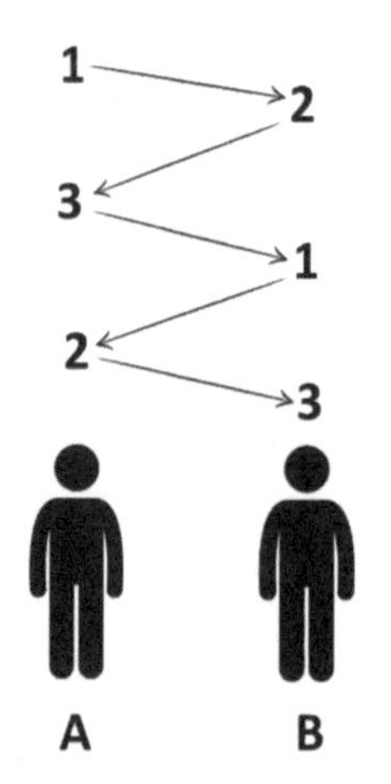

whose turn it is to say two will now jump instead. Now, the sequence looks like this: Person A will clap; person B will jump; person A will say “three”; person B will clap, etc. Allow them to continue for a few minutes.

When the team has become proficient in the above sequence, a new replacement will be added. The participant whose turn it is to say three will now say his birthplace instead. Now the sequence looks like this: Person A will clap; person B will jump; person A will say his birthplace; person B will clap; person A will jump; person B will say his birthplace, etc. Again, let them continue for a few minutes.

To make the exercise more challenging, the participants will now form trios instead of duos. Let them decide who will be person A, person B, and person C. Now the trios will count to four. The numbers one, two, and three still have the same replacements. The number four is, for now, just the number four. The sequence will now look like this: Person A will clap; person B will jump; person C will say his birthplace; person A will say “four”; Person B will clap, etc.

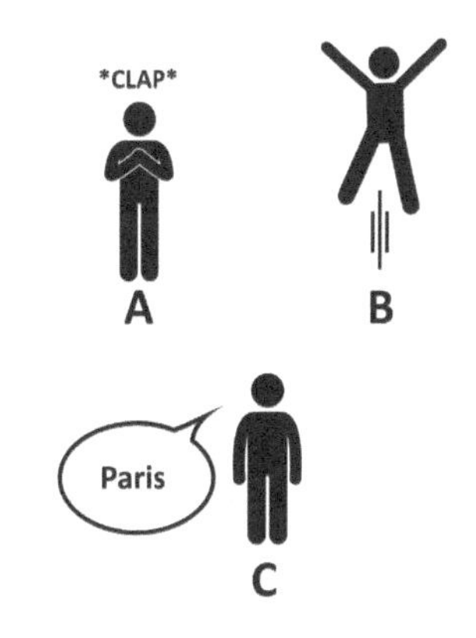

When the participants can perform this easily, the number four will be replaced by a clap, jump, or birthplace. The person who has to say the number four can decide if he claps, jumps, or says his birthplace. Because a jump, clap, or birthplace will occur twice in the sequence, the participants have to stay extra focused to keep track of where they are. Now the sequence can look like this: Person A will clap; person B will jump; person C will say his birthplace; person A will clap (random choice); person B will clap; person C will jump; person A will say his birthplace; person B will jump (random choice), etc.

Let the team practice this round until they perform the sequence correctly.

Variations

1. Instead of replacing number four with a random choice, you can make it easier by telling them to replace it with something else. They can replace number four for example with their favorite solo artist or band, favorite vacation place, or the number of siblings they have.

2. If you are working with a big group, it is also possible to make groups of more than three people. Make sure that the number they are counting to is equal to the amount of people in the group plus one. So, if there are five people, they will count to six. In this way, each participant has to say something different each time it is his turn.

3. Instead of counting to a number that is one number higher than the amount of people in a group, they can also count to a higher number. For example, a duo can count to five. Make sure it is an uneven number. Otherwise, in each sequence, it can be the case that the same person can just say the same number; that would be too easy.

4. You can also turn the last round into a competition. Each time a trio makes a mistake, they get a point. When a trio makes three mistakes, it is out of the game. Let them play until one trip is still in the game and wins.

5. After the exercise, you can form a circle with the group and discuss the exercise. Encourage the discussion by asking them the following questions: How do you focus most efficiently and keep track of where you are in the sequence? How does this exercise relate to working together in real life?

Why you should use this exercise

This exercise will help the group improve both concentration and cooperation. Because each round will be more challenging, they have to cooperate with a great focus. Being focused and working together at the same time on a common goal will increase team spirit.
To know at all times what to say when, they have to listen carefully to their partners. This will train their listening skills.
Successfully establishing a flow in which they can maintain the sequence, will engender positive feelings among the participants.
This positive energy will contribute to the group chemistry.
Because the exercise feels like a game, it is a great energizer with which to start the day.

Scan this QR code to see an animated example video of this exercise:

You can also type: **team exercise 37 1, 2, 3** into YouTube's search bar to find the video.

Team Exercise 38 - The keyring

"To bring anything into your life, imagine that it's already there."
- Richard Bach

Necessities: Every participant has to bring at least four of their keys.

In this exercise, the participants will get to know each other through each other's keys. Tell the group beforehand that they should bring their keys. To start the exercise, the team will sit in a circle and everyone will take out their key rings. Tell the group that each participant will pick two keys about which he would like to tell stories. Let them think about the stories for a minute. After a minute, you select someone to start the exercise. It is up to him what kind of story he will tell. It can be a purely factual story about what you can open with the key, or it can be a more personal story about what the key means to him. After he tells the stories about two keys, the other participants may now ask questions about the stories. They can be questions about the facts of the story or personal questions to get to know the storyteller in a deeper way. Tell them that the people who want to ask questions can raise their hands. You pick three people to ask a question. After the questions are answered, the person to the left of the first storyteller will do the same. He will tell stories about two of his keys and will answer the three questions asked by the other participants. You continue by going clockwise around the circle until each person from the group has told a story based on two keys and answered three questions from the other participants.

Next, the second part of the exercise starts. Tell the group that each participant will tell a story based on two other keys from his keyring. They will now tell the rest of the group what they had to do to achieve these keys. Tell them it can be a short story, for example, "This key is from my bicycle. I bought it with the money I earned by working at a toothpick factory when I was fifteen years old". It can also be a long story, for example, how someone bought his first house. You point to a first random participant who will tell two stories. After he has told what he had to do to achieve the keys, three other participants ask questions as in the first round. After he has answered the questions, the person sitting to his left tells his stories. Go clockwise around the circle until all the participants have had a turn to tell their stories about how they achieved the keys and answered the three questions from the other participants.

In the final part of the exercise, the participants will fantasize about a nonexistent key they want to have ten years from now. Tell them they can be as creative as they want and that it can be a key to everything they want: the key to a big house, a new office, or an abstract thing like the key to someone's heart. They can have any type of wish as long as they are being truthful about their feelings. Let the group think about it for a minute before you point to a first participant who will tell where his fantasy key will lead him. After he has finished his story, three participants may now ask questions. After he has answered the three questions, the person sitting to his left now gets a turn.

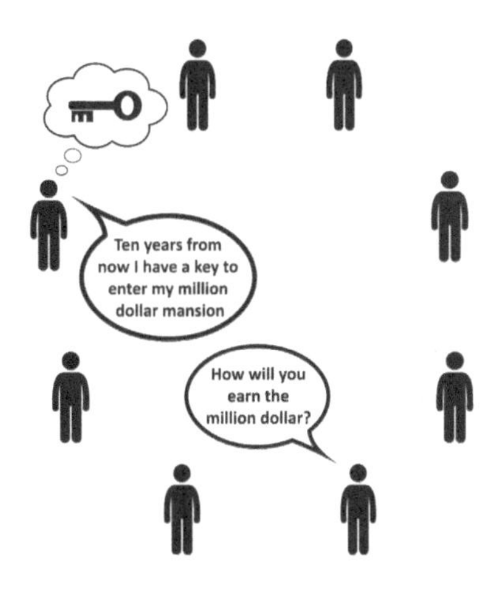

Go clockwise around the circle until each person has told his story about a key he would like to own ten years from now and has answered the three questions.

Variations

1. Instead of telling them to bring their keyrings, you can also let them bring their smartphones. In this case, you just play one round in which each participant tells a story about two applications on his phone. Participants can tell anything they want concerning why they have certain apps on their phones. These days, everyone has personal interest apps, so it will be easy to tell a fun or interesting personal story about them.

2. You can let the group do the same exercise with their wallets. In this case, the participants will tell a story about two cards they have in their wallets. For example, someone can tell why he has a discount card from a favorite store and why he has a library card. Just play one round for this variation.

3. In addition to letting the participants tell about their keys, you can instruct them to bring an object from their homes that has a special meaning. Each participant tells a story about his object and the other participants can ask questions about the object and the story.

4. As a fun bonus round, you can ask for a volunteer to tell a story about what key on his keyring he wants to get rid of. For example, someone might have a key to a car they don't like anymore. Again, the rest of the group can ask three questions. In this variation, not everyone needs a turn; not all people may have a key that they would like to get rid of.

Why you should use this exercise

This is a great exercise to enable the team to share some personal stories in a playful way. You can play this exercise as an icebreaker with people who don't know each other yet. Due to all of the stories and questions, people will quickly get to know each other. It is also a good exercise to do with people who are acquainted but want to discover new things about each other. The more people share and the more personal the stories are, the more the team will get to know each other at a deeper level.
Because everyone tells a story regarding a key, it will be easier for them to tell a story. People who are usually uncomfortable telling a story now have a base to start from.
The last round will stimulate each person's creativity and will help people visualize their goals.

Scan this QR code to see an animated example video of this exercise:

You can also type: **team exercise 38 the keyring** into YouTube's search bar to find the video.

Team Exercise 39 - Points for improvement

"Make improvements, not excuses."
- Roy T. Bennett

Necessities: Flip chart or whiteboard and a marker.

To start the exercise, you tell the team to form a circle. In this exercise, the team will determine what improvements could be made within the team concerning cooperation and communication. They will do this in three different ways. Tell them that first each participant will think of the improvements he would like to make within the whole team including him. Tell them that these improvements can be work relating topics like "being on time more often", but also more abstract topics like "being more open towards each other".
Give each participant a minute to think about what he would like to improve about the group including him. Tell the group they have to remember the improvement. If someone thinks he won't remember it, he can write it down.
Next, you tell them that each person now thinks of an improvement within the team excluding him. So an improvement of which he thinks that everyone except himself needs. Again, they will remember what they came up with or they write it down. Lastly, each person thinks about an improvement he alone needs to make. This should be an improvement that only applies to him and not for the rest of the group. Again, they can remember what they came up with or they can write it down.
After everyone has decided on these three improvements, you now select one participant to share his three points of improvement.
He first says what he would like to improve about the whole group including himself. You write this point of improvement on the whiteboard. He then shares what he would like to improve within the team excluding himself. Lastly, he shares what he alone would like to

improve upon. You don't need to write these last two improvements on the whiteboard. Now, tell this participant to point to other participants who will suggest solutions to make these three improvements a reality. First, he points at someone who will devise a solution for the just named improvement for the whole team including himself. The participant he points to now shares his suggestion. He can be as creative as possible as long he thinks it is a good suggestion for producing the desired improvement. Write the given suggestion on the whiteboard below the point of improvement. Now, the participant points at someone else to suggest a solution for the improvement for the team himself excluded. Lastly, he selects someone to come up with a suggestion for the just named improvement for himself alone. You don't have to write these last two solutions on the whiteboard.

Go clockwise around the circle to let each person share his three points of improvement and select others from the group to create suggestions for each improvement. Each time, you write on the whiteboard the solution for the improvement for the whole group. You write the given solution for that improvement below the improvement. Eventually, the number of improvements and solutions for the whole team will be equal to the number of participants.
All the participants can now see on the white board exactly what they can do to make these improvements happen.

Stop gossiping
Speak up if something bothers you

Work efficiently
Plan things in advance

Be on time
Treat the rest for coffee if you are late

Relax more often
Have drinks with the team once a week

Gain more costumers
Everyone makes a cold call every day

Variations

1. During the part in which someone has to create a solution for a named point of improvement, tell him to share if he agrees or disagrees with that point for improvement before he shares the suggestion. Let him explain why he agrees or disagrees before making the suggestion.

2. After all the improvements and suggestions have been written on the whiteboard, tell the group to take a photo with their phones of the whiteboard. They now have a record of what was said so they can read it later.

3. If there is no flip chart or whiteboard in the room, you can write the improvements and suggestions on your phone and send it to all the participants. In this way, they can read it during and after the exercise.

4. After the exercise, you can ask how the participants experienced sharing their points of improvement. Ask them the following questions to encourage the discussion: "Was it easier to share what you would like to improve in the team including yourself, or was it easier to say what you would like to improve in the team excluding yourself? And why do you think that is."

5. As a bonus round, in addition to the three types of improvements described in the exercise, you also can let the participants generate improvements for things outside of the team. For example, "What would you like to improve concerning the furniture in our office?", or "What would you like to improve concerning lunch?" Write these improvements and suggestions on the whiteboard or flip chart.

Why you should use this exercise

This is a suitable exercise to help everyone become aware of the differences among what someone would like to improve in the team including him, in the rest of the team excluding him, and what he would like to improve upon just himself. It is especially important to be aware of the nuances between "the whole team including myself" and "the whole team excluding myself". Often, when people say, "We have to improve communication", they actually mean "You, and not me, have to improve communication." When people learn to see this difference, people will become much more aware of what they really mean and how to communicate that.
Because the participants create suggestions on how to make each other's improvements happen, the team will become supportive and cohesive.
Writing the suggested solutions below the improvements on the whiteboard, will help everyone to see what the team can do to make the improvements happen.

Scan this QR code to see an animated example video of this exercise:

You can also type: **team exercise 39 points for improvement** into YouTube's search bar to find the video.

Team Exercise 40 - Who stands where

"Self knowledge is the beginning of self improvement."
- Baltasar Gracian

Necessities: Three topics that are relevant to the group and ten prepared statements for each topic.

Before you begin this exercise, you ask the participants for three topics they think are relevant to the group. For each topic, you prepare ten statements and write them on a piece of paper. For example, the group might suggest the topic: listening to each other. You will then write ten statements pertaining to the topic of listening. On the top of the paper you write the topic. Make sure that the statements pertaining to an overarching topic are all negative or all positive. Examples of negative statements for this topic could be: "I think people don't listen to me enough" or, "I don't say the things I want to say, because I don't feel heard." You can also choose to prepare all positive statements such as: "I think people listen very carefully to me" or, "I love to talk because everyone listens to me very well." It doesn't matter if the statements are all negative or all positive, as long as all the statements regarding the overarching topic are all negative or all positive. Do this for all three topics. Therefore, before you start the exercise, you will have three papers containing ten statements pertaining to each overarching topic. To begin the exercise, you tell the team to form a straight line on one side of the room. You now tell the group what the first topic will be and that you are going to read aloud ten statements belonging to that overarching topic. Tell them that each person who agrees with this statement will take one step forward into the room. Tell them everyone needs to remain silent during this exercise. You now read the first statement, and each person who agrees with the statement takes one step forward. Let the participants stand where they are for a few seconds before you read the second statement pertaining to the same topic. Again, the ones who agree with the statement take a step forward. Continue until you have read aloud all ten statements pertaining to the overarching topic. After all the ten statements pertaining to the first topic have been played, the participants will be standing at different spots in the room. Tell the group that everyone can now take a moment to look around and see how each person relates to the topic. If the statements you read were all positive, the further someone moved into the room the more positive he views the overarching topic. If all statements were negative, the further someone stands in the room the more negative he views the overarching topic. Tell them that everyone will now walk back to where they started and stand in a line.

You now play the second topic. One by one you read each of the ten statements aloud that pertain to the second topic. When someone agrees with a statement, he steps forward. Again everyone can now take a moment to look around and see how each person relates to the topic. After this second theme has been played, you follow the same procedure for the third theme. After the third theme has been played, you tell the team to sit in a circle and you will evaluate the exercise.

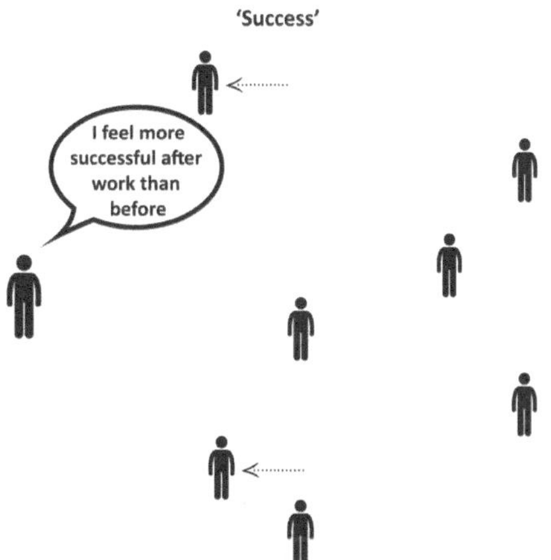

Ask them the following questions to encourage the conversation: What did you discover about yourself and others during the exercise? Were you surprised to see how you and the others relate to a certain topic? Was it a different experience to see everyone physically standing in the room instead of sitting and talking about a topic?

Variations

1. In addition to stepping forward when someone agrees with a statement, you can tell them to step backwards when they disagree with a statement. When they don't know if they agree or not, they can stay where they are. If you play this variation, the line has to start in the middle of the room; otherwise, they can't step backward.

2. After everyone stands in the appropriate place after all the ten statements have been read, you tell the group that the people who feel like describing how they relate to the theme can raise their hands. Each of these people can now elaborate on his choice.

3. While playing the second variation, you can let the other participants ask questions to the person who just described how he relates to the topic. Tell the team that the questions can only be asked out of curiosity and cannot be judgmental.

4. You can also let the group create statements themselves. You tell the group what topic is being played, for example, "being passionate". The group will stand in a straight line on one side of the room and a volunteer will say a statement pertaining to the topic "being passionate". An example might be "I love my job". The people who love their jobs take a step forward. Now a second person will say a statement. Make sure this is a positive statement as well, so at the end all the positions make sense. If the first person said a negative statement, all the others have to say negative statements for that topic.

Why you should use this exercise

This is a great, active exercise to give the participants insight into how they relate to a certain topic. Because they only have to step forward in silence without explaining anything, it is easier for them to show how they relate to a certain statement. They don't have to justify their feelings using words.
After all the ten statements pertaining to a certain topic have been played, everybody can see clearly where everyone literally stands regarding the topic.
This exercise is great to break the ice when you talk about certain topics. After playing this exercise, it will be easier for people to talk about how they relate to a certain topic. They already show physically how they relate to the topic, so talking about it will just be a small step.

Scan this QR code to see an animated example video of this exercise:

You can also type: **team exercise 40 who stands where** into YouTube's search bar to find the video.

Team Exercise 41 - Musical chairs

"Energy is the key to creativity. Energy is the key to life."
- William Shatner

Necessities: Chairs equal to the number of participants plus one.

To start the exercise, you tell the group to sit on chairs in a circle. Tell them to place the chairs two-arm's length apart. You will stand next to the circle and tell the group that you will say a sentence starting with the words "I love people who..." and that you will end the sentence by naming a characteristic based on appearance. Tell them that all the participants who think that they fit that characteristic will switch chairs. Each person who stands up because he fits the characteristic, is required to switch chairs. He cannot go back to his own chair anymore. You now state the characteristic, for example, "I love people who... wear jeans". Now, all the participants wearing jeans switch chairs. The ones who are not wearing jeans just keep sitting on their chairs. If three people fit the characteristic, these three people have to switch chairs.

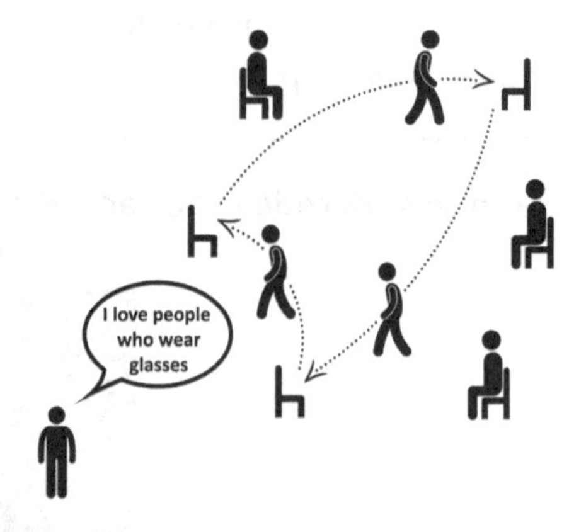

Each of the three people will have to move to a new chair. In this case it cannot be the case that two people exchange chairs with each other. The third person then won't have a new chair to sit on. Together they have to figure out how to change chairs in such a way that everyone who fits the characteristic moves to a new chair. If everyone who recognized himself in the characteristic changed chairs, you will say a new "I love people who..." sentence with a characteristic based on appearance. Again, everyone who thinks they fit the characteristic changes chairs. Continue playing this round for around five minutes with different characteristics based on appearance. After the team has warmed up and has successfully mastered switching chairs, you will now announce characteristics based on personality. An example could be, “I love people who... stand up for themselves”. The participants who think they stand up for themselves switch chairs in the same way as in the first round. Because these characteristics are personal, it might take more time for the participants to determine if they fit the characteristic. However, because they get used to it, they will be faster each time a characteristic is played. Continue playing this round for around five minutes with all different types of characteristics based on personality.

You will now start the last part of the exercise. You tell the team that a game element will be added which will accelerate the exercise. To start the game, you will now join the exercise by standing in the center of the circle. You begin by saying a sentence with a characteristic you identify with. An example could be, “I love people who... like team building sessions”. The moment you have ended the sentence all the participants who like team building sessions as well switch chairs as quickly as possible. Because you are now joining the exercise, you will also try to find a chair to sit on as quickly as possible. Now, there will be one more participant than there are chairs. This means that after the chair exchange, one participant remains standing and has no chair. The one who remains standing is the next one to stand in the center of the circle. He will say a statement that applies to him starting with “I love people who...”. He can say any type of characteristic that fits him. Again, the participants that recognize themselves in the statement switch chairs as quickly as possible. Continue this for five minutes until everyone has been the last man standing once and has expressed a statement.

Variations

1. During the game round, you can instruct the participants to only announce characteristics based on personality. This will make the game round more in-depth.

2. You may not want to play during the game in the last part of the exercise. If that is the case, before you start the second part of the exercise, you can remove a chair and tell one of the participants to stand in the center of the circle. By doing this, there is one less chair than there are participants, and the game can be played without you.

3. You can remove persons who didn't find a chair on time from the game. After someone is removed from the game, you remove an extra chair. Therefore, there will still be one less chair than there are participants. The person who was removed from the game now calls out a new characteristic based on personality, but he is now standing next to the circle and won't play the chair game himself anymore. Continue playing this until there are three people left. These three people are the winners.

4. In the first part of the exercise, after the round in which you named characteristics based on appearance, you can add a round in which you mix up characteristics based on appearance with characteristics based on personality. Let the characteristics based on personality predominate until there are only characteristics based on personality left. By doing this, you smoothly transition into the round in which only characteristics based on personality are being used.

Why you should use this exercise

This is a great energizing exercise to play with people who don't know each other that well yet. Because each person has to choose whether a certain characteristic fits him, each person will quickly gain some insight into himself and others.
It is also interesting to play with people who already know each other. Because the group will physically move from chair to chair, this exercise is a great warm up to energize people at the beginning of the day.
When the game element is being added to the exercise, it will accelerate the pace. The participants will react on their initial impulses and think less. Because everyone will respond to their first physical reaction to a certain characteristic their choices will be more honest.

Scan this QR code to see an animated example video of this exercise:

You can also type: **team exercise 41 musical chairs** into YouTube's search bar to find the video.

Team Exercise 42 - What happened?

"Problem solving is hunting. It is savage pleasure and we are born to it. "
- Thomas Harris

Necessities: A prepared situation.

To start the exercise, you will sit in a circle with the participants. Tell the participants that you will describe a situation, and they will have to guess the details and discover what happened. It can be a funny situation, but to excite the participants a thrilling situation would be better. By selecting a thriller, the participants can uncover the plot by being detectives. Tell them each person can ask one question at a time. By asking the questions they will try to discover what happened. Tell them the questions should be closed questions that can only be answered with yes or no. If the answer to the question is yes, the person who asked the question can ask another question. If the answer is no, the next person in the circle will have a turn to ask a question. You now tell the team the mystery that they have to solve. A good example of a mystery is the following: In the forest, at the foot of a mountain, lies a dead man surrounded by bags containing sand. What happened? What has happened is a secret to the group. They have to try to unveil the secret as quickly as possible using as few questions as possible. (What happened is that the man was flying with his family in a hot air balloon. They were flying towards a mountain. They needed to increase the altitude of the balloon, or the balloon would crash into the mountain. The man threw all the sandbags out of the balloon, but they were still flying too low to get over the mountain. The man knew that if they crashed into the mountain, they would all die. So, he sacrificed himself by jumping out of the balloon so the balloon would gain altitude and fly over the mountain.)
Of course, you don't tell the group what happened; they have to guess. Moving clockwise, the participants will ask closed questions which you can only answer with yes or no. You point to a random participant

who will begin the questioning. The first participant might ask if the man was murdered. You now answer with a simple yes or no. In this case, the answer is no. Because the answer is no, the next participant sitting to his left can ask a question.

For example, he might ask if the man committed suicide. In this case, your answer is yes. Because the answer is yes, the participant who asked the question can ask another question. Continue going clockwise around the circle and letting them ask questions until someone solves the mystery. It usually takes about one hundred questions to discover what has happened. If someone thinks he has enough information to solve the mystery, he can only offer his solution when it is his turn to ask a question. He has to ask a questions in the same way as the other questions; it has to be a closed questions. He could phrase the questions in the following manner: Was the man flying in a hot air balloon with his wife and children? (You answer yes) Were they flying towards a mountain that he thought they were going to crash into? (yes) Did he throw sandbags out of the balloon to increase altitude so that they could fly over the mountain. (yes) Did that fail?(yes) Did he jump out of the balloon to decrease the weight so the balloon could fly over the mountain? (yes) In this case, the answer is yes each time and the whole story has been revealed. The one who guessed the plot wins the game and now has to suggest another situation. He can be as creative as he wants. Now, the others will ask him closed questions to find out what happened.

Variations

1. Instead of a thrilling situation, you can also create a lighthearted situation. This is better when, for example, you do the exercise with children for whom it is too scary to play a thrilling situation.

2. When you work with a big group, you can divide the group into smaller groups and walk from one group to the other. Each group asks you a yes/no question they come up with together and you answer it. If the answer is no you walk to the next group. Make sure the groups can't hear each other's questions and answers. The group that guesses the cause of the situation the fastest wins the game.

3. You can make the stories funny by putting famous characters in the story, for example, Mickey Mouse or Brad Pitt. This will make the story hilarious.

4. Instead of the story mentioned in the exercise, you can also use another story to start the exercise. Another example of an interesting situation is the following: A woman walks into a library and opens a book. Soon after, she leaves the library with tears running down her face. What happened?
The woman is the author of the book. She had left five 20-euro notes in random pages of the book. When she opened the book, they were still there. She is sad because she now knows that no one has read her book.

5. If you need more of these stories and their answers, just Google "black stories" and you will find a lot more of them.

Why you should use this exercise

This exercise teaches the team how to ask questions in an effective way. Because they have to find out as quickly as possible what has happened, their questions need to be effective.
Each question is of equal importance, so each individual's input will contribute to the final solution. Because they have to come to a solution together, the group will feel a cooperative spirit.
Since everyone gets a turn to ask a question, even the more quiet people will be heard.
It is also a very enjoyable exercise. When they come up with the right solution a cheerful moment will occur in the group. Because of all the extraordinary stories and solutions that they will share, they will laugh together a lot. This is good for the group chemistry.

Scan this QR code to see an animated example video of this exercise:

You can also type: **team exercise 42 what happened** into YouTube's search bar to find the video.

Team Exercise 43 - Is this it?

Every act of communication is a miracle of translation." **- Ken Liu**

Necessities: None.

To begin the exercise, you instruct the team to form duos. Tell them to form duos with someone they don't know well, or with someone with whom they want more effective cooperation. All the duos decide who will be person A and who will be person B. Instruct them to sit down in a half circle on one side of the room.
Before you start the exercise you give them the following instructions: Tell the group that you are going to choose a duo and that person B will close his eyes. Tell them that the other participants will point to a random object while person B has his eyes closed so only person A will see what the object is. When person B will open his eyes again, person A will point to objects one by one while asking person B if the object he points to is the one selected by the others. Because person B didn't see what object the other participants picked, it will be impossible for person B to know what object was chosen by the group.
Tell them that before the group chooses an object, the selected duo will leave the room to invent a secret code together. The code will make person B know if the object person A points to is the chosen object. Tell them it can be any kind of code. For example, when person A coughs before he points to an object, it is the correct one. Another example of a code can be that when person A points to a black object asking if it is the chosen object, the object he points to right after that is the selected object. Of course, now it will be easy for person B to identify the chosen object. Tell them that the code has to be complex, so the others won't be able to easily decipher it. The goal of the other participants will be to guess the duo's secret code as quickly as possible.
After you told them these instructions, you will start the exercise. You pick a duo and tell the duo to go out of the room to invent a code.

After the duo invents the secret code, they return to the room. You now tell person B to close his eyes, and you point to a random person from the half circle who will point to an object in the room. He makes sure that person A and the rest of the group see the object he points to. Now person B opens his eyes and person A points one by one to objects in the room asking if it is the chosen object. He starts the sentence with "Is it...?" For example, "Is it... the little table in the corner?" Person B answers with a simple yes or no. Person A can point to unchosen objects as long as he wants before he points to the correct object. He can also choose to point to the chosen object immediately. The moment person A points to the chosen object, person B confirms by saying yes. After person B has confirmed that it is the chosen object, the rest of the group will now try to guess what their secret communication code is. Let each participant make a guess. If no one guesses correctly, person B closes his eyes again and you point to someone from the group who will choose another object. Person A sees what it is, person B opens his eyes and the same game will be played. Continue playing the game until someone correctly guesses the code.

Now, you point to another duo that will leave the room and devise a new secret code.

The game will continue and follow the same procedure. Continue until each duo has invented a secret code and has played the game.

Variations

1. You can implement a game element. Each time person B guesses the right object without the group guessing the secret code, the duo gets a point. At the end of the exercise, the duo with the most points wins.

2. You can implement a maximum time for the guessing rounds. This way the exercise won't take too long and the duos won't take up too much time. For example, you can limit the guessing rounds to ten. If the audience has not guessed the code after ten tries, the duo can reveal their secret code or keep their secret code a secret. If they decided not to reveal their code, after the day of the exercise they can continue showing their trick to their colleagues in daily life, just as long until someone cracks the code.

3. To increase the difficulty of creating a code, you can implement a new rule. After person A and person B discuss the code, they are not allowed to talk anymore. They can only point to objects while the other person nods yes or no. By doing this, the participants have to create a code that doesn't concern language and is only physical. For example, after person B touches his nose, the next object person A points to is the chosen object.

4. You can also instruct person B to keep his eyes closed while person A points to different objects. This way, the duo has to devise a code just based on language or tone of voice.

5. If you have a small group they can play the game again, but now each duo switch roles. This way each person has been the pointer and the guesser once.

Why you should use this exercise

This is a great exercise to enable people to practice communicating with each other. This will be especially useful if they don't know each other well or if they need better cooperation skills. Because person A and person B must create a code together, they will form a bond. This will quickly break the ice between the two.
It is an exciting exercise because each round all the participants watching the duo will try to figure out the secret code.
You can use this exercise when you want to talk with the group about communication. In daily communication, many codes are also used. For example, little jokes people share, the way people laugh, or certain accents. You can make the connection between this exercise and daily life by talking with the group about these communication codes.

Scan this QR code to see an animated example video of this exercise:

You can also type: **team exercise 43 is this it** into YouTube's search bar to find the video.

Team Exercise 44 - Brainstorming

"If at first the idea is not absurd, then there is no hope for it. "
- Albert Einstein

Necessities: Pens and pieces of paper equal to the number of participants, a whiteboard or flip chart, and a couple of books.

To start this exercise, you tell the participants to form a circle. You ask the group what group goal they would like to achieve. They have to unanimously decide what the group goal is. An example of a common group goal might be to obtain more customers. You now give each participant a piece of paper on which he draws a vertical line in the middle. Tell them to write on the left side of the line three ideas that would achieve the opposite of their goals. For example, you might have a group of dance teachers from a dance school who want more customers. Since they are writing opposite suggestions for their goals, they might suggest putting a big lock on the dance school door to block people from entering. Next, each person writes the opposite of each negative idea on the right side of the line. The opposite of putting a big lock on the door and blocking entry could be organizing an open house in order to show people the school. When everyone is done writing the three positive opposite ideas on the right side of the line, everyone now shares their positive ideas. After each person has shared his three positive ideas, the group will now vote for the best three ideas. One by one, each person reads his three positive ideas aloud again. After each idea, the people who think it is the best of all the participant's ideas raise their hands. The three ideas with the most votes win and you write these three ideas on the whiteboard. Make sure to keep space for another sentence below each idea.

Now, the next part of the brainstorming session begins. You instruct the group to form groups of three. Each trio takes one of the books. One member of the trio opens the book to a random page. Another member of the trio will say two random numbers. The numbers should be between one and fifteen. The first number represents the number of the sentence on the page, and the second number represents the location of the word in the sentence. For example, when someone says the numbers five and twelve, they are selecting the twelfth word of the fifth sentence on that page. If that word happens to be an article such as "a" or "the", or another word that doesn't mean anything by itself, the first word after that word will be picked. Using that word, the trio will now think of a way to put the first idea on the whiteboard into practice. For example, if the word they find is "bag", they come up with a suggestion to put the first positive idea on the whiteboard into practice by using the word bag. For example, "During the open house for our school, we can distribute bags with goodies in them. In addition to those goodies, we can add application forms so people can apply to our dance school." Each trio follows the same procedure for the second and third positive ideas. When this is done, the groups come together and each trio shares their three suggestions for the ideas on the whiteboard. After each trio has shared their suggestions, the group will now vote for the best suggestion. One by one, each trio shares their suggestions for the first idea again. For each suggestion, the others raise their hands if they think that is the best suggestion. The suggestion with the most votes wins and you write that suggestion on the whiteboard below the idea. They will do the same for the second and the third suggestions. When this is done, there will be three positive ideas on the whiteboard with below each idea the best suggestion to make it happen.

Variations

1. In the first round, you can also let each person read their negative idea aloud before they read their corresponding opposite idea. This can cause amusement and a lot of laughter within the group. Of course, the participants only vote for the positive ideas.

2. You can tell the group before the exercise starts that it is impossible to do things wrong. Tell them that every idea or suggestion someone creates is perfect. This will allow the team to freely brainstorm without judging themselves or being afraid of being judged by others.

3. It is possible that during the vote round there are multiple ideas, or in the second part of the exercise suggestions, that have the same amount of votes. In this case, you can take the ideas or suggestions that have the same amount of votes and let the group vote again. You can practise this voting procedure as long as there are three ideas or suggestions that have received the most votes.

4. Instead of bringing books to the exercise, you can bring magazines or newspapers. These will work just as well for the second round. You can also tell the team to open random news articles on their phones or laptops to find words to use for the solutions. By doing this, you don't have to carry books with you.

5. At the end of the exercise, let people take a picture of the whiteboard with their phones. This will allow them to review their three ideas and three suggestions whenever they want.

Why you should use this exercise

This is a great exercise when a group wants to devise new and creative ideas for a common goal.
The first part of the exercise is counterintuitive, because the team generates ideas that will result in the opposite of what they want to achieve. This forces the brain to take a different route while forming thoughts and ideas. They won't be afraid of writing down something wrong because everything they write down is intentionally wrong. Therefore, there won't be any fear of failure, which is great when you do a brainstorming session. When they write the exact opposite on the other side of the line, surprisingly good ideas will form easily.
The free association with the book pushes the team to think outside of the box. At first glance, it might seem impossible to make a connection between a word and a suggestion. However, after a bit of brainstorming, something unexpected always arises. During this exercise, every group can experience the ease in which new ideas can be created.

Scan this QR code to see an animated example video of this exercise:

You can also type: **team exercise 44 brainstorming** into YouTube's search bar to find the video.

Team Exercise 45 - The empty chair

"In walking, the will and the muscles are so accustomed to working together and performing their task with so little expenditure of force that the intellect is left comparatively free. "
- Oliver Wendell Holmes

Necessities: Chairs equal to the number of participants.

To start the exercise, you tell everyone in the group to grab his chair. Instruct them to occupy the whole room by spreading out. Each person sits on his chair. Tell the group that this is a silent exercise and no one is allowed to talk. You now select one participant who will stand up and walk to a point in the room as far away from his chair as possible. Tell the team that this person is going to reclaim his seat by walking at a normal pace back to his original chair. His goal is to sit down again in the empty chair. The goal of the other participants is to prevent the walker from sitting down. The moment the walker will start walking to the empty chair, another participant will leave his own chair, walk quickly to the empty chair that the walker is heading to, and sit on it before the walker gets the chance. The group is not allowed to discuss who this person will be; they will have to sense that.
After you have given the group these instructions, you now tell the walker to start walking.
The moment the walker starts walking towards his chair, one person stands up and walks as quickly as possible to the empty chair before the walker gets there. The moment someone rises from his current seat to go towards the empty chair to prevent the walker from being there first, he is not allowed to reseat himself in his

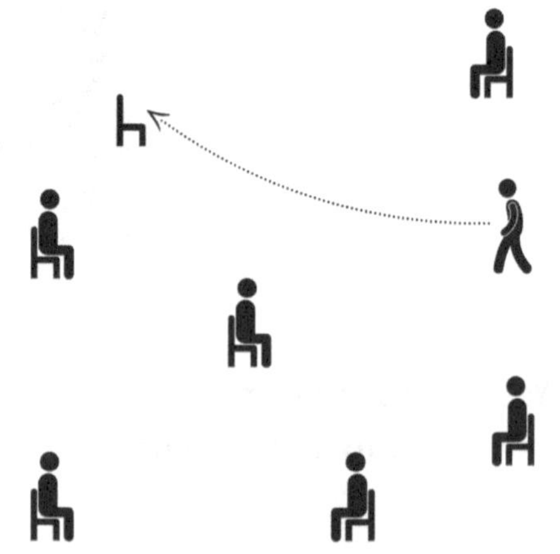

vacated chair. The moment this person stands up there are two empty chairs. The walker can now choose which chair he will walk to trying to sit down. The person who just got up can not go back to his own chair. So if the walker decides to walk to the chair of the person that just got up, a new participant will have to stand up and protect this new empty chair by trying to sit on it before the walker does.
It might be the case that more than one participant will stand up and try to protect the empty chair. In this case, the walker has three or more empty chairs to choose from. He can walk to the closest chair or to the chair that he thinks is the easiest to capture. In this case, one of the people who got up will walk towards the empty chair that the walker is moving towards. The other(s) can claim a chair they didn't just left.

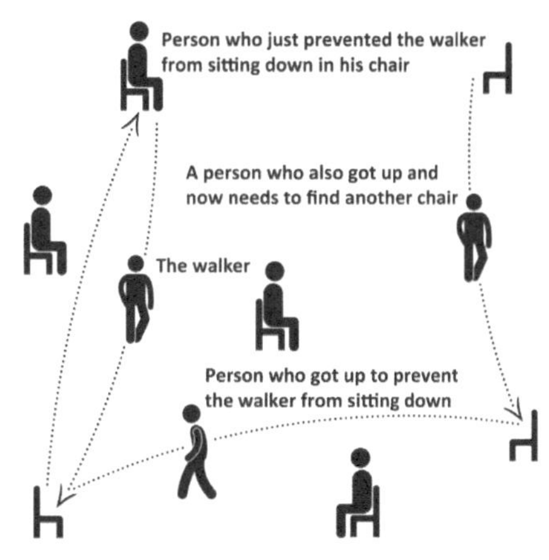

Because verbal communication is not allowed, the people who got up at the same time have to intuitively decide who moves towards the empty chair that the walking participant is approaching and who takes another chair.
If finally the walker succeeds and sits in an empty chair, the participant who has left that chair last will now be the new walker. The others all go back to sit on a chair, so there will be one empty chair left.
The new walker walks to a point in the room as far away from the new empty chair as possible. He then starts walking towards his chair trying to sit down. The same procedure is followed as the other participants try to prevent the walker from sitting.
Continue playing this game until everyone has been the walker once.

Variations

1. If the group masters the exercise, you can allow the walker to accelerate the pace. This will make the exercise more exciting. The walker and the person who tries to prevent him from sitting down, will now run as quickly as possible towards the empty chair. Of course, make sure the exercise remains safe by alerting the participants to be aware of their surroundings when running to a chair.

2. If you play variation one, tell them that the one who touches the empty chair first can sit down on it. This makes it safer because they won't try to sit down at the same time.

3. You can turn the exercise into a game. You time how long it takes a walker to sit in a chair. The walker who succeeds the fastest wins the game.

4. You can play some music during the exercise. This will spice up the exercise. Playing music will also help the group react impulsively because they will think less.

5. You can record this exercise with a camera or your phone. This is especially fun to do when you play music during the exercise. It will look like an interesting geographic dance and will be fun to watch back as a group.

6. If you have a big group you can start the game with two walkers. This means you start with two empty chairs. At the same time the two walkers start walking to one of the empty chairs. Each walker can walk to either of the chairs. In the same way the others try to prevent the walkers from sitting down. The round is over if both walkers succeeded to sit down on a chair.

Why you should use this exercise

This is a great exercise to do as a physical warm up or energizer. During the exercise, the group is working together to prevent the walker from sitting on the empty chair. To do this, the participants have to use their senses without talking to determine who will stand up when. This will improve the sensitivity of the group. The participants will have to intuitively make quick decisions as a group. This will stimulate the group's focus and decisiveness. The participants will move a lot during the exercise. Therefore an active energy will occur in the group. When you play this exercise at the beginning of the day, the group will be warmed up fast. Because it is exciting to see how long the group can prevent a walker from sitting down, the participants will experience the exercise as a game and will have a lot of fun.

Scan this QR code to see an animated example video of this exercise:

You can also type: **team exercise 45 the empty chair** into YouTube's search bar to find the video.

Team Exercise 46 - The drawing

"I sometimes think there is nothing so delightful as drawing."
- Vincent van Gogh

Necessities: One big rectangular shaped white paper, a pencil and eraser, and drawing materials such as crayons or markers.

In this exercise, the participants sit next to each other on one side of a long table. You lay a big white paper or a canvas that is suitable for drawing or painting on the table. Let the paper fill the part of the table at which the participants are sitting. A rectangular piece of paper will probably work best. You now ask the participants to choose a topic or theme that has been the most relevant recently concerning their communication. For example, a group can say that a relevant theme is that they can use more positivity in their communication. If so, this will be the theme of the drawing they are going to make together. You will now draw four evenly wide lines with the pencil vertically on the part of the paper that is in front of each participant; so for each person three strips will be formed. Make sure the widths of the strips you make are all the same size. Also, make sure that all three strips are accessible to the person who is sitting in front of them to draw on. Everyone sitting in front of the paper now draws something in his first empty strip that he associates with positivity. This can be something concrete or abstract. Encourage the group to use their imagination, and tell them that there are no "incorrect" drawings. Give them about five minutes to draw something. When everyone is done drawing in his first strip, you tell them that everyone now moves one seat to the right. The person sitting on the far right moves to the seat on the far left. Now, everyone sits behind two new empty

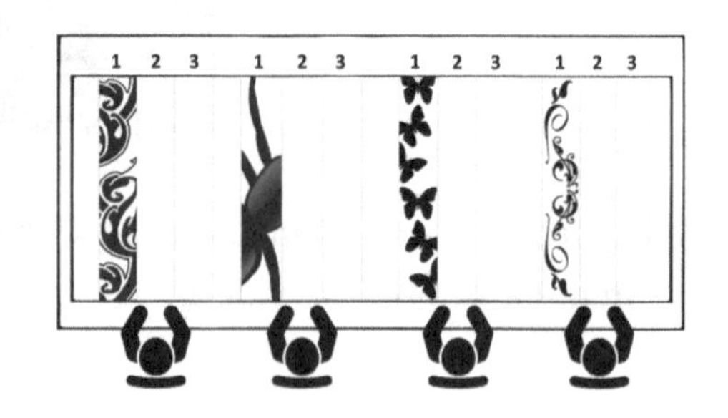

strips that he can draw on. Each person now draws something new in the second strip that connects to the drawing in the first strip made by the previous person. They draw whatever they want as long as it connects to the first strip. If there is an abstract image in the first strip, the drawing doesn't have to stay abstract; it can blend into a concrete drawing and vise versa. After about five minutes, when everyone is done drawing in his second strip, you tell them that everyone will now move one seat to the right again. Again the far right person moves to the far left seat.

Each person is now sitting behind three strips of which two are already painted. He now makes a drawing in the third strip connecting to the second strip that was made by the previous person. Now, all three strips are full of drawings. To finish the whole drawing, you tell the participants to move one seat to the right again. The person sitting on the far right goes to the far left seat again. Tell them to create a drawing in the empty space between the third strip in front of them and the first stripe on its right side. The participant who is now sitting on the far right will not be drawing this round. When the drawing is complete, everyone will write their names in the remaining empty space on the left side of the paper. Now, ask each person what he personally sees in the complete picture and how it relates to the positivity theme. Let everyone share and explain their thoughts. Each person now writes his interpretation in one sentence in the remaining empty space on the right side of the paper. If you still see any lines between the drawings, you can remove them with the eraser. Now, the drawing is finished and can be displayed in their workplace as a reminder to keep communicating and interacting in a positive manner.

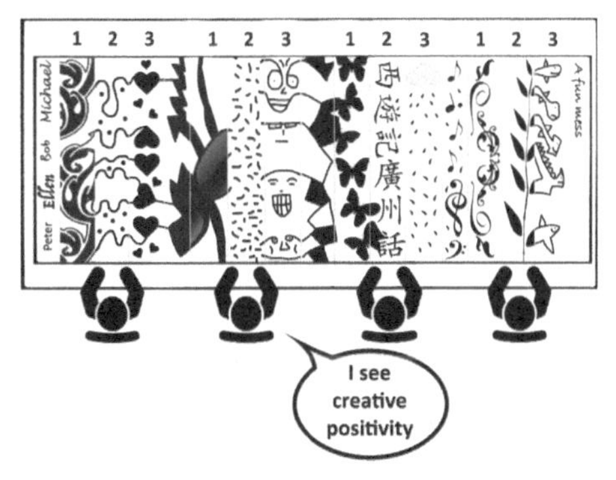

Variations

1. When you are working with a big group, you can split the team into two groups. In this way, they can contribute to the drawing from both sides of the table. In this case, you draw one horizontal line towards all the vertical lines. Each side of the table will now have their own strips. Make sure that the people sitting opposite each other now also connect the top of their drawing in their strip to the bottom of the drawing in the strip of the person opposite them. Of course, some things will be upside down. When the drawing is finished you can decide which side will be the top and which side will be the bottom.

2. If the team can't unanimously agree on a suitable theme for the drawing, you can play a vote round. Let each person suggest a theme regarding communication and let everyone raise their hands who think it is a good theme to use for the painting. The theme with the most votes will be the theme for the drawing.

3. In addition to putting the drawing up in their workplace, you can also take a photo of the drawing and send it to each participant. In this way, everyone has his own copy of the drawing. Suggest that they all put it as their background on their computer screen.

4. You can let the group work with a variety of materials. In addition to crayons, you can also let them use markers or paint. The rest of the exercise will be played in the same way.

5. You can also let them make a collage. Give them scissors and glue and let them cut out images or shapes from magazines to paste onto the paper.

Why you should use this exercise

In this exercise, the team will collaborate in a creative way by collectively making a drawing. This will help the group work together as a team and have fun at the same time.
Because each person contribute to the drawing, each person's creativity will be stimulated. Working on the same artistic endeavor will enhance their spirit of cooperation.
In a lighthearted way, this work of art will provide the team with a representation of their theme. At the end of the exercise, each person will share what he sees in the drawing and how they think that relates to the common theme. It will be interesting to hear everyone's different views of the painting.
Putting the finished piece on a wall in the workplace, will remind them of the time that they made the painting together. This pleasant memory will reinforce that spirit of cooperation.

Scan this QR code to see an animated example video of this exercise:

You can also type: **team exercise 46 the drawing** into YouTube's search bar to find the video.

Team Exercise 47 - Team constellations

"Don't wait for the stars to align, reach up and rearrange them the way you want...create your own constellation" - **Pharrell Williams**

Necessities: None

This exercise works best with a group of people who already know each other. To begin the exercise, you tell the participants to sit on one side of the room. You select one participant from the group to start the exercise. Tell him he is going to place everyone in the room on a spot that makes sense based on his intuition. He starts by putting himself somewhere in the room. Tell him he is not literally going to place himself into the room, but that he will use you to represent him. This means that you will be the surrogate for the constellation creator. For example, he can place you in the center of the room because he feels that he belongs in the heart of the organization. After he has placed you somewhere in the room to represents him, he now explains to the other participants why he put "himself" in that particular spot. Tell him that explaining aloud why he chose that particular spot is optional; he doesn't have to tell it if he doesn't want to. After he has placed you somewhere in the room to represent him, he now chooses a random participant and puts him somewhere in the room relative to you (his surrogate). This person doesn't represent anyone else, but is just himself. Tell the constellation creator that he can take his time to intuitively feel where he wants this person to put in the room. For example, if he is very close to that person, he will place that person next to you (his surrogate). Alternatively, if he feels emotionally distant from that person, he can place that person far

away from you (his surrogate). Again, if he wants to, he can elaborate on why he put that person in that particular spot. When he feels that he has put that person into the correct place, he chooses another participant and follows the same procedure. After he has placed each person from the group in a spot somewhere in the room, he switches places with you. Now, he is standing in his own spot. Let him silently stand there for a while to observe how that feels. When he is ready, he shares how he feels standing there. For example, he might say, "I feel strong in the center, but I also feel that I don't have a good overview of what's happening behind my back." After he has elaborated on how he feels, you tell the others they can also share how they feel standing in that particular spot. For example, someone might say, "I like having an overview standing in the corner, but I also feel a bit alone." After each person has shared his feelings, you will switch places with the constellation creator and you will be his surrogate again. You now tell him that he may place everyone in the room in a way that would represent his ideal situation. One by one, he tells each person standing in the room to which spot he should move. When everyone is standing in their new spot, you switch places with him again. He will stand in his own spot for a moment before telling the group how this new constellation makes him feel. Again, he is free to remain silent if he is more comfortable keeping his feelings to himself. When he is done sharing his feelings, the other participants also share how these new spots feel compared with the previous spots. After everyone has shared their experiences, they all may sit down. Now, it is another participant's turn to create a constellation. You point to a new random person who will follow the same procedure. Continue the exercise until everyone has had a turn to create a constellation and adjust it to his ideal standard.

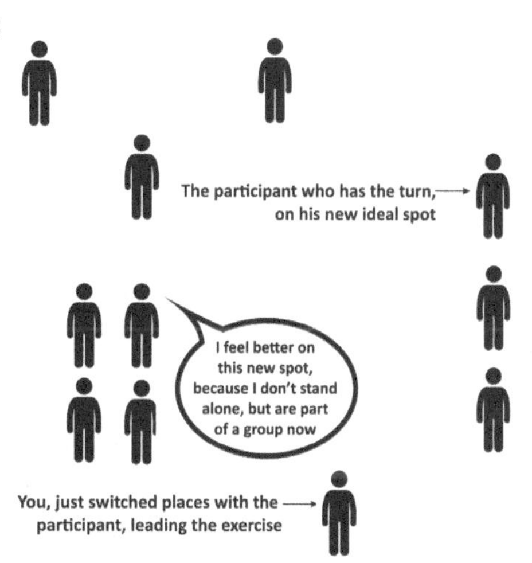

Variations

1. You can tell the group that in addition to putting people in a standing position somewhere in the room, they can also put people in other positions. For example, sitting on the ground or leaning against a wall. This removes limitations. Of course, the constellation maker will explain why he chose to put someone in a certain position.

2. After the constellation creator has placed everyone in his ideal position, and everyone has shared how he feels in this new spot, you can ask them how this constellation and these new positive feelings could be transferred to a real world situation.
The constellation creator and the other participants can individually generate ideas. If someone doesn't have an idea, you can ask him questions. For example, someone was first standing alone. After the changes, he is standing close to the group, which, according to him, made him feel better. A good question to ask would be, "What is a specific action that you could perform in real life to become closer to the group?"

3. You can also do this exercise with actors. Now, the constellation creator doesn't place his colleagues around the room. Instead, he uses the actors to represent himself and the others. The actors are now the surrogates for the constellation creator and the other participants. In this way, all the participants can observe from the sidelines where they are being put in the room. They can clearly see from a distance how the constellation creator is perceiving them. In this case, it is very interesting to ask the actors how they each feel about their positions. Everyone will be stunned by how much the person that the actor represents will recognize in the feelings shared by the actors.

Why you should use this exercise

During this exercise, the team gets a vivid image of how the constellation maker sees himself and others relative to the rest of the group. Because the exercise is based on intuitive feelings, each person gets an honest and clear view of everyone's perception of the team.
The exercise will be revealing to people who never realized why they felt a particular way in the group. The participants will gain insight into where these feelings might come from.
The participants will also gain insight into how they would like to see the positions in the group in a different way and how that would make them feel. This revelation can be the beginning of a positive change in the group's chemistry.

Scan this QR code to see an animated example video of this exercise:

You can also type: **team exercise 47 team constellations** into YouTube's search bar to find the video.

Team Exercise 48 - Decision making

"The elegance under pressure is the result of fearlessness."

- Ashish Patel

Necessities: Fifteen pieces of paper or cards, with on each of them one of the objects described in the exercise.

To start the exercise, the team sits in a circle. You tell the participants that you are going to tell them a fictional story. Tell them they were all going on a vacation together to Hawaii, and that unfortunately their airplane crashed on an uninhabited island. The airplane is in flames and will explode within ten minutes. Tell them that there are fifteen objects in the airplane, but they can only remove three of them before the airplane explodes. Before the exercise, you wrote the names of the objects on pieces of paper. The following objects are written on the pieces of paper: a box of matches, a crate of beer, a crate of twelve bottles of water, five warm sweaters, a first aid kit, a transistor radio, an ax, a gun with twenty bullets, a bag with twenty-five magazines, an inflatable lifeboat for four people, a compass, insecticide spray, a sewing kit, a flashlight, and a bag with five big blankets. You now put all fifteen papers face up in the center of the circle. Tell the group that they now have to unanimously decide which three objects they will remove from the airplane before it explodes. Tell them that if they don't make a unanimous decision within ten minutes, the airplane will explode and they will have nothing at all. The team has to unanimously choose which three objects should be removed from the airplane. During the discussion, each person tries to convince the others why a certain object must be removed from the airplane.

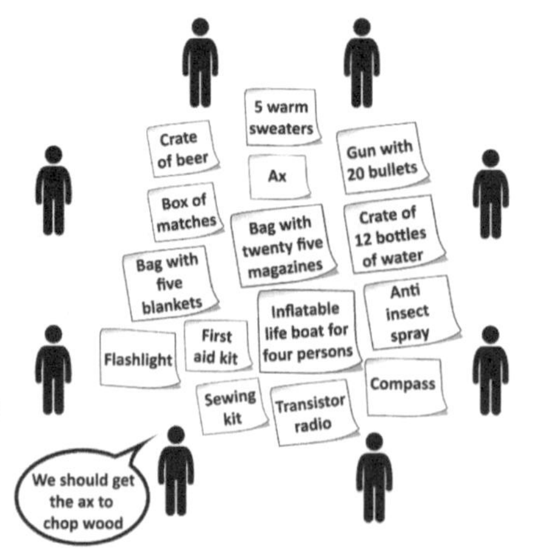

After the team makes a unanimous decision, you tell them that the three objects they chose were good choices.
You continue the story by telling them that they have been living on the island now for a few weeks. Luckily, they are spotted by a pilot flying over the island. The pilot lands with his airplane on the island and takes all the participants with him to bring them home.
However, when the participants are in the airplane and flying home, they discover that the airplane is almost out of kerosene. Other than the pilot, only one other person can stay on the airplane. If they all stay, no one will survive. That means that four people have to sacrifice themselves by jumping out of the airplane. Tell the participants that they now have to unanimously decide which person can stay in the airplane. Again, they have to make a decision within ten minutes; otherwise, the airplane will crash.
Tell them that each person can plead for himself or for someone else to be the survivor. During the discussion, each person tries to convince the others why a particular person deserves to survive. You will increase the pressure by keeping track of the time and announcing each minute how many minutes they have left until a unanimous decision has to be made.

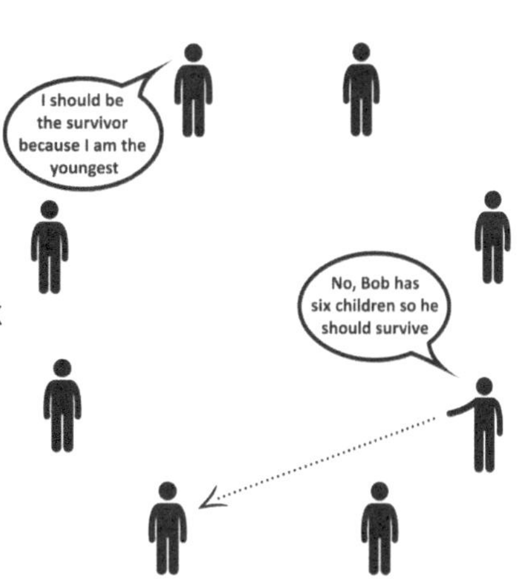

When the team has made a unanimous decision and has told you who will survive, you tell them that the pilot has discovered another can of kerosene in the airplane. Therefore, everyone can stay and will be home safely.
Now the group will evaluate their performance. Ask them the following questions to encourage the evaluation: Was it easy to come to a unanimous decision together? What worked and what didn't work? Who took the lead, and who preferred to be led? How can you quickly make a decision without losing the quality of the decision?

Variations

1. When you have a very big group, you can split it up into smaller groups. Each group performs the same exercise at the same time. You tell the stories aloud so all the small groups can hear you. After the exercise has finished, you can mingle the groups and do the same exercise again. The stories can be the same. Because the groups have different compositions, the exercise will feel new again for everyone. In this way, everyone can experience how different making a discussion can be with different people.

2. You can vary the time limits. For example, you can change the ten-minute time limit into a five-minute time limit. You can make it very difficult by giving them only a one-minute time limit. You can set a different time limit for each part of the exercise. For example, the object part has a ten minute time limit and the airplane part has a one minute time limit.

3. After the fictional exercise has been played, you can do the exercise again using a real life situation. Because they are already warmed up, real life, unanimous decisions will now be easier to make. First, you let the group unanimously decide on a topic about which they think they need to make a decision. Give them one minute to decide on a topic. An example might be, "What kind of team event are we going to organize?"
Now, they will have to make a unanimous decision. Tell them that they have a ten-minute time limit and if they don't meet it, there will be consequences. This will help motivate them. Give them a fun consequence. For example, if they can't produce a unanimous decision within ten minutes, they have to watch a bad movie three times in a row for a team day event.

Why you should use this exercise

In this exercise, the group will improve their decision making skills by making choices within time constraints. Because they have to come to a unanimous decision, they will all feel the responsibility as a group to constructively discuss all the options.
Of course, the participants know it is just a fictional story and not a real situation. However, the process of making unanimous decisions stays the same and will have a positive effect on their decision-making processes in general. It will will help the group generate decisions in real life without obsessing about the pros and cons of certain situations. These skills will be beneficial in situations in which a decision must be made quickly.
Because this story is fictional, it is also a very enjoyable exercise. The team will experience a serious decision making exercise and a fun game at the same time.

Scan this QR code to see an animated example video of this exercise:

You can also type: **team exercise 48 decision making** into YouTube's search bar to find the video.

Team Exercise 49 - Transferring

“Communication works for those who work at it.” **- John Powell**

Necessities: None

To start the exercise, you tell the participants to divide themselves into two lines facing each other. Tell them which is line A and which is line B. Tell them that all the people in line A are going to call out a color to the person directly in front of them in line B. The only colors they can choose are red, white, and blue. Using a normal volume, all the people in line A call out a color. Each person from line B listens carefully to the color that the person in line A is saying to him. Because all the duos are performing the exercise and are talking at the same time, the people in line B have to pay close attention so as not to be distracted by the noise around them. Now, all the people from line B respond by repeating the color aloud that was sent to them by the person in line A. Now, the roles switch and it is person B’s turn to call out a color to the person A in front of him. Person A then repeats the color aloud.

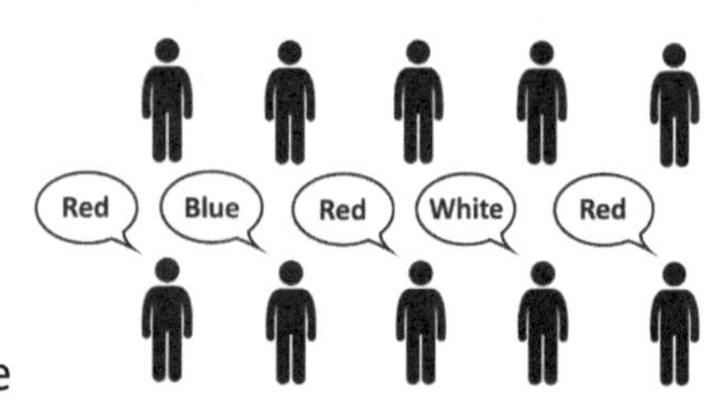

After they have called out colors back and forth for a minute, both lines will take a step backward. They will repeat the procedure without changing their volumes. Again, each person focuses on the person in front of him and tries to ignore the noise around him. Continue in this manner for a minute.

Now, you tell them that they don’t have to stick to the colors red, white, or blue; they can call out any color they want. Tell them they still have to talk at the same volume as in the first round. In the same way as before, they call out the random colors back and forth for a minute. Due to the variety of colors, it will be more difficult for the listener to hear what the person in front of him is saying. After this goes well for

a minute, you instruct everyone to take three big steps backwards. By doing this, the game will be played at an even greater distance. However, in addition to verbally communicating the color, they can also use other ways to communicate. Give them a few examples to clarify what you mean. For example, tell them they can articulate excessively so the listener can read the lips of the person saying the color. They can also illustrate the word. For example, they can look sad when they say blue, or look angry when they say red. Now, person A communicates the color to person B, and person B returns the communication to person A. When they both think they have the same color in mind, they switch roles. Let them continue for one minute.
Now, you tell the participants to name an animal instead of a color to the person in front of them in the same manner. After person A has communicated the animal name to person B, person B repeats the animal name. They keep repeating the name until they both think they have the same animal in mind. For one minute, have them communicate animal names back and forth. In the last part of the exercise, person A and person B are going to stand as far away from each other as possible while still being able to see each other. Using the same volumes, they will now communicate a random word. It can be anything. Because the listener doesn't know the word category, it will be even more difficult to communicate. There will be a good chance that they will have to illustrate the word with body language. Person A communicates the word, and person B returns the communication until they both think they have the same word in mind. After a minute, you tell everyone to walk towards each other and check if the words actually were the same. Instruct them to also discuss what went well and what communication issues they discovered during the exercise.

Variations

1. You can tell the participants that they can speak as loudly as they like. They will discover that talking louder doesn't necessarily guarantee clearer communication. Since everyone is talking louder, the noise level will increase, and no one will be able to hear each other anymore. They will discover that in this case talking very loudly doesn't help people hear you better.

2. During the last part, you can make it a bit easier by giving them a theme for the random words, for example, "countries".

3. If there is a duo that finds it very difficult to communicate words, tell them they can form letters with their hands to illustrate the letters of the words.

4. During the last round, you can challenge them to communicate random sentences to each other. In this way, the exercise becomes more challenging.

5. You can play a bonus round in which everyone forms new duos. Let the new duos start with the last round of the exercise. They will stand as far away from each other as possible while communicating random words. They will experience that communication will be more difficult with a new partner. Because they were not with this person in the beginning, they have to become accustomed to him. After trying to perform this last round for one minute, tell them to do the exercise with their new partner from the beginning while following the original instructions. They will see that when they get to the last round again it will now be easier to communicate.

Why you should use this exercise

During the exercise, the team will experience in a playful way the basics of communication. There will be a sender, a receiver, and noise. Just as in real life, those three elements together form communication. Everyone talking at the same time makes this exercise challenging. The group will experience how both sender and receiver experience can miscommunication and how that can be resolved.
Gradually, everyone will stand farther away from each other. Because the noise will become louder than the sound of the person's voice someone has to listen to, communication will be more difficult to maintain. The participants will now experience how important nonverbal communication is to maintaining clear communication when there is noise.
You will see that if they have to illustrate a word, they will easily go outside their comfort zone. They won't care how they look while illustrating the word. At that moment, it will be more important to them to be clear about the word.
In a fun and lighthearted way, people will be amused when they share the word that they both had in mind to find out if is the same word.

Scan this QR code to see an animated example video of this exercise:

You can also type: **team exercise 49 transferring** into YouTube's search bar to find the video.

Team Exercise 50 - Yes, maybe, no

"Not making a decision means forgoing an opportunity." **- Auliq Ice**

Necessities: Tape to divide the room, a whiteboard, and pens and pieces of paper equal to the number of participants.

To start the exercise, you ask the participants what improvements they would like to achieve within the group. When they unanimously agree on an improvement, you give each person a piece of paper and a pen. Tell them to write down three ideas on how to achieve the improvement. After everyone has written three ideas, you collect all the papers. Using tape, you divide the room into three sections - a "yes" section, a "maybe" section, and a "no" section. You tell the team to stand up and you read all the ideas one by one. After you read an idea, each person who agrees with the idea will stand in the "yes" section. Each person who doesn't agree with the idea will stand in the "no" section. Each person who has doubts about the idea will stand in the "maybe" section. After the participants have chosen their sections, you tell the people standing in the "maybe" section that eventually they will have to move to a "'yes" or "no" section. The people in the "yes" and "no" sections will now try to convince the people standing in the "maybe" section to go into their section. They do this by devising arguments to convince the participants. The people in the "yes" section will create arguments as to why the idea is very good. The people in the "no" section will create arguments as to why the idea is terrible. You start the battle by asking a participant in the "yes" section to present an argument to the people in the "maybe" section.

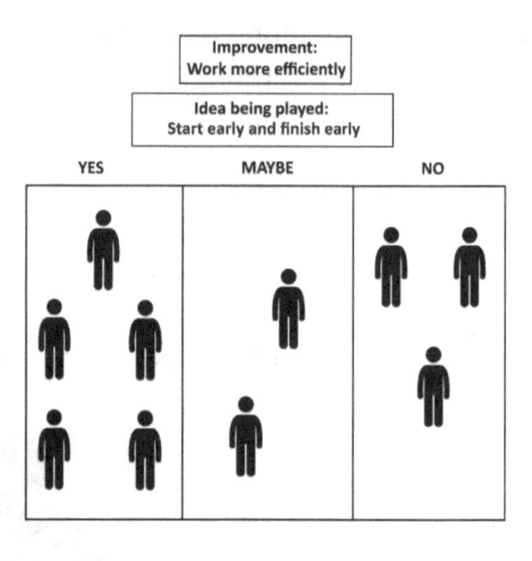

When he is done presenting the argument, you ask a participant from the "no" section to present an argument. After both sections have presented their arguments, the people in the "maybe" section can now choose a side. It might be possible that not all persons in the maybe section were convinced by the arguments to walk over to the "yes" or "no" section. If there are still people standing in the "maybe" section, they still have to decide which side to choose. The people in the other two sections are now free to call out arguments whenever they want. Tell them not to talk at the same time, so the participants in the "maybe" section can still hear and understand the arguments. Tell the participants standing in the "maybe" section that they all need to make a choice within two minutes. This time limit will cause the participants in the "yes" and "no" sections to be more enthusiastic in their attempts at persuasion. Within two minutes, all the participants will now be in either the "yes" or "no" section. You now count the number of participants in the "yes" section and the number of participants in the "no" section. When there are more participants in the "yes" section than in the "no" section, you write the idea they were playing on the whiteboard. Next to the idea, you write the number of people standing in the "yes" section. You tell the participants to leave the sections.

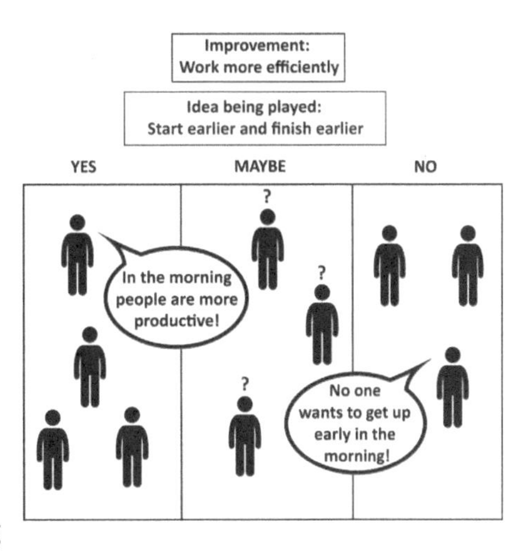

Now the next idea will be played following the same procedure. Continue playing this game until you have used every idea written on the pieces of paper. When the exercise has been completed, the number of ideas on the whiteboard will be three times the number of participants. They can now see all the ideas with the number of votes next to them. The idea with the most votes can be used to achieve the improvement that the group suggested at the beginning of the exercise.

Variations

1. It is possible that there might be a tie for the highest number of votes; no one idea has the most votes. If that is the case, in the same way they will vote to see which idea wins. You ask the participants, "Out of the ideas with the same highest votes, do you want idea number one to be the final winner?" Again, each person will stand in the "yes", "maybe", or "no" section. Again, the people in the "yes" and "no" sections will try to convince the people in the "maybe" section to come to their section. You do the same for the other ideas that have the same highest number. In the end, the idea for which the most people were standing in the "yes" section has the most points and wins and will be used to achieve the improvement.

2. In addition to doing the exercise with themes relevant to the team's improvement, you can also use this exercise to practice making quick decisions regarding other sorts of single questions. For example, "Do you want the company to introduce a bonus system?" The exercise will be played in the same way.

3. After luring the people from the "maybe" section into the "yes" or "no" section, there might be an equal number of people in the "yes" and "no" sections. Tell the team that there must be a different number of people in the "yes" and "no" sections. Now, the people in the "yes" and "no" sections can try to lure people over to their sides. When it is the case that there is a majority of people standing in the "yes" section, the idea will be written down on the whiteboard. If no one moves and there will still be the same amount of people in each section, the idea won't be written down on the whiteboard.

Why you should use this exercise

For each idea written by the participants, the team will playfully discover who agrees with the idea, who disagrees with the idea and who questions the idea. Standing in different sections will provide a clear visual representation of everyone's feelings concerning a particular idea.
For people who are reserved, the exercise can be very helpful. It can be less intimidating for them to walk to a "yes", "maybe" or "no" section, than to share their opinions aloud.
It is also a great exercise for outspoken people. They can try to fervently convince the participants standing in the "maybe" section to come the section they are standing in.
During the battle to convince the people in the "maybe" section a fun atmosphere will be created. This will be good for team spirit.
At the end of the exercise, everyone sees the democratically chosen most popular idea on the white board. The group now knows exactly what to do to achieve the desired improvement.

Scan this QR code to see an animated example video of this exercise:

You can also type: **team exercise 50 yes, maybe, no** into YouTube's search bar to find the video.

Team Exercise 51 - The wishing well

"Know what it is that drives you - motivates you - and pursue it. Endeavor to work to make it happen."
- Peggy Whitson

Necessities: None.

During the exercise, the participants will stand in a circle. To start the exercise you tell them they are standing around a wishing well. Since there is no real wishing well, you tell the team they have to imagine they are standing around one. You tell the group that you will point to a person who will call aloud into the wishing well what he wishes to improve regarding the team. Every person who agrees with the improvement will repeat the statement like an echo.
Give each person a minute to think about what he wants to improve within the team. You now point to a random person who will bow his head towards the wishing well and loudly announce what he would like to improve within the team. After he has announced his wish, everyone who agrees with the improvement repeats it. In this way, it will sound like an echo returning from the wishing well. Tell them the person who shared the wish doesn't repeat his own wish. If many people have the same wish and agree with the improvement they just heard, there will be a loud echo returning from the wishing well. If fewer people have the same wish, the echo will not be very loud because not that many people in the circle will repeat the wish. It is possible that no one from the circle agrees. In this case, no echo will come out of the wishing well at all.

After the first person has called out his wish into the well, the person standing on his left side now calls out his wish for a team improvement. In the same way he announces his wish into the well. Again, each person who agrees with the wish repeats the wish aloud so an echo returns from the well. Go clockwise around the circle until each person has announced his wish into the well and learned based on the echo to what extent the others agree. The wish that produces the loudest echo is the winner and will be used to play the next round.

In the second round, you tell the group to suggest ideas on how the winning wish from the first round can be achieved. First, let the group think for a minute about an idea to achieve the improvement. You now point to the first person who announces his idea into the wishing well. As in the first round, everyone who thinks it is a good idea repeats the idea like an echo returning from the wishing well. If many people think it is a good idea, a loud echo will return from the well. If few people think it is a good idea, a softer echo will return from the well.

After the first person has announced his idea into the well, the person standing on his left side will announce his idea into the wishing well. Again, the participants who think it is a good idea will repeat the idea like an echo. Continue until everyone has called his idea into the wishing well.

The idea with the strongest echo is the winner and can be carried out to let the wish with the loudest echo come true.

Variations

1. After all the wishes or ideas have been stated, you might recall a few echoes with the same volume. It may not be clear which one had the loudest echo. In this case, you can play the loudest ones again, and ask the people who repeat the echo to also raise their hands. In this way, it will be clear how many people are repeating the wish or idea and which one got the most support.

2. After a wish or idea has been announced, you can write it on a whiteboard and give the volume of the echo a grade. In this way, it is easy to see which wish or idea earned the highest grade and had the loudest echo.

3. You can do this exercise at the beginning of the day and ask what everyone wants to achieve during the day. Each person calls out his achievement aloud in the wishing well. The people who want to achieve the same thing repeat the achievement. In this way, you know what the team thinks is important during the day.

4. Instead of calling out a wish for an improvement, you can also play the exercise with other types of questions. First ask the group what question they would like answered. After they unanimously come up with a question, for example, "What kind of present shall we buy for our manager?", you play the idea round. In this case, one by one each person calls out a present into the wishing well. In the same way, the people that agree with the present repeat it as if it is an echo returning from the well. The present with the loudest echo wins and the group will buy it for the manager.

Why you should use this exercise

During this exercise everyone will learn about each others wishes, so the group will get to know each other on a deeper level. Visualizing a wishing well will unite the group and will make the exercise playful and lighthearted.
Because all the improvements and ideas will be announced loudly, all the participants will use their voices. This will ensure that all the participants will be engaged in the exercise.
Each person from the group will learn at what level the rest of the group agrees with his wish for a team improvement. In the second round, each person will learn at what level the group agrees with a certain idea to achieve an improvement. Playing this exercise is a fun way to democratically reach an idea for an improvement that most people would like to see happen. After the exercise, they knows exactly what to do to make this improvement happen.

Scan this QR code to see an animated example video of this exercise:

You can also type: **team exercise 51 the wishing well** into YouTube's search bar to find the video.

Team Exercise 52 - Counting down

"The whole is other than the sum of the parts." - **Kurt Koffka**

Necessities: A stopwatch and an empty room.

To start the exercise, you tell the participants to stand in a straight line at one side of the room. You tell them that when you say "now!" and hit your stopwatch, everyone will silently count down from ten to zero. Tell them each individual participant will take one step forward exactly at the moment he thinks ten seconds have passed.
At a random moment you say "now!" and start the stopwatch.
Everyone will step forward when he thinks ten seconds have passed.
You check the stopwatch to see exactly when ten seconds have passed.
Now, you can see which participant stepped forward the closest to ten seconds. Don't let the participants know when ten seconds have passed. If they see you stop the stopwatch at ten seconds, everyone will know ten seconds have passed and will take a step forward to be on time. So, just look at the stopwatch to see when the ten seconds have passed. You wait until everyone has stepped forward before you stop the stopwatch. You now tell the group which person stepped forward closest to the ten seconds. This person is the winner.

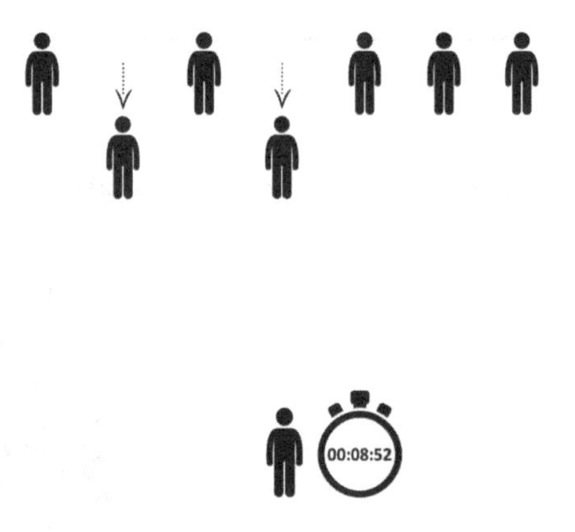

Now, you start the second round. You play the same game in the same way. Only now, the participants will step forward the moment they think twenty seconds have passed. In the same way you look at the stopwatch to see when twenty seconds have passed. Observe who made the closest estimate to how long twenty seconds lasts. This is the winner.
In the third round, you play the same game for thirty seconds. You play

it in the same way. When there is a winner, you proceed to the fourth round playing the game for forty seconds. In the fifth round, you play the game for fifty seconds, and in the sixth and final round, you play it for one minute. After you have played the one minute game, you proceed to the second part of the exercise.

Tell the team to return to the line at one side of the room. You tell the team they will now have to step forward together at the same moment. They will have to collectively sense when twenty seconds have passed. Of course, everyone has a different sense of how long twenty seconds is, but they still need to try to step forward at the same time. There is no talking allowed, so they have to step forward together based on their collective intuition.

You also tell them that a new game element will be added to this round. Tell them that when they succeeded to step forward after twenty seconds with a deviation less than a second they succeeded the round. This means that if they step forward between twenty seconds and twenty-one seconds, they will have succeeded. If they stepped forward between nineteen and twenty seconds, they will have succeeded as well. If they are under nineteen seconds or over twenty-one seconds, they will have to play the twenty second round again. You say "now!" the moment you hit the stopwatch. Observe how close they are to the twenty seconds the moment they collectively step forward. If they succeed, you proceed to the next round by increasing the number of seconds by ten seconds. Play the round in the same way. After a successful round, you increase the number by ten seconds just as long they can sense together how long one minute lasts with a deviation less than one second. When they are able to finish the one minute round, they have completed the game.

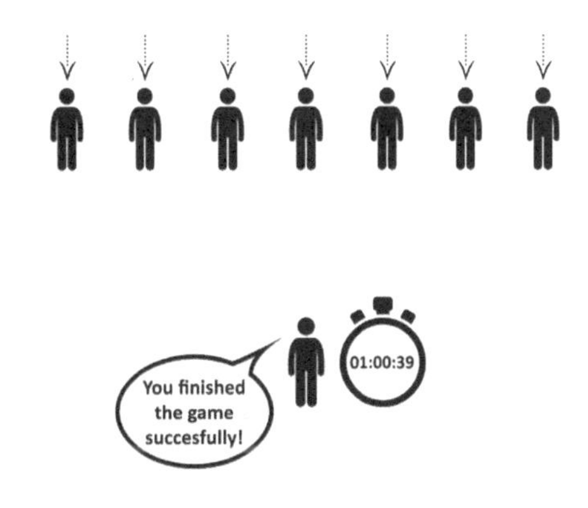

Variations

1. In addition to letting the team stay in line and take a step forward, you can also instruct the team to walk across the room. Each person stands still when he senses that the seconds being played are reached. Again, in the first part of the exercise, each individual stands still at the moment the seconds are reached. In the second part of the exercise, they all have to stand still at the same time.

2. You can play a bonus round. The team stands in a line, you say "now!", and start the stopwatch. At a random moment, they all have to step forward at the same time. After they have taken the step forward, you ask each individual how long he thinks it took before they took a step forward. Because you tracked time with the stopwatch, you know whose guess is the closest to the real time. This person is the winner.

3. When you play the second variation, you can ask the whole group how long they think it took before they stepped forward. They unanimously have to agree to a number of seconds. If they are right within a deviation of one second, they have won this bonus round.

4. If the group finds it difficult to step forward together in the second round, you can let the participants first count aloud from ten to zero. In this way, everyone can sense how long a second is. Next, they will count silently; this will now be easier since they have practiced counting aloud.

Why you should use this exercise

This is a great exercise to stimulate group feeling. In this exercise, the group will experience the difference between sensing something individually and sensing something as a group.
The first round is a fun competition to see who most accurately predicts time.
In the second part of the exercise they all have to step forward at the same. Therefore they together have to sense when the step needs to be taken. There might be more hesitation in the beginning. However, the more they practice, the better their timing and coordination will be. They will learn that it is easier to be accurate when they step forward as a whole group than when someone tries to step forward at the right moment on his own. Just like the more people sing a song together, the more on key it sounds. This group cohesiveness will enhance the team spirit; they all have the same goal in mind and will think like one group. Because of the game elements, the exercise is fun and entertaining. Therefore, you can play this exercise as a warm up or energizer.

Scan this QR code to see an animated example video of this exercise:

You can also type: **team exercise 52 counting down** into YouTube's search bar to find the video.

Team Exercise 53 - Distance

"The only healthy communication style is assertive communication."
- Jim Rohn

Necessities: None.

To start the exercise, you tell the group to split up and to stand in two straight lines facing each other. One line stands on the left side of the room, and the other line stands on the right side. Tell them which is line A and which is line B. Tell them that each person from line A now starts to walk slowly towards the person standing directly in front of him in line B. Person B stays where he is. Person A will continue walking towards person B until person B feels that person A is too close. The moment person B feels uncomfortable with the proximity of person A he tells person A not to come any closer. Person B can word this request in any way he wants. When person B says this to person A, person A immediately stops walking, stands still for a second, and walks back to where he came from.

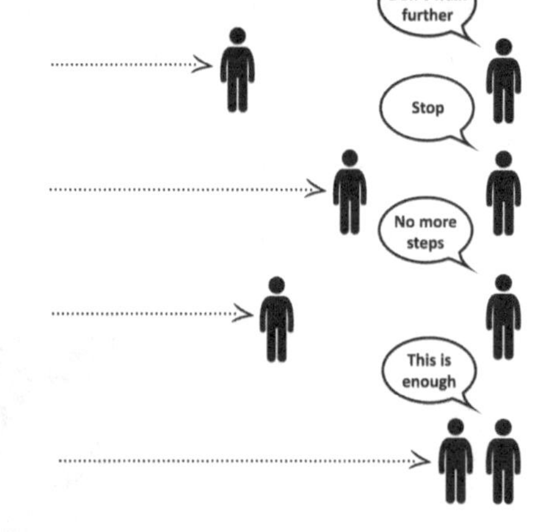

Now they switch roles. Person B now walks towards person A. Person A will tell person B when he feels uncomfortable with the proximity of person B and when he wants him to stop walking. Person B stops walking and returns to the spot he came from. Now all the people in line A shift one place to the right. The person standing in the far right spot in line A moves all the way to the far left spot. The people in line B stay where they are. Everyone now stands in front of a new person. Again, person A walks towards person B. This time person B only uses body language to let person A know that he is getting too close. For example, person B can use a hand gesture or a facial expression to let person A know that he is getting too close. At this point, person A shouldn't advance any farther. Person A stops walking and returns to the spot he came from. They switch roles and person B now walks towards person A. Person B continues walking until person A uses body language to make him aware that he is getting too close. Person B then walks back to where he came from. All the people in line A shift one spot to the right again. Now, person A and person B silently walk towards each other at the same time. They need to sense when they have reached the distance that is appropriate for both of them. They stand still for a few seconds. After a few seconds, either person A or person B walks calmly towards the other person. The other person walks backwards so the distance remains the same. At a random moment, the person walking backwards now walks forward and the other person walks backwards to maintain the same distance. All the duos keep moving back and forth on the same line for a minute while maintaining the same distance. After a minute, you tell the duos they can leave their lines to walk together through the room while remaining the same distance apart. Both people will intuitively determine the directions they walk. They do this in silence and without someone being the leader. After this has been going well for a while, the group may now switch partners while walking. The new duos will determine a new distance they both feel comfortable with. They will sense this intuitively without talking. After walking around for a while, the people who feel like it can switch partners again at a self-chosen moment. It is possible that some people change partners and others keep on walking with the same partner a bit longer.

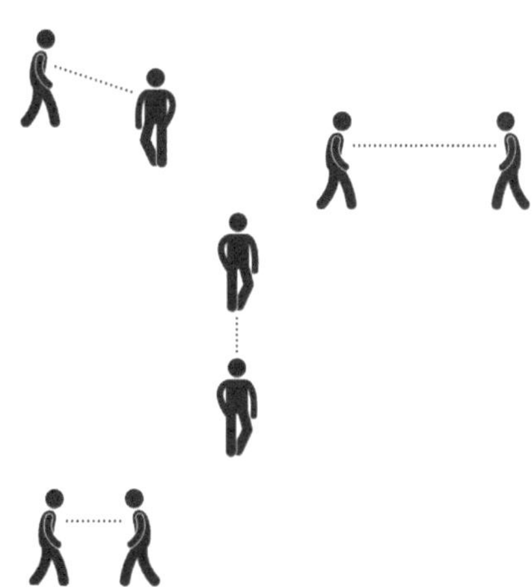

They continue doing this until everyone has switched partners a few times.

Variations

1. In the first part of the exercise, after the participants have walked towards each other and determined a comfortable distance, you can tell them to do it again. However, this time they need to do it with their eyes closed. Now, they will have to sense what distance is comfortable. Of course, they keep their hands a bit in front of them so they don't bump into each other.

2. Tell the participants to walk towards each other in two different ways. First, tell them to look into each other's eyes while walking. While doing this, they both have to determine a comfortable distance. Next, have them walk towards each other while avoiding each other's eyes. Let them experience the difference. It might be different for everyone. After they have walked towards each other in these two different ways, ask them if they feel a difference between the two variations and which time they feel they can endure a smaller distance.

3. You can do this exercise at the beginning and at the end of the day. If people bond during the day, they might feel more comfortable being in closer proximity to each other than they did in the beginning of the day. The distances between them might have gotten smaller.

4. After a few minutes of walking and changing partners, everyone stands in a circle and evaluates the exercise. Encourage the discussion by asking the following questions: Was it more powerful to let the other person know with words or with body language that he was too close? Was the distance with a different partner almost the same? Or was there a big difference?

Why you should use this exercise

During the exercise, the participants will improve their assertiveness. They will learn how to determine their personal boundaries and how to communicate that to others.
Each participant will experience how it feels if someone comes too close, and how it feels if he comes too close to someone else. They practice announcing their borders verbally by expressing themselves aloud and nonverbally by using body language. Each person will discover what works better for him.
Because they switch partners during the exercise, the participants will learn that there can be a difference in the desired distances between various people.
When people walk towards each other at the same moment, both people will feel what distance feels comfortable to both of them. This way, each person will learn how to discover a comfortable distance for himself and for the other at the same time.

Scan this QR code to see an animated example video of this exercise:

You can also type: **team exercise 53 distance** into YouTube's search bar to find the video.

Team Exercise 54 - Questioning

"Part of being successful is about asking questions and listening to the answers." - **Anne Burrell**

Necessities: None.

To start the exercise, you tell the participants to form pairs. Let them decide who is person A and who is person B. You give them a topic and tell them they are going to develop questions regarding that topic of which the think the answers will give them insights into how they see the other person. For example, a good topic might be, living as roommates in a house. They will now try to determine if they want to be roommates with their partners. Tell them that person A now asks person B one open-ended question to help him decide if he wants person B as a roommate. Explain that an open-ended question can be answered in any way. Tell them they can ask only one open-ended question. For example, "What does your favorite day look like?" Person B now answers the question. Next, they switch roles and person B asks person A one open-ended question to learn what kind of roommate person A would be. For example, "How would you describe your personality?" Person A answers the question.

In the second round, you give all the duos another topic. For example, a good topic might be, working together as business partners. Now, person A will ask person B one closed question to determine what kind of business partner person B would be. Explain that a closed question can only be answered with "yes" or "no". In this case an example of a closed question can be "Do you think money is more important than good cooperation?"

Person B now answers the question with "yes" or "no". Now person B will ask person A a closed question to determine if person A would be a good business partner. Person A answers the question.

In the third round, you tell the duos that person A now generates a topic himself. He can ask one open-ended or closed question to determine how he sees person B regarding that topic. This time person B will not know based on what topic the question is asked so he can't anticipate giving the right answer.

Explain them that an answer can have a different effect depending on what topic the question is based on. For example, person A might ask person B if he can drink a lot of alcohol. A "yes" answer could have a negative effect if person A wants to know if person B would make a good employee. However, a "yes" answer could have a positive effect if person A is looking for someone to party with.

After person B has answered the question, the roles switch. Now, person B asks person A a question regarding a self- chosen topic. Again, person A doesn't know what the topic is. After person A answers the question, they both guess what the other was trying to find out. After they both guess what the underlying topic was, they tell each other what the actual topic was.

Now you tell everyone to sit in a circle to evaluate the exercise. Ask the participants the following questions to encourage the conversation: Is it more effective to ask an open-ended question or a closed question to find out how you see someone regarding a certain topic? Did you prefer to keep your topic a secret, or did you prefer that your partner knows what the topic is? When you were answering a question did you prefer to know what the other one was trying to find out? Or did you prefer not to know his agenda to be more honest by not been able to anticipate on the topic?

Variations

1. In addition to the topics in the first round, you can also create other topics. Some good examples include the following: Who would make a good potential lover? Would you go to war with a particular person? Can you trust a particular person? Is a certain person a good manager? Is a certain person a good dog owner?

2. Let the participants switch partners after each round. This way everyone gets to know each other better and people can experience the differences between working with different partners.

3. During the third round in which the answerer doesn't know the topic, he can guess after each question what the topic is. The questioner will continue asking questions until the answerer guesses what the topic is. The faster he guesses what the topic of questioning is, the better. This will train the participants to be aware of motivations when someone asks questions. This will improve people's skills in giving the most advantageous answers. These skills are helpful during job interviews.

4. In the exercise, the participants ask only one question per topic. You can also let them ask more than one question in each round. Let the participants discover how many questions they need in order to learn how they see someone regarding a certain topic. Ask them during the evaluation round if it is always better to ask multiple questions, or that focussing on just one question might also have its benefits?

Why you should use this exercise

This exercise is great to use when it comes to interviewing techniques. They will practice how to be most effective when they want to get to know someone regarding a certain topic.
Because they can only ask one question regarding a certain topic, the questioner is forced to think very carefully about the question. The one answering have to be very precise about his answer. This teaches them both to think in a sharp and fast way.
The participants will discover the difference between an open-ended and a closed question. They will learn that the answer to a closed question is different from the answer to an open-ended question.
In addition, they will experience the difference between asking a question when the listener knows the topic and when the listener doesn't know the topic.
Next to practicing interviewing skills, the group gets to know each other better in a fun and playful way.
During the evaluation, everyone will form an opinion about their favorite way of asking questions.

Scan this QR code to see an animated example video of this exercise:

You can also type: **team exercise 54 questioning** into YouTube's search bar to find the video.

Team Exercise 55 - Change

"Anything looked at closely becomes wonderful."
- A. R. Ammons

Necessities: None.

To start the exercise, you tell the participants to split the group in half and stand in two lines facing each other. Tell them both lines should have an arm's length distance between them. Designate one row A and the other row B. Tell them that each person will now look at the person directly in front of him and remember as much of the other person's appearance as possible. You tell the group that when you clap your hands, all the participants will turn around at the same time. This way each person stands with his back towards his partner. After you have clapped your hands and they have turned around, you tell the group that they have one minute to change three things about their appearances. It can be anything. For example, they can remove earrings, put glasses on or take them off, or roll up sleeves. The only rule is that the changes must be visible. After they are done changing the three things, they turn around again. When each person has turned back and faces the person in front of him, you tell them that they have one minute to see what their partners have changed. Person A starts sharing with person B the changes in appearance that they notice. When he is done, person B tells person A which things he guessed correctly. Now, person B shares with person A what they thinks he changed regarding his appearances. Person A now tells what things person B guessed correctly. It is rare that both person

A and B will guess all three things correctly. If there are incorrect guesses, both people turn around again. The recipient of the incorrect guesses knows what the other person didn't notice. He now returns these unnoticed changes to their original positions.
Next everyone turns around and faces their partners again. The people who at first didn't spot all three changes now have the chance to find what they missed the first time. They will look for the things their partners just changed back to normal again. If some people still don't spot all three changes, they both turn around again. They change the things that are still not discovered in the same way as they did the first time. They both turn back and let their partners guess again.
They continue like this until each person has finally guessed the three changes his partner made. Tell them each person should remember how many turns it took to notice the three changes.
Next instruct row B to shift one spot to the right and the far right person in row B to shift to the far left spot. The people in row A stay in place. Everyone is now standing in front of a new person. Everyone turns around and changes the same three things about their appearances as they did in the first round, and the same game will be played. After everyone has spotted the three things their partners changed about themselves, they add the number of turns from both rounds. Again, row B shifts one spot to the right and the same game will be played. Again, everyone adds up the number of turns it took to guess the three changes to the turns of the previous rounds. Continue in the same way until all the people from row B have stood in front of all the people from row A. Now, everyone reports his final number of turns. The one with the lowest number of turns is the winner of the game.

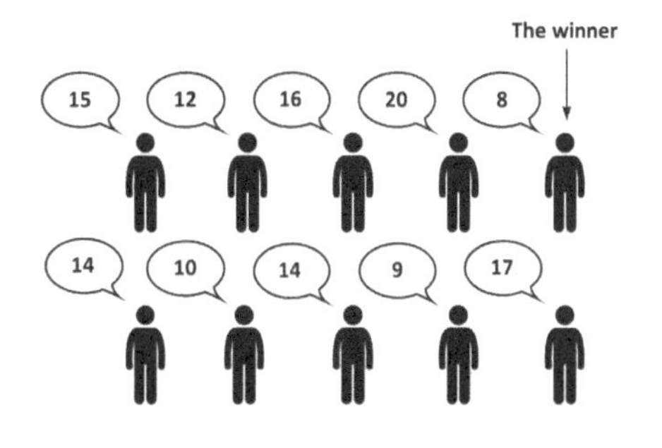

Variations

1. You can also just let everyone change one thing about themselves. This will make the exercise easier and faster to play. Play the exercise in the same way.

2. You can also let everyone change four or more things about themselves. This will make the exercise harder. Play the exercise in the same way.

3. When there is a final winner, the winner of the game can stand in front of all the other participants who are standing in a straight line. The winner observes all the other participants as precisely as possible. The winner turns around and all the other participants change one thing about themselves. The winner turns around again and tries to describe what each participant has changed about himself.

4. If you don't want the exercise to take too long, you can limit the number of times they can turn around and guess to three times per round. If during the third time people still don't spot all three things, they can give each other hints and eventually tell what the three things are.

5. In the original exercise, after the participants change partners, they change the same three things about themselves. You can also instruct each participant to change three different things for each new partner. In this way, their creativity will be stimulated.

Why you should use this exercise

This is a great exercise to do as a fun energizer game. Because the participants have to examine each other closely, the participants increase their powers of concentration and observation. Everyone will be scrutinized. This will make the participants will feel noticed by their colleagues. Each person will pay a lot of attention to the person in front of him and will receive a lot of attention himself. Because everyone looks at each other in a technical way to try to discover changes, they will make contact in a lighthearted and nonjudgmental way.
It is a good exercise to do at the beginning of a team day because the participants will interact with each other in a playful way.
The game element will make the participants stay focused and interested during the whole exercise.

Scan this QR code to see an animated example video of this exercise:

You can also type: **team exercise 55 change** into YouTube's search bar to find the video.

Team Exercise 56 - For or against

"Ask yourself the question why you are a great public speaker and you will always find the answer." - **Herman Otten**

Necessities: None.

During the exercise, the participants will sit on chairs in a half circle on one side of the room. You tell the team that each participant will think of a subject he is either for or against. Tell them it can be anything from big issues like politics to smaller issues like the behaviour of people in the subway. Anything is allowed as long as people can present arguments for or against it. Give everyone a few minutes to form an opinion regarding a certain topic and to think of a few arguments to support his opinion.
You now ask the group for a volunteer to come in front of the group to present his opinion. This person will provide examples, arguments, and statements that will support his opinion. For example, if he argues against animal testing, he must use good examples as to why animal testing is wrong. His argument should be as strong and convincing as possible. After his presentation is complete, the participants will disagree with his opinion and will ask him critical questions about his statement. It is possible that some people might agree with him. However, for the sake of argument, the people who agree will pretend that they disagree so they can ask critical questions as well. After a critical question, the speaker will answer the question. During the question period, you will tell the speaker how to deal with these questions. Tell the speaker to address his answer to the whole audience and not to just the questioner. The speaker should

look at everyone so that they know he is addressing all of them. Also, tell him to keep his answer brief and to let the answer after a few sentences transition into his original presentation. This way he goes back to the things he wants to tell and won't be distracted by the question. Continue until everyone has asked a critical question and the speaker has answered all of them.

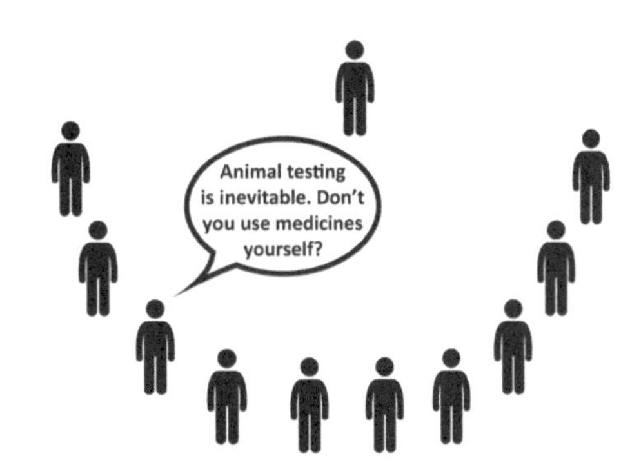

Now, you tell the speaker to give a second presentation about the same subject. Only this time, he will present arguments for the opposite opinion. If, in his first presentation he pleaded against animal testing, in his second presentation, he will present an argument for animal testing. Of course he doesn't really believe this, but he will pretend to believe in the opposite statement. Tell him he can use the earlier critical questions from the audience as an inspiration for his opposite opinion. This presentation will last for a few minutes. After this presentation, the audience doesn't ask questions.

When this presenter has finished his argument, another participant will present his argument. In the same way he will answer the critical questions from the audience and then give his second presentation based on the opposite opinion. Continue in this manner until each person has given a presentation, answered the questions, and presented the opposite opinion.

Now, tell them to sit in a circle and evaluate the exercise. You ask the team the following questions: Was it difficult to present the opposite opinion when you didn't agree with it? Or, was it easier because it wasn't real and you felt less vulnerable? Did the participants feel the critical questions as a personal attack, or did they see it only as an attack on the subject itself? Did it help to just give short answers to the critical questions and then continue with the original presentation?

Variations

1. You can tell the group that at the end of the exercise, you will choose someone who will try to give exactly the same presentation as one of the other participants. He must be as precise as possible. This will make the participants pay close attention to each presentation, because they might have to copy the presentation. At the end, you will point to someone and tell him which presentation he will copy and present to the audience.

2. You can make cards ahead of time in case there are people who can't think of topics themselves. Maker these topics about moral issues, for example, meat eating. If a participant draws this card, he will then give a spontaneous presentation on why he is for or against the topic. The rest of the exercise remains the same.

3. You can tell the first presenter to choose the next person who will give a presentation. In this way, you don't have to wait until a person volunteers.

4. You can give the first person a topic on which to share his opinion. After he gives a presentation and answers the questions, he chooses a new person and gives him the next topic. This new person must spontaneously think of an argument regarding that topic. He then gives his presentation in front of the audience. After he completes his presentation, he chooses the next person and gives him a topic. Continue with this variation until everyone has had a turn.

5. You can also tell the audience to call out comments instead of asking questions. This will make it more difficult for the speaker to respond and stay on task.

Why you should use this exercise

This is a great exercise to practice debating and public speaking. The participants learn that they don't have to enter into a discussion with every questioner. They experience that they also can respond with a few sentences and then continue with what they want to say. By doing this, they won't be distracted by questions and can focus their attention on their own presentation. By looking at the whole audience while answering, attention is diverted away from the questioner. In this way, the questioner is not the most important person in the audience anymore; he is just an audience member. This enables the speaker to focus on his own thoughts.
The exercise also stimulates group bonding, because the participants get to learn more about each other by hearing each other's opinions. The group will be very amused when they present their opposite opinions as if they were real.

Scan this QR code to see an animated example video of this exercise:

You can also type: **team exercise 56 for or against** into YouTube's search bar to find the video.

Team Exercise 57 - Strings

"Sometimes, reaching out and taking someone's hand is the beginning of a journey. At other times, it is allowing another to take yours."
- Vera Nazarian

Necessities: A ball of yarn, a smartphone, and a selfie stick.

To start the exercise, you tell the participants to stand or sit in a circle. You give a random person from the circle a ball of yarn. This person holds the ball of yarn and you tell him to share what he would like to improve within the group. Let him think about it for a moment. Tell him his wish for improvement can be anything. It can be a lighthearted topic such as having more fun in the workplace or a more serious topic such as making more revenue. After he thinks of an improvement, he will now tell the others who is the first person he needs to implement this improvement. Lastly, he explains why he needs that particular person to make it happen. For example, a participant can say, "I want us to invest more time into social media marketing. This will make our company more modern and will be good for our revenue. Ted is the first person I need to make this happen. The reason I choose Ted is that Ted is the head of marketing and he needs to give me the authority to get the marketing department to do more with social media."

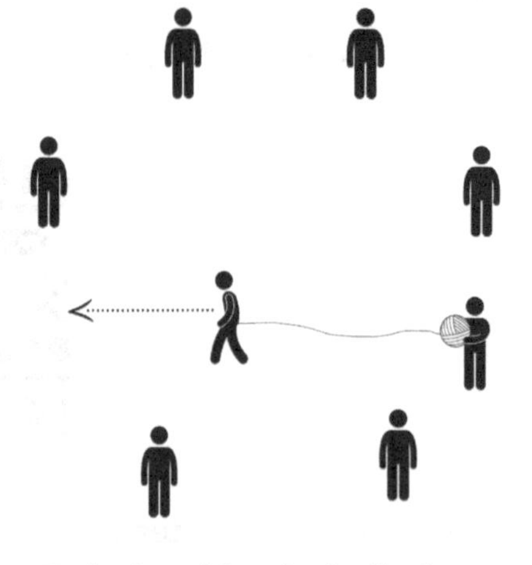

After he is done talking, you tell him that he can now give the ball of yarn to the person he just mentioned. He walks to Ted, gives him the ball of yarn, and returns to his original spot while holding the beginning of the string of the ball of yarn. The person he gave the ball of yarn to holds the ball loosely in his hands. This way, the ball of yarn will be unrolled

and a line of wool will be stretched between the person who just shared his wish and the person he first needs to fulfill his wish.
The person who has received the ball of yarn now does the same. He shares what he would like to improve within the group, who is the first person in this circle he needs to make that actually happen, and the reason why he needs that particular person. He walks up to the person he first needs to implement his wish and gives him the ball of yarn. Before he returns to his own spot, you tell him that he should hold the thread of wool between his fingers just before it goes into the ball of yarn. The person who just got the ball of yarn holds it loosely in his hands. This way, when the person who just delivered the ball of yarn returns to his own spot, a thread of wool is spun between him and the third person. Now, the third person who just received the ball of yarn follows the same procedure. Tell the team to continue this until each participant has received the ball of yarn at least once and has given it to someone else. The participants will notice that after a while, it will be harder to walk towards each other because there will be more and more strings between the participants. Therefore, they will have to step over the already stretched lines when they want to give the ball of yarn to a new person and when they return to their own spots. At the end of the exercise, a beautiful spider web that connects all their wishes for team improvement will have been created. You now take a photo of the circle of participants with the spider web between them. You can use your selfie stick for this. Take the picture from above so everyone and the web is in the picture. By doing this, the participants will have a nice memory to look at and will see all the connections between the people of the group.

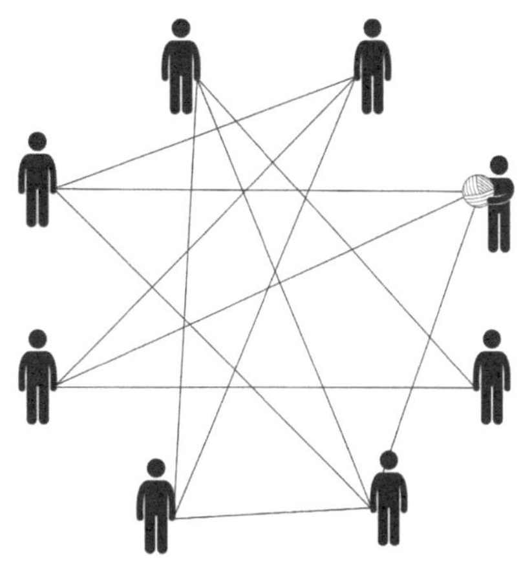

Variations

1. If you don't want to play the exercise with a ball of yarn, you can go outside and play the exercise with sidewalk chalk instead of wool. The exercise will be played in the same way, but when someone walks to the person he first needs to fulfill his wish, he draws a line on the ground with the chalk. He gives the piece of chalk to the person he walked to and walks back. This person does the same. So, in the end, a lot of lines will be drawn on the ground.

2. After the exercise, the group can make a copy of the spider web with pins and wool. They can create this on a wall at their workplace. They can copy the lines from the picture you took. By doing this, the participants have a nice piece of art to look at.

3. Instead of letting the participants stand in a circle, you can also let them stand in different places around the room. The strings between the people can be longer during this variation, so make sure the ball of yarn is big enough.

4. In addition to letting the participants think of what they want to improve within the team, you can also do this exercise with different kinds of content. For example, if you do the exercise at the end of the day, each person can tell who he thinks supported him the most during the day. He can then give the ball of yarn to the person who supported him the most. The person who receives the ball does the same. They keep on playing the exercise until everyone gave the ball to someone and the construction of the spider web is created.

Why you should use this exercise

In a playful way, each participant will find out what he would like to improve within the team, who is the first person he needs to do that, and why he needs that particular person first.
Passing around the ball of yarn is a fun way to make the connections between the participants visible.
This exercise is very helpful to people who think it is difficult to ask someone for a favor. In this playful way, they get a chance to say what they want and who they need as a first step.
During the exercise, each person will also find out who needs him as the first person to fulfill his wish for improvement. After the exercise, people now know what they can do to fulfill someone else's wish.
You will see that it will be more and more difficult to walk up to someone because of all the lines between the participants. This will add a fun element to the exercise, because the participants have to step very carefully over all the lines without stumbling.

Scan this QR code to see an animated example video of this exercise:

You can also type: **team exercise 57 for or against** into YouTube's search bar to find the video.

Team Exercise 58 - Photos

"Share your life with others. You will have a joyful life."
- Lailah Gifty Akita

Necessities: Photos the participants will bring to this exercise.

A few days before the exercise, you tell the team that each participant has to bring two photos to the exercise. One should be a childhood photo of himself. The other should be a photo that engenders a positive memory.
You start the exercise by telling the team to stand or sit in a circle. Everyone puts the childhood pictures of themselves face down in the center of the circle. By doing this, no one knows who placed which picture where. You mix the childhood pictures by shuffling them, so no one knows which picture belongs to whom.
Now, you point to someone from the circle who will grab a random picture. You tell him to look at the picture and guess who it is. He can take his time by looking around the group to see who most resembles the kid in the photo. Tell him to show the picture to the rest of the group, so they can also think about who it is. The others think about it in silence. After he has decided who he thinks is in the picture, he says that person's name. While he announces the name, he also points to that person. The chosen person tells the group if the guesser is correct. If it isn't correct, he says it isn't him in the picture and the person who is in the picture now reveals himself.

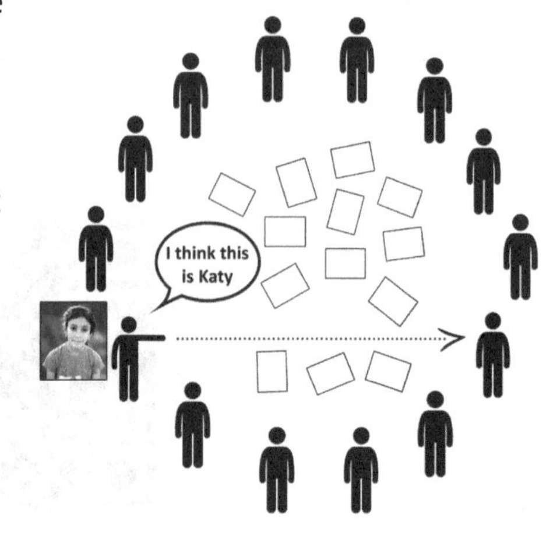

The person who picked the picture now gives the photo back to the original owner. Now, the person who just received his picture grabs a new random picture. He shows it to the rest of the group, examines it closely and looks around the group to see whom he thinks is in the picture. While pointing to the person he thinks is in the photo, he says his name. Again, the person who is in the photo reveals himself, retrieves his photo, and takes another random photo. Continue this until each person has chosen a photo and has gotten his own photo back. The longer the group plays this part of the exercise, the easier it becomes, because each round there will be less photos and people to choose from regarding who is in the picture.

Now the second part of the exercise starts. You point to someone who will show the picture about his positive memory to the group. He holds it up while he describes this memory. If the group is too large to see the picture clearly, he can have the participants pass the picture around while he describes his memory. Tell him to take the group back to the moment in the picture by graphically describing what happened. For example, if there is a mountain in the picture, just saying, "I walked on a mountain once", isn't enough. Tell them to describe the situation very vividly with many details, so everyone in the group gets a clear image of the positive memory. This will help the listeners experience the positive memory too.

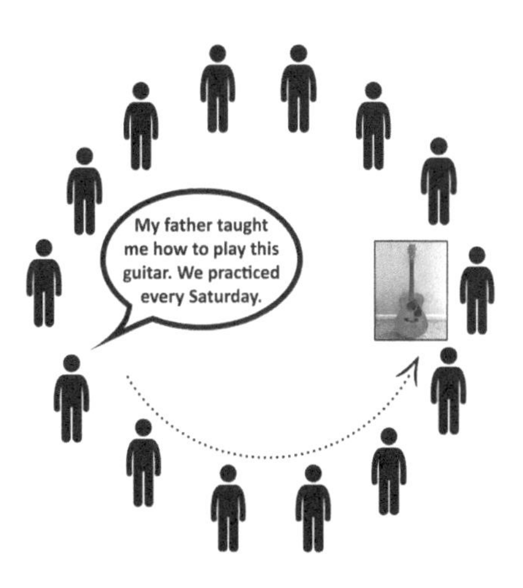

When everyone has seen the photo, he now points to someone else who will show his photo of his positive memory. Using the same procedure, he describes his positive memory regarding the photo. When he is done, he points to another person who will do the same.

Repeat this until everyone has had a turn to share his positive memory regarding his photo.

Variations

1. When someone is done talking about his positive memory, you can encourage the others to ask questions about the memory. By having more interaction, more information will be shared.

2. In addition to a photo of a positive memory, you can also instruct each participant to bring an emotionally significant photo to the exercise. Tell them it can be something cheerful, but it may also be something beautiful or sad. The photo must be of something that has an emotional impact; it must be something that touches the person who brought it. As in the previous exercise, while the picture goes around the circle, the owner of the picture describes this memory.

3. In addition to a photo, you can also instruct the participants to bring a random object to the exercise. This object should remind them of a positive memory. You can begin the exercise by collecting all the objects before people enter the room. Put them in the center of the circle. By doing this, no one knows which object belongs to whom. As in the original exercise, one by one, each person will grab an object. Next, they guess whom it belongs to and why they think it belongs to that particular person. Then the owner of the object reveals himself. In the second part of this variation, each person passes his object around the circle while he tells about the object and his positive memory.

4. To play a bonus round, you can instruct the participants to bring a piece of music that reminds them of a positive memory. One by one, they let the others hear the music they brought. While the music plays, the person who brought the piece of music describes the memory.

Why you should use this exercise

Sharing personal pictures is a fun and easy way to open up and break the ice among people.
You can play the exercise as an icebreaker with a group of people who are meeting for the first time. They will get to know each other very fast in a personal way.
It is also a good exercise for people who already know each other and want to get to know each other at a deeper level.
Guessing the identities of the participants creates a lighthearted atmosphere. There will be times people will guess wrongly who is on a picture which will create amusement and laughter in the group. When someone guesses correctly a cheerful vibe will occur.
In the second part of the exercise, people will form connections based on feelings. All the positive memories will create a shared positive energy within the group.

Scan this QR code to see an animated example video of this exercise:

You can also type: **team exercise 58 photos** into YouTube's search bar to find the video.

Team Exercise 59 - The dictionary game

"The creation of something new is not accomplished by the intellect but by the play instinct." - **Carl Jung**

Necessities: A dictionary, and pieces of paper and pens equal to the number of participants.

During the exercise, the participants sit in a circle. You hand out a piece of paper and a pen to each participant. You point to someone from the group who will be the first game leader. You give the dictionary to the game leader and tell him that he can choose a word from the dictionary that he thinks no one knows the definition of. Tell him it can be any type of word. When he finds a word, he writes the word on his paper and reads the word aloud. He does not tell the group the meaning of the word. Now, each participant writes this word on the top of his paper. Below the word, each person writes what he thinks the definition of the word is. Most of the time, no one knows what the real definition is. Tell them that each person have to create a definition that sounds like a real definition of the word. Tell them they can be as creative as they like and can invent any definition they want. However, their definition has to sound legit to fool the other participants later in the game thinking it is the real definition.
If someone might know the real definition of the word, he can write that word down. However, if the game leader tries his best to find a difficult word, most people won't know the meaning. Let them think for a minute to create a definition and write it on the piece of paper. The game leader writes the real definition below the word on his own piece of paper. After everyone has written a definition, the game leader collects all the papers.
The game leader now reads aloud all the meanings in a random order including the real one he wrote down himself. He must use a neutral tone of voice when he reads the definitions. He doesn't want his voice to reveal the real definition. After each definition, participants

who believe it is the real one, raise their hands. Of course, the game leader doesn't raise his hand; he already knows what the real definition is. When everyone except the game leader has made his choice, all the participants now earn points based on their choices. There are points to be earned for different achievements. The game leader earns one point for each player who didn't guess the real meaning. Each player earns one point when he raised his hand at the correct definition of the word. Each player also earns one point for each other player who chose his fake description as the correct description. That is why it is smart for the players to write believable definitions that will fool the other players. Everyone remembers the number of points he earns during this first round. The game leader now returns the papers to their owners. He points to a new person who will be the new game leader. This new game leader gets the dictionary and the game will be played in the same way. During the second round, each participant writes the word and his definition below the definition he wrote down in the first round. After this round has been played, everyone adds up his earned points to the points he earned in the first round. Again, the game leader chooses a new game leader. Continue playing rounds with new game leaders until everyone has been a game leader once. At the end of all the rounds, the participant who earns the most points wins the game.

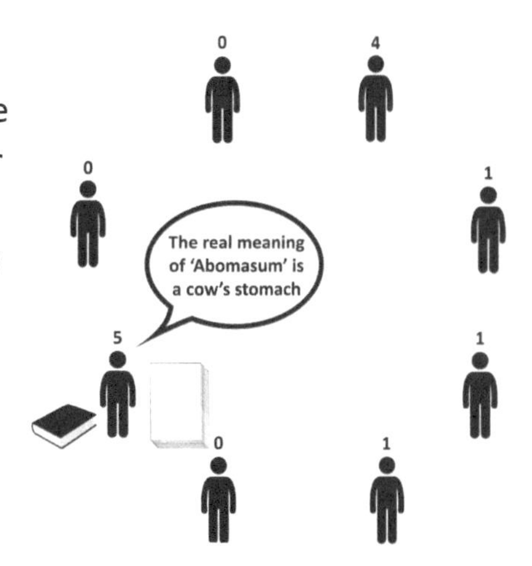

Variations

1. The game leader can earn a bonus point. When no one guesses the correct meaning of the word, the game leader gets an additional point. This encourages the game leader to choose a word whose real meaning is very hard to guess.

2. The players can earn a bonus point. Each player who writes the correct meaning of the word himself gets an extra bonus point.

3. You can play the exercise in a reversed way. The game leader chooses a definition of a word he thinks no one knows. Each participant now writes a fictitious word that sounds legit to fool the other participants later in the game thinking it is the real word. The game leader writes down the actual word. The exercise is played in the same way.

4. When you do the exercise with a very big group, you can divide the group into smaller groups of five people. The winners from each group play against each other in a new round until there is one final winner.

5. You don't need to have a real dictionary. The game leader can also use his smartphone to pick a word and its definition. However, to create an old-fashioned feeling, a real dictionary can add a nice touch to the exercise.

6. If you play this exercise with children or in a language class, you can do this with easy words too. In this way, people will learn words in a fun and playful way.

Why you should use this exercise

This exercise stimulates the participant's creativity because each round they have to generate new creative definitions.
Different types of people can succeed playing this exercise. Participants who are linguistic can earn points by picking the correct definition. People who are proficient at making up credible definitions can earn points by tricking people into thinking their definitions are correct.
Because of the game element, it is a great exercise for getting to know each other better in a fun and lighthearted way. People often write very funny definitions. When the game leader reads all the definitions aloud, there is often a lot of laughter.
At the end of each round the participants will share an exciting moment when the game leader reveals the real definition.

Scan this QR code to see an animated example video of this exercise:

You can also type: **team exercise 59 the dictionary game** into YouTube's search bar to find the video.

Team Exercise 60 - Positive language

"Communication is your ticket to success, if you pay attention and learn to do it effectively." **- Theo Gold**

Necessities: None.

Before you start the exercise, you tell the team that during this exercise they are going to practice how to use language in a positive way. Tell them that in this case the word "positive" is not meant in a moralistic optimistic way but in a linguistic way. In this exercise, "positive" means saying what you want to say without the words "not" or "don't".
By saying things in a positive way, you directly say what you mean because the negative words that might be confusing aren't there. For example, "I don't think he is a nice person" isn't positive language. "I think that he is annoying" is a positive statement. "I think that is not a bad thing to do" isn't positive language. "I think that is a good thing to do" is a positive statement. Explain to the team that if someone uses positive language in a sentence, the listener has a clearer view of what someone means. Sentences using negative language could cause misunderstandings.
Now, you start the exercise by telling the group to form trios. Each group now decides who will be person A, person B, and person C. Tell them that person A is the speaker who tells a story. Person B is the interviewer who asks person A questions during his story. Person C is the monitor who notifies the speaker when he uses negative language. Person C does this by immediately saying, "stop" when negative language is used. He then tells person A why the sentence he just said contains negative language. After person C interrupts person A because of the use of negative language, person A repeats that particular sentence, but now only using positive language. Tell the trios that in the first round, person A starts the exercise by describing a memorable holiday. They play the exercise following the above instructions. Person A describes his holiday and person B asks questions about that holiday.

Each time person A forms a negative sentence, person C notifies him by saying, “stop”. He then explains why the sentence was negative. For example, “the mountains weren’t that big” is negative language. Person A then repeats his own sentence in a positive way, for example, “the mountains were small”.

After two minutes of doing this, they switch roles. Person A, who was the speaker, now becomes the interviewer. Person B becomes the monitor who checks the language. Person C becomes the new speaker. Tell them that during this second round, person C will speak about what he would like to achieve in life. Person A asks questions about what person C says. Person B notifies person C when he uses negative language. For example, “I don’t want to work at an office my whole life” is negative language. After person B intervened, Person C now repeats the sentence using only positive language, for example, “I want to have a job that gives me the opportunity to be outside half of the time.”

After two minutes, they switch roles again. Person B now becomes the speaker. Person C becomes the interviewer, and person A becomes the monitor. Tell them that now the speaker will talk about something he would like to improve within this team. They play the game in the same way for about two minutes.

After everyone has filled each role, all the participants sit in a circle and evaluate the exercise. Ask them the following questions to encourage a discussion: Which forms of negative language did you notice during the exercise? Was it difficult to talk only in positive language? What is the benefit of only using positive language?

Variations

1. It is possible that a speaker might disagree with the monitor. The monitor might say that a sentence is negative, but the speaker thinks it is positive. If that happens, they can write the sentence down. In this way, you can discuss it during the evaluation and resolve the issue. The whole group can help clarify the dispute.

2. You can turn the exercise into a game. The speaker gets a point each time he is interrupted for using negative communication. At the end of the exercise, the one with the least points wins.

3. When there are multiple winners at the end of the above-described game variation, the winners will do a presentation in front of the group. You give them a topic to talk about, for example, their youths. Each person in the audience will now be a monitor and will interrupt the speaker when he uses negative language. The winner who can talk the longest without using negative language is the final winner.

4. You can also play the exercise without a specific speaker and interviewer. Two of the three people just have a conversation about a certain topic. The third person is the monitor and interrupts them when they use negative language.

5. A week after the exercise, ask the group if they noticed of how many times people used negative language. Also, ask them if they noticed when they did it themselves. Ask them if they noticed a difference in their communication when they used positive language instead of negative.

Why you should use this exercise

During this exercise, the participants learn that positive communication doesn't necessarily means optimistic communication, but that it means to communicate in a direct way. They learn the effect of positive communication and how it can improve overall interaction and cooperation among people. They can immediately implement this technique in real life to check in what way positive communication can make a difference. Because everyone will be the monitor once, each person also learns how to carefully listen to what words someone is using. Everyone talks about multiple topics. Therefore the participants get to know each other at a deeper level.
The participants will have fun noticing how often people use negative language without even being aware of it.

Scan this QR code to see an animated example video of this exercise:

You can also type: **team exercise 60 positive language** into YouTube's search bar to find the video.

Team Exercise 61 - Find the object

"Communication is everyone's panacea for everything." - **Tom Peters**

Necessities: Objects and blindfolds equal to a third of the participants.

To begin the exercise, you tell the team to form groups of three. Each trio stands together somewhere in the room and decides who will be person A, who will be person B, and who will be person C. Tell them that all the A people will now put on a blindfold and will be the searchers. All the B people will be the instructors, and all the C people will be the messengers. Tell them that each instructor now silently places an object somewhere in the room as far as possible from the searcher and messenger of his group. He then walks back to his searcher and messenger. The instructor will now stand facing the object in such a way he can see it. The messenger is standing next to the instructor with his back towards the object so he can't see the object. Tell them the goal of each trio is to help the searcher find the object as quickly as possible with as few instructions as possible. First, the instructor whispers a walking instruction into the ear of the messenger. The messenger needs to carefully listen to the instruction that the instructor whispers in his ear. Since the messenger's back is to the object, he can't see the object. If he gives the searcher the wrong instruction, the searcher could go in the wrong direction. The messenger repeats the instruction aloud, so the blindfolded searcher knows how to walk towards the object. Tell the group that the instructions should be as clear as possible. For example, "go a bit to the left" is not as clear as "go two feet to the left". The searcher follows the instruction. Because there are multiple trios in the same room performing the exercise

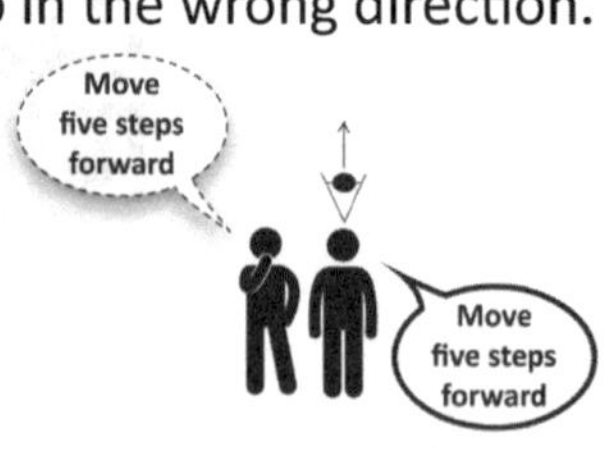

it is important that the searcher only listens to his own messenger. Because the messenger has his back towards the searcher, he repeats the instruction in the opposite direction of the searcher. This makes it especially difficult for the searcher to hear the voice of his messenger. Of course, you walk around during the exercise to make sure that nobody bumps into each other.
After the searcher has followed the first instruction as accurately as possible, the instructor now whispers the next instruction into the ear of the messenger. Again, the messenger repeats the instruction aloud and the searcher follows the instruction as accurately as possible.
The closer the searcher comes to the object he needs to find, the farther he will be away from his messenger. Due to the increasing distance, it will be more difficult for the searcher to hear the instructions of his messenger. It also increases the difficulty to differentiate the voice of his messenger from all the other messengers. Each trio continues this process until the searcher finally finds the object. After the searcher finds the object, he removes his blindfold and waits at that spot until all the other searchers have found their objects.

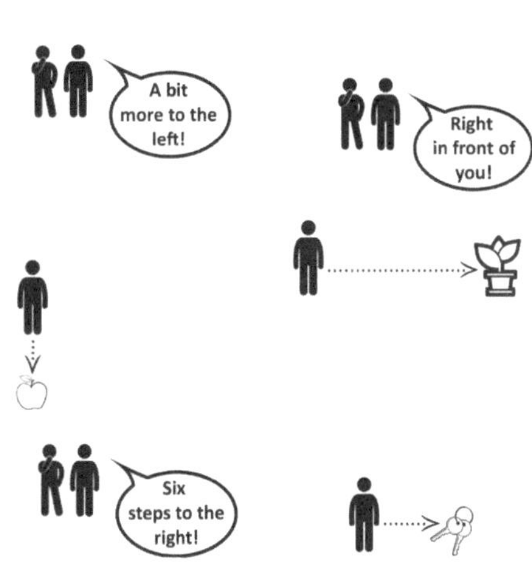

After all searchers have found their objects, they return to their instructors and messengers. Each trio now switches roles. Person A becomes the instructor, person B becomes the messenger, and person C becomes the searcher. The game will be played again in the same way. After they have played the game for the second time, each trio switches roles again. Person A becomes the messenger, person B becomes the searcher, and person C becomes the messenger. They play the game again so that everyone has experienced each role once.

Variations

1. You can turn the exercise into a competition. Each trio counts per round how many instructions it took them to find the object. The total points of these three rounds are their final score. The trio with the lowest score wins the game.

2. If you have a big group, you can play this exercise with groups of five or more. For this variation, there are people standing in a row between the instructor and the messenger. They stand with their backs towards the object. The instructor whispers his instruction into the ear of the first person who stands between the messenger and him. This person whispers that instruction into the ear of the second person standing between the instructor and the messenger. They continue until the last person standing between the instructor and the messenger whispers the instruction into the messenger's ear. Passing the instruction from one person to another will create more chances for miscommunications. This will make the exercise more challenging.

3. Tell all trios to stand on one side of the room. After each searcher is blindfolded, you place just one object somewhere in the room. Following the same procedure, all the trios try to capture the object as quickly as possible. The first searcher who finds the object wins the game for his trio.

4. You can give them hints how to make the voice of each messenger recognisable for his searcher. For example, the messengers can speak in a weird voice, say the name of the searcher before giving an instruction, or make a strange noise before giving an instruction. In this way, the searcher can differentiate the voice of his messenger from the other sounds.

Why you should use this exercise

This is a great exercise for practicing communication and experiencing how to deal with noise while communicating. Because all the trios play the exercise in the same room, noise will interfere with their communication. The noise makes the communication a challenge and makes it easy to become distracted. Therefore each trio has to cooperate to clearly and effectively communicate to the searcher what to do to find the object as quickly as possible.
During the process, the team will experience miscommunications. This will cause laughter within the group, which will be good for team spirit.
When the searcher finally finds an object, people will feel joyful. This will create a positive atmosphere for the group.
Because the participants walk through the room, the exercise can also be seen as an active energizer. If you add the competitive variation No. 1 to the exercise, it will increase the fun. The competitive factor will make the exercise more like a game.

Scan this QR code to see an animated example video of this exercise:

You can also type: **team exercise 61 find the object** into YouTube's search bar to find the video.

Team Exercise 62 - The maze

“Increased physical activity enhances positive energy.”
- Lailah Gifty Akita

Necessities: A stopwatch.

You start the exercise by telling the group they are going to play a special kind of tag. First, you ask volunteers to be the catcher and the runner. After they decide who will be the catcher and who will be the runner, you instruct the other participants to form a square of parallel lines with their arms widely spread. In this way, the people in the lines will remain a double arm’s length distance with their fingertips slightly touching. The maze should at least contain three lines with three people in them - nine people total. Ideally, the number of lines is equal to the number of people standing in each line. For example, four lines with four people in each line would be good. If that is not possible because of the number of people in the group, the lines can contain an uneven number of people as well. For example, if you have nineteen people, they van make four rows of four people and one row of three people. The distance between the different lines should be equal to the distance between two people in a line. That would be about two arm’s lengths. This way, a convenient walking path is formed between the lines.
You now appoint a random person who is standing in one of the lines to be the changer. Tell him he will be able to change the maze by saying “left” or “right”. The moment the changer will say “left” everyone who is standing in the lines will make a quarter turn to the left while keeping their arms spread. When the changer will say “right”, everyone who is standing in the lines makes a quarter turn to the right. In this way, all the paths in the maze change. Of course, it doesn’t really matter whether the participants turn left or right; the maze changes in the same way. However, during the game it is a fun element to let all the participants turn in the same direction to change the maze.

To start the chase, you tell the catcher to stand at one corner of the maze. Tell the runner to stand at the opposite corner from where the catcher is standing. The goal of the catcher is to catch the runner as quickly as possible. The goal of the runner is to elude the catcher for as long as possible. When you say, "go" you start the stopwatch and the catcher starts chasing the runner. He can chase the runner around the maze and towards the maze. The same thing applies to the runner. He can run around the maze, but he can also run in the maze to elude the catcher. After the chase has begun, at a random moment the changer calls out "left" or "right". Now, everyone standing in the maze makes a quarter turn to the side the changer just announced. Now the paths in the maze have changed. Encourage the changer to change the maze at a moment when the catcher and/or runner are in the maze. Changing the paths when they are in the maze can directly change the distance between the catcher and the runner. All of a sudden the catcher can end up being closer to the runner or farther away. The chase continues and at a random moment, the changer calls out "left" or "right" again. They continue in this manner until the catcher finally catches the runner. You stop the stopwatch and inform the runner how long it took the catcher to catch him.

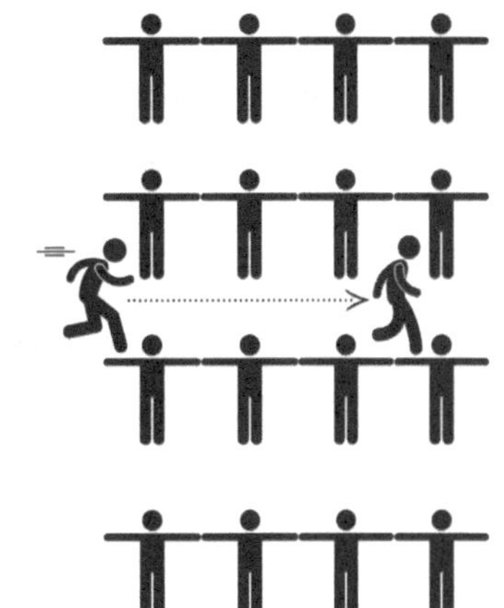

Now you choose two new people to be the catcher and the runner. You also choose a new person to be the changer. Continue with this until everyone has been the runner once. The person who was able to elude the catcher for the longest amount of time is the winner of the game.

Variations

1. You can add the rule that the catcher can also change the maze by calling out right or left. In this way, he can anticipate the runner's moves and catch him sooner.

2. You can also add the rule that the runner can call out right or left. In this way, he can anticipate how he can effectively evade the catcher.

3. When you let the participants form the maze, you can let a few participants stand at different angles than the others. In this way, it will have actual corners like a real maze. As in the original exercise, the changer calls out "left" or "right" which will make the maze change completely.

4. If catching someone is too physical for a group, you can have the catcher "catch" the runner by tapping him on the shoulder. People might be more comfortable being tapped on the shoulder than being grabbed by the arm.

5. To make sure people don't bump into each other, instruct the runner and the catcher to stand still when the directions are called. By doing this, the people in the maze have enough time to change their angles. The moment everyone has changed the angles, you clap your hands to signal that the chase will continue.

6. You can film the game with your phone. After the exercise is done, the participants will enjoy watching it.

Why you should use this exercise

This is a great team building exercise to do as a fun game or as a warm-up. The physical movements are good for creating energy. Everyone standing in the maze has to listen carefully to the changer and move at the same moment in a specific direction. This will generate a cooperative energy in the group.
Because the runner needs to elude the catcher for as long as possible, it will be an exciting game to play. Everyone will be amused to see the catcher finally catching the runner.
The competitive element will encourage people to do their best while running to elude the catcher. They will try to evade the catcher for as long as possible.

Scan this QR code to see an animated example video of this exercise:

You can also type: **team exercise 62 the maze** into YouTube's search bar to find the video.

Team Exercise 63 - Copy the building

"Communication is a skill that you can learn. It's like riding a bicycle or typing. If you're willing to work at it, you can rapidly improve the quality of every part of your life."
- **Brian Tracy**

Necessities: As many Lego bricks as possible and a watch or stopwatch.

To start the exercise, you tell the participants to form groups of three. Tell them that all trios will now stand at one side of the room. There should be enough distance between each trio to keep the trios from hearing each other. You now create a Lego structure with some of the bricks and place it somewhere at the opposite of the room where the can't see it. Make sure it is a complex creation so it is not easy to rebuild. You now tell the trios that they are going to recreate the Lego structure as quickly and as accurately as possible. Next, you give many random Lego bricks to each trio. Make sure that each trio has enough Lego bricks in every shape and color to recreate the Lego creation you just built. It is advisable to give them as many Lego bricks as possible so they don't know which bricks have to be used to recreate the original Lego structure. Tell them that one person of each trio is the instructor and the other two are the builders. Tell them the builders have to copy the Lego creation as quickly as possible. However, only the instructor can walk back and forth to the original creation. You start recording the time as each instructor walks to the original Lego creation, takes a close look at it, and remembers as much as possible of what he sees. Each instructor now walks back to his two builders and instructs them in

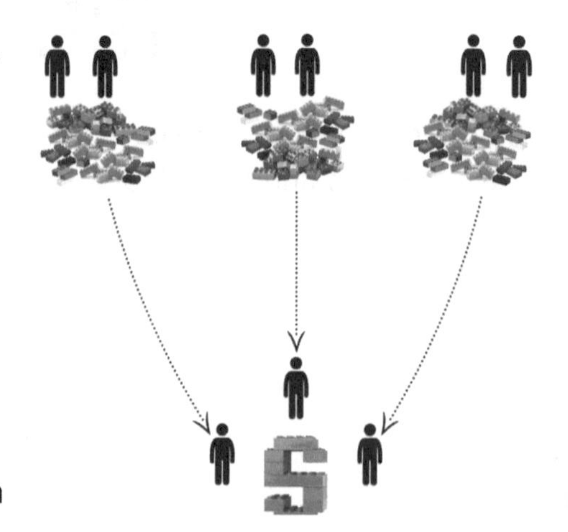

recreating the original structure. The instructor is only allowed to give verbal instructions. He can't point or help them by building as well. The builders are not allowed to talk. After the two builders have built the replica according to the instructor's directions, the instructor can decide to stop the process if he thinks the replica is accurate. He will then ask you to write down the time of completion. However, if the instructor thinks that the replica has some mistakes, he can return to the original structure to check. When he is at the original Lego creation again, he will check what he thinks is divergent compared with his builder's replica. He walks back to the two builders and tells them what he thinks should be corrected to make the replica as accurate as possible. Again, he is only allowed to give verbal instructions.

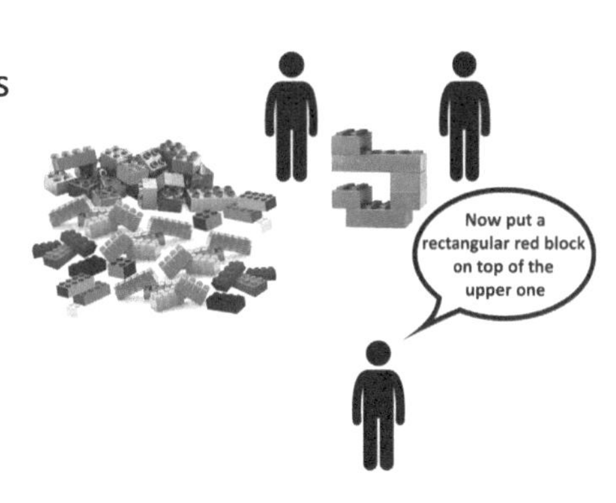

The builders change the replica according to the instructions they hear. If the instructor thinks that the replica is accurate, he stops the process by telling you to write down their time. If he still has doubts, he returns to the original Lego structure and checks for differences. Each trio continues this process until they all think they have built the replica as accurately as possible. When each group thinks that they have accurately recreated the original structure, they convene and all the replicas will be checked for accuracy. The trio that copied the Lego creation the most accurately wins the game. It might be possible that multiple groups built accurate replicas. In that case, the trio that built an accurate copy within the shortest time wins the game. All the participants will now sit in a circle to evaluate the exercise. Ask them the following questions to encourage the discussion: Is it more efficient to give lengthy instructions so you don't have to walk back and forth all the time? Or, is it better to give short instructions and walk back and forth many times to check the accuracy of the copy? What kind of miscommunication occured? And how could this be improved?

Variations

1. If a trio violates a rule, you can add a time penalty of ten seconds to their final time. Violations are: the instructor pointing to a Lego piece, building himself to help the builders, or the builders talking.

2. You can skip recording the time. Instead, add a limit on the number of times the instructor can walk back and forth to the original Lego structure. For example, after three tries, the trio who has most accurately recreated the original structure wins.

3. You can skip recording the time. Instead, tell the trios to count the number of times the instructor walked back and forth to the original Lego structure. The trio with an accurate copy of the building and with the instructor who checked the original structure the least wins the game.

4. Tell each trio to make a Lego creation for the other trios to copy. Tell them to make the creation as complicated as possible. However, tell them there is a maximum of Lego bricks that they can use. If you allow them an unlimited number of pieces, the structure might be too difficult to copy. For example, they can use a maximum of twelve Lego bricks. One by one, each trio puts their creation somewhere in the room where the others can't see it and chooses another trio to recreate their Lego creation. The trio who makes the most accurate copy the fastest wins.

5. As a bonus round, you can let them create a final Lego creation together using all the Lego pieces they want. Make a picture of the creation to send them after the exercise so they have a nice memory of the game to look at.

Why you should use this exercise

This exercise is great to use as an energizer game, but also as a more serious communication exercise. Because there is a time challenge, the instructions need to be as accurate as possible without any miscommunication. This will encourage the instructors to communicate as effectively as possible.
To make the best use of time, the builders need to listen attentively so as not make any mistakes. By doing this, the group will train to communicate as effectively possible.
The game element will create a stimulating, lighthearted, and competitive energy which will make the team be engaged during the exercise.

Scan this QR code to see an animated example video of this exercise:

You can also type: **team exercise 63 copy the building** into YouTube's search bar to find the video.

Team Exercise 64 - The word game

"Improvisation is the power of spontaneous observation."
- Wyatt Pringle

Necessities: A tennis ball.

To start the exercise, you tell the team to stand in a circle at equal distances from each other. You give one person a tennis ball. This person throws the ball to someone in the group and says the first random word that occurs to him, for example, "car". The person who catches the ball now throws the ball to another random person in the circle. He says the first random word that occurs to him regarding the word car, for example, "wheel". The person who catches the ball now throws the ball to another person in the circle. He says the first word that occurs to him regarding the word wheel, for example, "circle". Continue this part of the exercise for a few minutes.

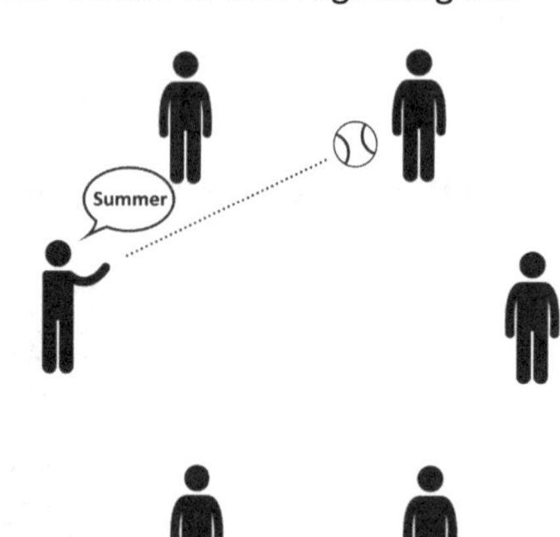

When the team is proficient, tell the one who has the ball to hold the ball. You now start the second round.
In this round, the participants produce words that rhyme with the word they receive. You will count the number of rhyming words they produce. Tell them they are not allowed to say the same word twice. Everyone remains silent except the person throwing the ball. The word can be multisyllabic as long as it rhymes with the previous word. While saying a word, the person holding the ball throws the ball to a random person in the circle. For example, he could say the word "ball". Now, the person who catches the ball throws the ball to another random person in the circle while saying a word that rhymes with the word ball. For example, he could say the word "hall". The person who catches the

ball throws it to someone while saying a word that rhymes with the word hall, for example, "rainfall". They continue playing this round until someone isn't able to provide a rhyming word. Then, the round is over and you tell them the number of rhyming words they produced. This is their final score. You tell the team they can try again and try to break their own record. Let the team play this round about five times.
Now the last round of the word game begins. The team will now form existing words starting with the last syllable of the word they receive. For example, someone from the circle throws the ball to a random person and says a random word, for example "toilet". The catcher now throws the ball to another random person from the group. Since the last syllable of the word "toilet" is "let", he will call out one or more syllables that, when you place it after the syllable let, form a new word. For example: "ter". This together forms the word letter. The participant who catches the ball now throws the ball to another random person. He says one or more syllables that, when you place it after the syllable "ter", form a new word. For example: "rific" (terrific). The person who received the ball now does the same with the syllable "fic" and for example calls out "tion" (fiction). When someone can't generate a word after a syllable, the number of times they have been throwing the ball around will be noted and you tell them their score. The team starts over again and tries each round to break their own record. Continue playing this syllable round for about five rounds. After the game, you ask each participant what he thinks was easier: producing a random word on the spot as in the first round, or producing a word they need to think about as in the second and third rounds. Let each person give an answer and elaborate on his choice.

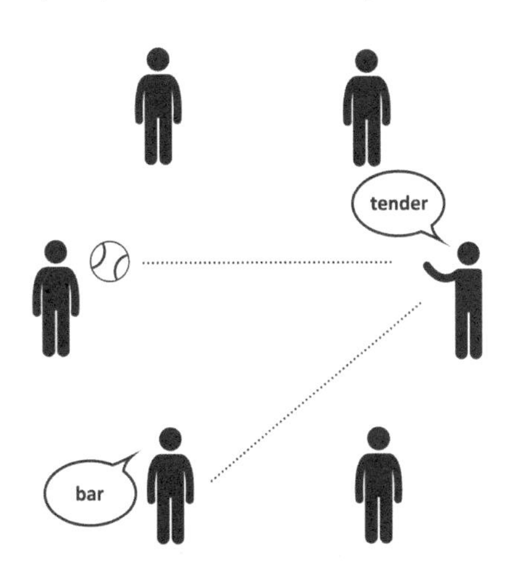

Variations

1. During the second round in which they say rhyming words, they are not allowed to say the same word twice. To make sure they don't do this, you can write the words they say on a whiteboard. Each time someone says a word, you check the whiteboard to make sure it is not said before. If they repeat a word, you tell them their final score and they have to start over.

2. Play an extra round in which the first person throwing the ball says a random word, for example, "table". The person who catches the ball throws it to the next random person while saying a word starting with the last letter of the word he just received, for example, "experience". When the team becomes proficient, you can choose a word category, for example, animals. They play the round in the same way, but are now just allowed to say animal names. A sequence can be: bird, dog, gazelle, etc.

3. You can let the team create a fictional story one word at a time. The first person throwing the ball contributes the first word of the story, for example, "there". The catcher throws it to a random person while contributing the second word of the story, for example, "was". They continue until they complete a fictional story together.

4. Play a positive bonus round in which the first person throwing the ball says a positive characteristic that describes the catcher, for example, "inspiring". The person who catches the ball throws it to a random person while saying a positive characteristic describing the person he throws the ball to. Because they are already warmed up, giving each other compliments will go smoother than ever before.

Why you should use this exercise

During this exercise, the creativity of the participants will be stimulated. Their word association skills will be enhanced, because they say the first thing that occurs to them when hearing a word. Because the exercise stimulates creativity, it will open their minds to new ideas. Therefore, this exercise is great to do just before a brainstorming session.
This exercise also gives insight into people's personalities. When you ask each person during the evaluation if he prefers saying random things or words he has to consider, you will learn about the different preferences in the group. Some participants are better at improvising and others are better at considering the right word before they say it aloud.

Scan this QR code to see an animated example video of this exercise:

You can also type: **team exercise 64 the word game** into YouTube's search bar to find the video.

Team Exercise 65 - The numbers game

"Only through focus can you do world-class things,
no matter how capable you are."
- Bill Gates

Necessities: None.

To start the exercise, you tell the participants to stand in a circle. Tell them that they will count clockwise to the number one hundred by each saying a number aloud. You point to a random participant in the circle who starts by saying the number one. The person on his left side says the number two; the next person says number three, and so on until they reach the number one hundred. When they finish this first simple task, you now tell the team that they will play the second round. In the second round, they will count to the number one hundred again. There is one difference. Tell them that when it is someone's turn to say the number seven or a multiple of the number seven - such as fourteen - this participant won't say that number aloud; he will clap his hands instead. Each person will now have to pay close attention to when he claps instead of saying a number. Tell them that next to calling out numbers or doing a gesture they are not allowed to talk or help each other. You choose a new person to start this round. This participant now begins the sequence by saying the number one. In the same way they count clockwise around the circle. The new sequence now looks like this: one, two, three, four, five, six, clap, eight, nine, ten, eleven, twelve, thirteen, clap, etc. They continue in this manner until they reach the number one hundred. If someone makes a mistake, they have to start over again at number one. In this case, you point to a new random person who

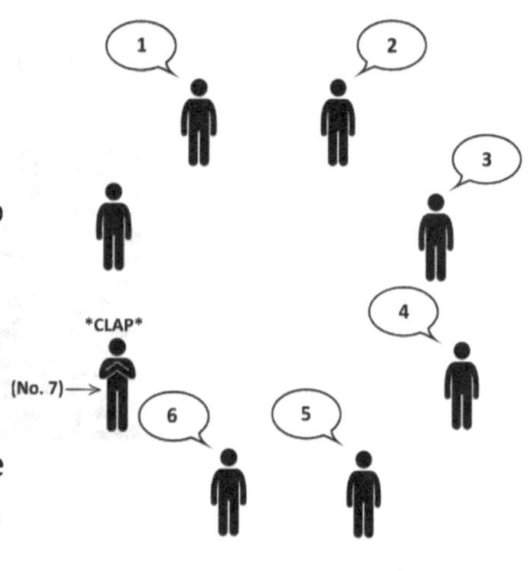

will start by saying the number one. This will change the sequence of who will say what, so they can't get used to the order of the sequence. In this way, each turn will be just as difficult as the previous one. The group tries repeatedly until they reach the number one hundred. If they succeed, another rule will be added to the game and the third round will be played.

You tell the team that the number four or a multiple of the number four will now be replaced by a jump. Now there will be a few moments that multiple gestures belong to the same number. If that is the case, the person that has the turn will do all the gestures belonging to that number at the same time. This will now happen at the numbers twenty-eight, fifty-six, and eighty-four. These numbers are a multiple of both four and seven. You point to a new person who will start the counting. Now the sequence will look like this: one, two, three, jump, five, six, clap, jump, nine, ten, eleven, jump, thirteen, clap, and so on until the number one hundred. When they reach the number one hundred, the fourth round will be played.

You now tell them that the number three or a multiple of the number three will be replaced by a cough. Now for more numbers it will be the case that multiple gestures should be done at the same time. The person whose turn it is at number eighty-four now even has to do all three gestures at once. He will jump, cough and clap his hands at the same time. Again you point to a new person who will start the counting. Now the sequence looks like this: one, two, cough, jump, five, cough, clap, jump, cough, ten, eleven, jump and cough, thirteen, clap, fifteen, jump, seventeen, etc. until the number one hundred. When the team has reached the number one hundred without making any mistakes, they have completed the game.

Variations

1. If you have a very big group, you can split the group into smaller groups and let them compete against each other. Each group counts all their attempts to complete all four rounds. Make each group start every new attempt with a different person, so they can't get used to the sequence. The group with the lowest number of attempts to complete all the rounds wins the game.

2. In addition to replacing a number and the multiple of that number, you can instruct the participants that the replacement will also occur for a number in which that number appears. For example, when the number seven or a multiple of the number seven is replaced, the numbers seventeen, twenty-seven, thirty-seven, etc. will also be replaced. Only play this variation when the team is good at the original exercise.

3. To make the game even more difficult, you can replace a number, multiple of that number, and number in which the number appears, by the same gesture as a previous number you replaced. For example, seven, a multiple of seven and the number in which seven occurs will be replaced by a scream. However, eight, a multiple of eight, and a number in which eight occurs will also be replaced by a scream.

4. Tell them that if a participant makes a mistake, he is out of the game. In this way, the more mistakes that are made the smaller the circle gets. If there are only two people left and someone makes a mistake before they reach number one hundred, all the participants can come back and they try again. This will make it easier to finish a round because they don't need to start over each time they make a mistake.

Why you should use this exercise

During this exercise, the focus and concentration of the team will improve. By setting a clear goal - counting to one hundred without making mistakes - you give the team members a common objective. If a participant loses his concentration and says the wrong number, they all have to start over. Therefore, each participant will feel the responsibility to achieve the common team goal. This team goal will encourage them to work together and create an atmosphere of cooperation.
Because each round there will be more numbers replaced by a gesture, it will be more difficult for them to reach the number one hundred. This will challenge the group and will keep them sharp during the whole exercise. Because of the game element, it is an enjoyable exercise to do. The team will have a lot of fun together. Each round, they will celebrate when they reach one hundred. This will create a lot of positive energy.

Scan this QR code to see an animated example video of this exercise:

You can also type: **team exercise 65 the numbers game** into YouTube's search bar to find the video.

Team Exercise 66 - Filler words

"A good orator is pointed and impassioned." - **Marcus T. Cicero**

Necessities: None.

Before you start the exercise, you first tell the participants some information about the use of filler words and saying "um". Tell them that filler words are words that are used to fill up sentences without actually meaning anything. For example, filler words can be "you know", "like", "okay" and "actually" if they are used in a sentence without adding any meaning to the sentence. For example, I enjoy drinking coffee **like** the whole day. In this case, "like" doesn't have any meaning. When you repeat a word, it also counts as a filler word. For example, I, I, I have worked here over ten years. Now you ask each participant why he thinks people use filler words and say "um". After everyone has given an answer, you tell them there are several reasons why people use them. For example, someone might wants to buy time to think of the next thing he is going to say. Another reason can be that someone wants to let other people know he is still talking so he won't be interrupted. Many people use filler words or say 'um' unintentionally. Tell them it is better not to use filler words. It is better to just use the words you need to say what you mean, so the communication stays pure.
Now, you tell the participants that they are going to do an exercise that will raise their level of awareness of the filler words they use. Tell them this will help them eliminate their filler words and improve their communication skills. You now start the exercise by telling the group to form trios. Each trio will sit somewhere in the room and decide who is person A, who is person B, and who is person C. The participants will now practice talking without using filler words and saying "um". Tell them person A will tell person B a story about something he would like to achieve within the team. Person B can ask questions about the

things person A tells him. When person A says "um" or uses a filler word, person C claps his hands. So when he would say: "I would like to cooperate in a more effective way, you know." person C claps his hands and tells person A the reason he clapped his hands. In this case, he tells person A that he said, "you know" at the end of a sentence and that in this case "you know" doesn't add any meaning. The speaker now repeats the sentence without the filler word and continues. After two minutes, the roles switch. Now person B will tell person C what he would like to achieve within the team. Person A will now clap his hands the moment person B says "um" or uses a filler word. For example, person C asks person B a question and person B starts his answer with "well... um". Person A will immediately clap his hands and tell person B that he said "well... um", which are filler words. After two minutes, the roles switch again. Now person C tells person A what he would like to achieve within the team. Person B will be the notifier. For example, when person C says "We should be more positive towards each other, this... this..." person A claps his hands. He tells person C he clapped his hands because person C repeated the word "this", which makes it a filler word. Again, they continue for two minutes.

Now tell the team to sit in a circle and evaluate the exercise. Ask them the following questions to encourage the discussion: What filler words were discovered? Was it difficult to tell a story without using filler words? Did it help being notified of the filler words or was it more difficult to focus on the story? Let each participant share his experiences.

Variations

1. In addition to telling each other what they would like to change within the team, you can let the participants tell each other different kinds of stories. For example, they can also talk about a holiday that they remember or about something they know a lot about.

2. In addition to using handclaps, the monitor can use different sounds to alert the speaker to his filler words or "ums".
For example, when you want serious energy, you can let the monitor interrupt the speaker by just saying he used a filler word. When you want a more lighthearted energy, the monitor can make an "oink" or other funny sound.

3. In addition to telling the monitor to immediately interrupt the speaker when he says "um" or uses a filler word, you can instruct the monitor to also write down the filler words. In this way, the speaker can read back his own filler words, which makes him even more aware them.

4. As a bonus round, you can turn this exercise into a game. After you have sat in a circle and have evaluated the exercise with all the participants, you can let each participant tell a one-minute story. For example, a fun topic might be, what they have learned from this exercise. Without notifying the speaker, you write down the number of filler words and "ums" he says. After each participant has spoken for a minute, you tell each participant how many times he said a filler words or "um". The participant with the least amount of counts wins the game.

Why you should use this exercise

During this exercise, everyone will become aware of his filler words. Therefore, after the exercise they will be able to choose not to use them anymore. This will help them become better speakers and communicators. Instead of filling every pause with filler words, they will be more comfortable with silent pauses. During these pauses, it will be easier for listeners to process the speaker's words. The listeners won't be distracted by the filler words anymore.
In the exercise they practice not to use filler words, by discussing what they would like to achieve within the team. This will provide insight into their own goals and into the goals of the other team members. This insight will create a positive atmosphere between the team members.

Scan this QR code to see an animated example video of this exercise:

You can also type: **team exercise 66 filler words** into YouTube's search bar to find the video.

Team Exercise 67 - Who are you?

"Life is more fun if you play games." - **Roald Dahl**

Necessities: Stickers which contain the names of celebrities. Make sure the celebrities you choose are famous enough to be known by the whole group. There should be enough stickers for all participants.

To begin the exercise, you tell the team to sit in a circle. You instruct all the participants to close their eyes and you paste a sticker on each person's forehead. When you instruct them to open their eyes again, everyone sees the names on the stickers of all the other participants, but no one knows what name is written on the sticker on his own forehead.

You now tell the group the purpose of the game is for each participant to guess as quickly as possible what name is written on the sticker on his forehead. Tell them they will do this by asking closed questions of which the answer can only be "yes" or "no". You now point to a random person who will be the first one trying to find out what is written on his forehead. He will phrase the questions as if he is the celebrity whose name is stuck to his forehead. For example, a question can be: "Am I a famous television personality?" Everyone in the circle can answer the question at the same time. When the answer is "yes", the questioner can ask another question. If the answer is "no" the person sitting on his left side can start asking questions to discover which celebrity is written on the sticker on his forehead. If he gets a "no" answer, the person sitting on his left side will be the next one to get a turn. In this way they go clockwise around the circle.

Occasionally, people disagree with each other when the answer is partially true. Of course, it is difficult to discuss this without giving the answer away. For example, if the person who asked if he was a famous television personality has Bill Clinton on his sticker, the others may not be able to unanimously agree on an answer. Bill Clinton isn't a famous television personality, but he might be famous because people often see him on television. If there is no unanimous "yes" or "no", they have to unanimously determine a final answer. They have to do this without letting the questioner know who the celebrity is. If they can't come to a unanimous decision, you will ask the people who think the answer is "yes" to raise their hands. In this way, the questioner sees how many people think the answer to his question is "yes". If the majority of the group raises their hands, he can ask another question. For example: "Am I a famous actor?" In this case, the answer is "no". The next person in the circle now asks a question to find out which celebrity is on his forehead.

Tell them it is important for the questioner to remember the answers, so when he gets other turns, he doesn't have to ask the same questions again. If a participant thinks he knows who he is, he asks, "Am I...?". He will complete the sentence with the name of the celebrity he thinks is on his sticker. He can only ask this when he has the turn. For example: "Am I Amy Winehouse?" If the answer is "no", the next person in the circle can ask a question. If the answer is "yes", he is out of the game. The first person who guesses correctly is the winner. He will stay seated in the circle to answer other people's questions.

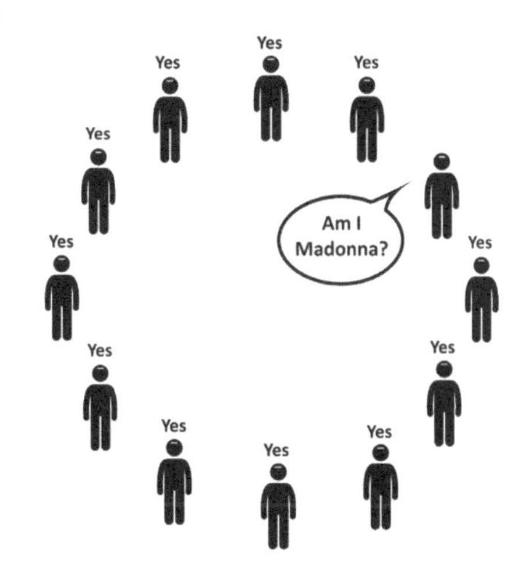

The rest of the group continues the game until each participant discovers which name is written on his sticker.

Variations

1. Instead of continuing the game until each person discovers the name on his forehead, you can stop the game after the first person has discovered the name on his forehead. Then, let everyone look at their stickers and start a new round. By doing this, you have more time to play multiple rounds and no one has to wait until the game is over to play again. Of course, if you play multiple rounds, make sure you have enough stickers with celebrities on them.

2. Instead of your writing the names on the stickers in advance, you can let the participants write the names themselves. You give each participant a blank sticker. Each participant writes the name of a celebrity on the sticker and sticks the sticker on the forehead of another random participant. It is important that participants don't see the names being stuck on their foreheads. The game will be played in the same way.

3. In addition to famous people, you can also write things or unfamous people they all know on the stickers. You have to make sure that everyone knows the meaning of the word or the identity of the person you wrote. Some examples are: The Statue of Liberty, Donald Duck, Michael Mut (the manager who they all know), or Michigan.

4. You can give everyone one opportunity for a hint. They can choose from the first letter of the name on their stickers, the last letter of the name, or the number of letters the name contains. They can ask for this hint at a self-chosen moment.

Why you should use this exercise

This exercise gives the team the opportunity to practice asking closed questions. They learn how to narrow information down from a wide scale to a more specific scale. Normally, people begin asking global questions such as "Do I have blond hair?", or "Am I a man?" The closer they get to the final answer the more specific the questions they ask will be. For example, someone might ask if he won America's Got Talent two years ago. This will make them see the difference between global and specific questions.
It also is a fun exercise to do. Because people often don't have a clue what name is written on their foreheads, the questions will generate much laughter. This will create a lighthearted atmosphere. The moment someone finds out who is on his sticker will also be a cheerful moment. Laughing together creates group synergy and bonds among people.

Scan this QR code to see an animated example video of this exercise:

You can also type: **team exercise 67 who are you** into YouTube's search bar to find the video.

Team Exercise 68 - Negative to positive

"Life becomes easier and more beautiful when we can see the good in other people."
- Roy T. Bennett

Necessities: None.

To start the exercise, you tell the team to sit in a circle. You point to someone in the circle who will be person A. You instruct him to point to someone in the circle with whom he experienced a negative interaction. This doesn't necessarily have to be a very negative experience. As long as it felt a bit uncomfortable, it counts as a negative experience. The person he points to will be person B. This duo separates from the group and sits down together somewhere in the room. You now point to another person in the circle who will be person A and will do the same. He chooses someone with whom he experienced a negative interaction; this will be person B. This duo also separates from the group. Continue doing this until the team has divided into duos around the room.
Now, each person A tells each person B about the negative interaction. For example, "Last week I asked you to join me for lunch. I thought the way you said you were too busy was a bit curt. It made me feel rejected." Now, person A explains how the situation could have been more positive. For example, "I would like you to have said that you appreciated that I asked you for lunch before telling me you were too busy." While person A is talking, person B remains silent. When person A has finished his story, person B now tells how he experienced the situation. For example, "I recall your asking me for lunch. I was very busy at that

moment and that caused my reaction to be too curt. I didn't mean to cause any negative emotions." While person B is talking, person A remains silent. Now, person A expresses his appreciation concerning the interaction based on what person B just told him. For example, "I am happy that I now know why you reacted that way. What I appreciate is that you work very hard and I understand why that can sometimes interfere with socially desirable behavior."

After all the duos are finished performing the exercise, you tell everyone to sit in the circle again. You now point to a random person B and tell him that he can choose a person from the group with whom he experienced a negative interaction. He can choose anyone he wants; it doesn't matter if the one he points to was a person A or a person B in the first round. This duo separates from the group and sits down together somewhere in the room. Let every person B pick someone until there are no person B's left and the group is divided into duos again. If some person B's picked another person B it is possible that there might be a few person A's left. These persons will wait for now.
In the same way as in the first round, all new duos discuss the negative interactions. Person B tells his partner about the negative interaction, He then describes how the situation could have been more positive. The other person then describes how he experienced the situation. Person B then tells his partner what he appreciates about the reaction he just heard. When they are done, they return to the circle.
It is possible that there are person B's who haven't shared a negative experience and turned it into something positive yet. These people can now choose someone to speak with while the rest of the group waits. In this way, everyone had the opportunity to share their negative experiences, describe their desired alternatives, listen to the reactions of the other people, and reframe the situations in a positive way.

Variations

1. Instead of using the word "negative" when you talk about the interaction, you can talk about the interaction as something "you would like to have seen differently". The exercise will be the same only this time you avoid the word "negative".

2. After everyone has shared their negative experiences and transformed them into positive experiences, the group can evaluate the exercise. Ask the group the following questions to encourage a discussion: Was it a relief telling about the negative interaction? Did it help to hear the other person's version of the situation? Was it easy to turn it into something positive? Was it harder to tell someone about your negative experience with him or was it harder to hear someone else's negative experience with you? Why do you think that was?

3. If the team agrees, you can let the whole exercise take place in the circle. You point to someone who points to a person with whom he experienced a negative interaction. They do the original exercise in front of the other people. In this way, everyone can see and learn from each other. Next, the person sitting on the first person's left side does the same. Go clockwise around the circle until everyone has had a turn.

4. If someone doesn't have a negative interaction to discuss, you can tell him he can point to someone with whom he thinks the chemistry can be better. When they do the exercise, this person explains why he thinks their chemistry can be better. The other person describes how he sees their chemistry, and together they devise a solution to improve their chemistry.

Why you should use this exercise

This is a great exercise to clear the air between people in a group. When people have known each other for a long time, there are often suppressed feelings concerning past interactions. Because everyone chooses to speak with people with whom they had a negative interaction, they can honestly express their feelings. They can share what made them feel hurt. Because both sides of the story are heard and the negative situation will be turned into something positive, the group will experience a feeling of optimism. After this exercise, the group will experience the fresh feeling of starting with a clean slate.

Scan this QR code to see an animated example video of this exercise:

You can also type: **team exercise 68 negative to positive** into YouTube's search bar to find the video.

Team Exercise 69 - If you really knew me

“Every person on this planet has a story to tell, something that makes them unique adding to the whole.”
- Madisyn Taylor

Necessities: None.

To start the exercise, you tell the participants to sit in a circle. You tell the group that each person will now think of stories about himself that have a lot of meaning for him. These should be things of which they think the other persons in the circle don’t know yet. Tell them it can be anything, from very personal touching stories to fun facts. As long as they think no one in the group has ever heard the story before, any kind of story is allowed. Give them examples to stimulate their creativity. Tell them they can for example tell something about their family, about that one time they stole candy when they were a child, or that they once were are a big star wars fan.

Next, you tell them that each person can now choose which story he wants to share with the group. You ask a volunteer to share his story first. Instruct him to start his story with the sentence: “If you really knew me you would know that...” For example, someone says, “If you really knew me you would know that when I was fifteen years old I was a big fan of the zoo. I went there every Saturday with my father to see the animals.” While he tells his story, the rest of the participants remain silent and listen attentively. When he finishes his story, the other participants in the circle get a chance to ask questions about the story.

Tell the storyteller that he is not obliged to answer the questions; he only answers if he wants to. Tell them that if someone wants to say something or ask a question, he raises his hand. You point to a person who raises his hand and he asks his question. For example, "What were your favorite animals?" The storyteller will answer the question. For example, "I preferred the penguins." Let three people ask questions about the story.

Now, the next volunteer tells his untold story. When this person is finished talking, the others can now ask questions again. When three people have asked a question and the storyteller has answered the questions, a third person volunteers to tell his story. Continue in this manner until everyone in the group has shared an untold, personal story.

It is possible that someone thought of something after he shared his story that he thinks is interesting to share as well. Ask the group if there is anyone who wants to share something that he didn't share yet. If so, this person can share this story now. After he shares, the other participants can comment or ask questions in the same way as before.

After everyone shares his story, you tell the group to evaluate the exercise. Encourage the discussion by asking the following questions: Was it fun to hear some unexpected things about people you already know? Do you see some people in the group differently now that you know certain things about them? Do you think people will see you differently now they know new things about you? Give everyone the opportunity to answer the questions.

Variations

1. Tell them that if someone from the group already knows the story the storyteller is telling, he should let the storyteller know. The person who already knows the story will now finish the story. This will give the storyteller time to think of another story he believes no one knows. When the person who knew the first story is finished telling the first story, the storyteller now tells his second story.

2. When someone has finished his "if you really knew me..." story, you can instruct the other participants to react by telling a similar personal story about the same topic. It doesn't have to be exactly the same story. However, it has to be about something that story reminded them of. In this way, the person who shared his story feels supported by the others.

3. After the exercise and the evaluation round, ask each participant which person he got to know better by listening to his story. Point to a random participant to identify this storyteller and to tell why his personal story helped him get to know the storyteller better. Go clockwise around the circle so everyone gets a chance to tell which person he was able to know better and why.

4. When you have finished doing the above exercise, you can play a second round. Tell them that they can now tell a story the others already know, but of which they believe it deserves more attention. For example, "I sleep very badly at night. This is the reason I am not always paying complete attention at meetings." Again, the others can ask questions by raising their hands.

Why you should use this exercise

You can perform this exercise to help people who don't know each other well get acquainted. Since they are not well acquainted, stories the others don't know are easy to produce. It is also a great exercise to do with a group of people who know each other well. In this case, it might be more difficult for someone to produce a story no one knows. However, if they think of a new story, it can be very entertaining.
By sharing personal stories, people will immediately feel empathy towards each other. Therefore, this exercise is a great way to let the participants bond with each other and to create a group synergy.

Scan this QR code to see an animated example video of this exercise:

You can also type: **team exercise 69 if you really knew me** into YouTube's search bar to find the video.

Team Exercise 70 - Instructive feedback

"We all need people who will give us feedback. That's how we improve."- **Bill Gates**

Necessities: None.

To start the exercise, you tell the team to sit in a circle. You point to a random person and tell him that he is going to point to someone and give that person a compliment about his behavior or personality. Tell him the compliment can be anything as long as it is sincere and genuine. Tell him that secondly he is going to give that person feedback about something he feels that person can improve upon regarding his behavior or personality. And lastly, he will give that person a specific instruction that he can do immediately to put the feedback into practice. Tell the group that during the compliment, feedback, and instruction the only person who speaks will be the person who gives the feedback. The rest remain silent.

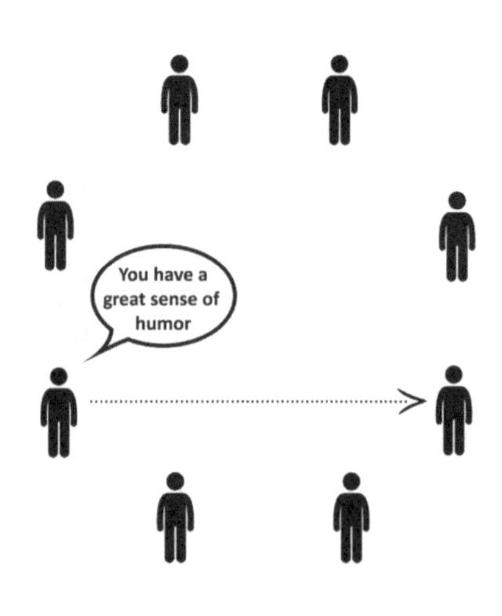

Let the person you pointed to think for a moment about which person he wants to give the compliment, feedback, and instruction. When he knows, he points to that person and gives him the compliment. For example he says, "I think you are very smart and you have a creative brain. If there is a problem with our computers, you can always fix it in an instance. This helps our team a lot." Next, he gives the same person the feedback about his personality or behavior he thinks he can improve upon. For example, "We always give you a lot of compliments about your being smart and your amazing work. I would like it if you sometimes can give us some compliments too." Now, he will give him a specific instruction that he

can execute immediately. In this case it must be an instruction that will promptly help him be more complimentary towards the others. For example, “Right now, I would like you to tell each participant in the group about something you think they excel in at work.”
In this way, the person who just received the feedback knows how to immediately implement the feedback in a productive way.
After the person who just received the compliment, feedback, and instruction has carried out the instruction, it is now his turn to choose someone from the group. He will give that person a compliment, feedback, and instruction in the same way. He starts with a compliment, for example, “I think you are very kind. You are always there for other people. If someone needs help, you are always the first to help.” Next, he gives this person feedback regarding a point to improve upon. For example, “Sometimes I think you are not comfortable asking other people for help. I think it would better if you asked for help more often.” Lastly, he gives him the specific instruction he can do immediately to put the feedback into practice. For example, “I now want you to ask someone from this group for a favor.” In this way, the person who received the feedback has a concrete instruction to implement immediately. After this person asks someone in the group for a favor, he now chooses another person in the circle. He will now give that person a compliment, feedback, and instruction.

Continue this until each participant in the group has received a compliment and feedback and has carried out a specific instruction.

Variations

1. In addition to an immediate instruction, the person giving the feedback can suggest an instruction that can be done in the future. There will now be two instructions - one for immediate use and one for the future. The one for immediate use can be executed at that very moment. The future instruction can be carried out later.

2. It might be the case that a participant can't devise a specific instruction to implement the feedback. If that happens, you can provide some suggestions. If the person agrees with one of the suggestions, he will give that instruction to the person he just gave the feedback to.

3. After the exercise, you can evaluate with the group. Encourage a discussion by asking the following questions: How did everyone experience the exercise? How did you feel about acting out the given instruction? How did you feel about creating an instruction? Was it easier to receive feedback or to give feedback?

4. It is possible that a participant doesn't feel comfortable carrying out the instruction. When this happens, you can ask the person who gave him the instruction to create another instruction. Just as long the other person agrees to the implementation of the new instruction.

5. If a participant declines to implement an instruction, you can ask him to create an instruction himself. He can then implement his own instruction to put the feedback into practise.

Why you should use this exercise

During this exercise, the team will learn how to give feedback combined with a specific instruction that can be immediately implemented. In this way, the person who receives the feedback knows how to immediately put the feedback into practise instead of just thinking or talking about it.
Because a compliment precedes the feedback, the person will be more receptive. The compliment creates a positive feeling; therefore, the receiver will deal with the feedback in a constructive way.
Because everyone will receive feedback and carry out an instruction, everyone will have the same experience. This will create a feeling of cohesiveness and openness within the group.

Scan this QR code to see an animated example video of this exercise:

You can also type: **team exercise 70 constructive feedback** into YouTube's search bar to find the video.

Team Exercise 71 - The puzzle

"To practice any art, no matter how well or badly, is a way to make your soul grow. So do it." - **Mary Lou Cook**

Necessities: Big blank pieces of paper, scissors and colored pencils boxes equal to the number of participants. A detailed, colored picture or image and glue. Before you start the exercise, make a copy or take a photo of the image.

Before the exercise, you cut the picture into as many pieces as there are participants in the group. Make sure none of the participants has seen the original picture. Don't make the puzzle pieces too complex, but don't cut them into exactly equal pieces. You can just cut out simple shapes, for example, a few squares and rectangles. Tell the group that the pieces you have cut out are puzzle pieces.
To start the exercise, you give each participant a puzzle piece, a big blank piece of paper, and a box of colored pencils. You now tell the participants to spread out through the room. Tell them each participant will sit alone somewhere in the room. They can sit on a chair at a table or on the ground. They need to sit where they are able to draw or paint on the paper. You tell them that now each person will cut the paper in the same shape as his puzzle piece. However, the participant needs to make his puzzle piece five times bigger than the original puzzle piece. Of course, they don't know exactly how much five times bigger is, so they will have to estimate. You now instruct each person to create a copy of his puzzle piece. They will do this by drawing the image that is on their puzzle piece onto the blank paper shape that they just cut out. Tell them they

need to do this as accurately as possible. Of course, they are allowed to give their own artistic touches to their drawings. For example, they can decorate the inside of an object with stripes or dots. As long as the shapes and figures in the drawing are the same size as in the original picture, the artistic touches are fine.

After each person has made his own enlarged copy of his small puzzle piece, the group convenes and everyone returns his original piece back to you. You tell the group that they will now try to recreate the original image by putting all the big pieces they created together. Therefore, an enlarged copy of the original image will be constructed. They put the puzzle pieces they just created on the ground or on a table and circle around them. If they put the puzzle pieces on a table, make sure the table is big enough for them to shift the puzzle pieces around.
Tell them they are not allowed to talk while puzzling. Because all the drawings are created in very different styles and they don't know what the original image looks like, it will be challenging for them to figure out which piece needs to be placed where. They continue shifting the pieces around until they unanimously agree that they have made an accurate, enlarged copy of the original image.
Now you show them the picture of the original image. They can now check if their copy is correct. They are only allowed to look just a few seconds at the original picture. If they didn't recreate the image correctly, they continue puzzling to make an accurate copy of the image. When they think they have made an accurate copy, they check again to see if it is correct. Let them continue puzzling until all the puzzle pieces fit together and form an accurate copy of the original image.

Variations

1. Instead of colored pencils, you can give everyone a normal, grey pencil. This will make it more difficult to create the final puzzle; they can't orientate based on colors.

2. To make the exercise more difficult, you can bring a black and white picture to the exercise and give each person a piece of the puzzle. Tell them that each person will draw the enlarged copy with colored pencils. This will stimulate their creativity even more and make it more challenging to put all the pieces together to form the big copy.

3. To make the exercise more difficult, you allow the participants to look for just one minute at the puzzle piece you gave them. Then, they have to return the piece to you. When they cut out the enlarged piece out of the blank paper and draw the enlarged copy, they won't have the original pieces to look at as an orientation point. They have to draw based on their memories. This will make it more challenging to create an accurate, enlarged copy. It will be more challenging to form the final puzzle with all the different pieces.

4. After they have finished the puzzle, they can glue their pieces onto another piece of paper and put the recreation in a frame as a reminder of the day. They can hang their art piece somewhere in the workplace as a nice memory to remind them what they created as a team.

5. If you frame their big copy, you can paste the original small piece somewhere in the corner of the big copy. This will provide an amusing touch to their work of art.

Why you should use this exercise

This exercise is great to stimulate the participants' creativity. Even if all the participants are not good drawers, they will do their best to make accurate, enlarged copies of their puzzle pieces. This way, each person will bring his own unique contribution to the exercise. Together, all the participants will use the individual creative pieces to form one big enlarged copy. This symbolizes teamwork; each person has his own creative personality that contributes to the bigger picture.

During the exercise they all have the same goal - to solve the puzzle together. This cooperative team effort will create a bond among the participants.

The energy of the group will be positive and upbeat when they succeed in creating an accurate copy of the image.

Scan this QR code to see an animated example video of this exercise:

You can also type: **team exercise 71 the puzzle** into YouTube's search bar to find the video.

Team Exercise 72 - The catching game

"If you want creative workers, give them enough time to play."
- John Cleese

Necessities: An empty room and blindfolds equal to the number of participants minus one.

To start the exercise, you tell the team they are going to play a blind folded catching game. You ask the group for a volunteer to be the first catcher. When someone volunteers, you blindfold that person and you place him in the center of the room. Instruct him to sit on his knees. You instruct all the other people to stand in a straight line on one side of the room and to kneel down too. Tell them that their goal is to make it to the other side of the room without being caught by the blindfolded catcher. A participant makes it to the other side of the room the moment he touches the wall at the other side of the room. Tell the participants that they have to walk on their knees. This way they move slowly and the exercise remains safe at all times. Tell them that if they prefer, they can walk on their knees and hands. At your signal, everyone will try to reach the other side of the room and the blindfolded catcher will try to catch as many people as possible. Because he is blindfolded, he will have to depend on his hearing and pay close attention to the sounds around him. To avoid being caught, the walkers will try to be as quiet as possible. When the catcher succeeds in catching someone, the caught person will sit down at the place he was caught. The other people continue trying to reach the other side while the blindfolded catcher tries to catch them.

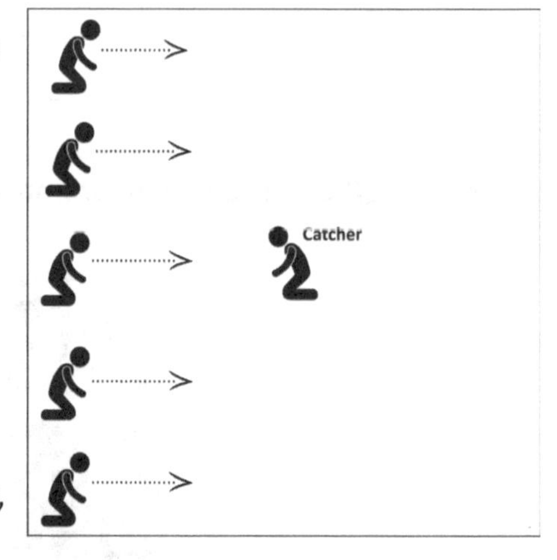

When the catcher catches another person, that person will sit down where he was caught as well. They continue until each person who has not been caught has made it to the other side. When this happens, you tell the people who made it to the other side of the room to stand in a straight line again. Tell the catcher he can now remove his blindfold. Now, give each caught person who is sitting on the ground a blindfold. Tell them they will now be catchers. Tell the catchers they can choose the most strategic launching point to catch the walkers trying to reach the other side. The catchers will now blindfold themselves and sit on their knees. At your signal, the walkers will try to walk to the other side of the room without being caught. Again, everyone walks on his knees or on his knees and hands. The walkers try to reach the other side and the catchers try to catch as many walkers as possible. When a walker has been caught, he sits down. The moment all the walkers who haven't been caught make it to the other side of the room by touching the wall, you play the next round. Again, the catchers remove their blindfolds. Each person who has been caught in the second round now also becomes a catcher and gets a blindfold. The catchers now strategically place themselves around the room and blindfold themselves. The walkers try to make it to the other side of the room again. Continue playing rounds like this until everyone has been caught or until there is only one walker left who has not been caught. This is the winner. One last time, he now tries to make it to the other side of the room.

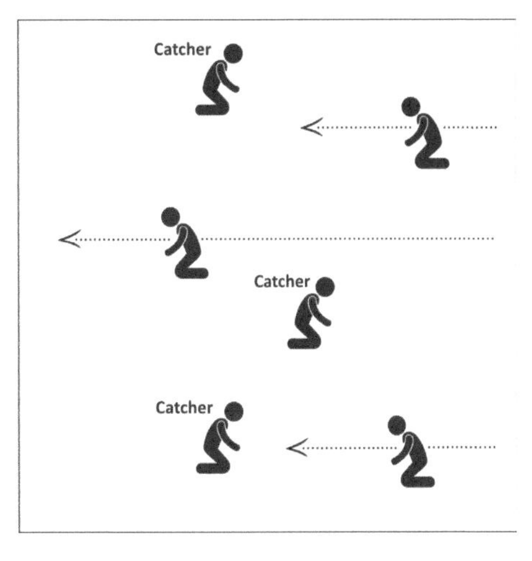

After he has reached the other side of the room or after he has been caught, the game is over. Tell all the catchers to remove their blindfolds to see who the winner is.

Variations

1. When there is one person left, he is the winner. However, you don't have to stop the game. You can let the winner continue to go from one side to the other side until he is caught. The moment one of the catchers catches him, the game is over.

2. It can be the case the blindfolded catchers become disorientated. This might causes them to go too near a wall. To prevent this from happening, you can place some participants at each side of the room. When a catcher comes close to bumping into a wall, the person who is standing nearby gently touches the catcher's shoulder. The catcher then knows he has to turn around.

3. If you don't have enough participants to put someone at each wall to prevent the catchers from bumping into a wall, you can keep watch yourself. Tell the team you will call out the name of the person who is too close to a wall. When he gets a warning, he knows he should turn around.

4. To make it more difficult for the catchers and easier for the walkers, you can play loud music. By doing this, it will be harder for the catchers to hear where the walkers are.

5. To make it easier for the catchers to know where a walker is, tell each walker to play a song on his phone. Each walker will put his phone in his pocket while the song plays aloud. The catchers can now hear where the walkers are. It will become more difficult for the walkers to make it to the other side and easier for the catchers to catch them.

Why you should use this exercise

This is a fun and energetic exercise to get the participants to physically interact. Because the participants move during the exercise, it is a great game to do as a warm up and for raising energy in the group.
All of the walkers have to move strategically from one side to the other while trying to avoid the catchers. Because they don't want to run into each other, each walker has to pay close attention to where the other walkers are. This will stimulate cooperation among the participants.
Each round the catchers have to strategically decide on which spots they will start to be able to catch as many walkers as possible. This will encourage their cooperation skills by coordinating efforts towards a common goal.
Because it is a competition, everyone will be motivated during the game to make it to the other side without being caught.
When at the end everyone removes their blindfolds, they will all be excited to see who is the winner. This will cause a shared positive energy in the group.

Scan this QR code to see an animated example video of this exercise:

You can also type: **team exercise 72 the catching game** into YouTube's search bar to find the video.

Team Exercise 73 - Animals

"In every animal there is a human and in every human there is an animal!" **- Mehmet Murat ildan**

Necessities: None.

To start the exercise, you tell the team to sit in a circle. You tell the team to think about the following question: If you were an animal, what animal would you be? And why would you be that animal? Tell them that each person can choose an animal based on one or more characteristics that he and that animal share. They can be characteristics based on appearance or based on personality. Give them a simple example to make it clear. For example, if someone thinks that he is faithful and likes to walk, he might choose to be a dog if he believes dogs are faithful and like to walk. Tell them this is just a simple example. If they want, they can make more in depth comparisons. For example, "I would be a horse because I can be strong, but I also like to help other people move forward like a horse carrying his rider." Tell them each person should think of at least one positive characteristic that he shares with the animal of his choice. They can also come up with characteristics they think they can improve upon. However, finding at least one positive characteristic will keep the exercise positive.

After they think about it for a minute, you now point to a random person who tells the group which animal he would be and why he chose that animal. When he has finished elaborating on his choice, the person sitting on his left can now tell what animal he chose and the reason he chose that animal. They go clockwise around the circle until

each person has shared his animal and the reason why he chose that particular animal.
Now, the second round of the exercise will start. You tell the group that in the second round, each participant will choose an animal for another participant. They will also explain why they chose that animal. You point to a random first person and you tell the others they can think for a minute about what animal they think this person would be and why. They choose an animal based on the characteristics of this person. Tell them they need to mention at least one positive characteristic belonging to this person and the animal they choose. By doing this, the exercise stays positive. After a minute, you point to someone from the group who will share which animal he thinks this person would be. He then explains why he chose that animal. Now, the next person sitting to his left side will do the same. He will also tell which animal he thinks this person would be and why. Go clockwise around the circle until each person has chosen an animal that he thinks suits this person and has elaborated on his choice.

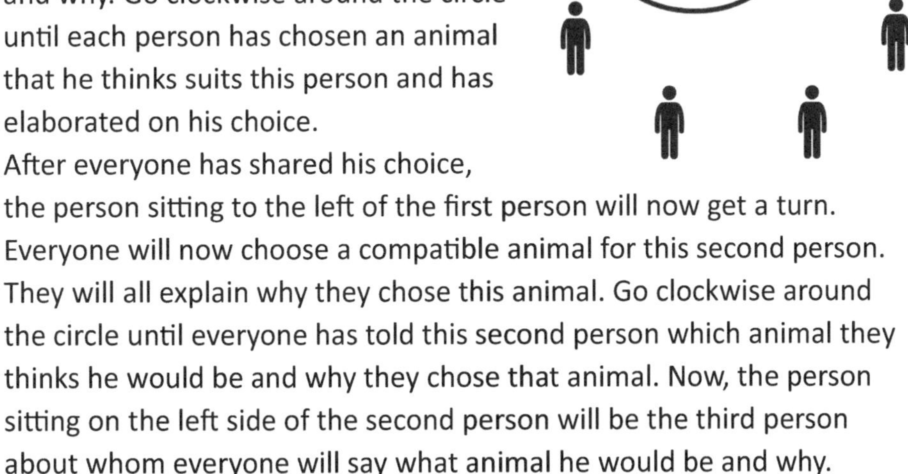

After everyone has shared his choice, the person sitting to the left of the first person will now get a turn. Everyone will now choose a compatible animal for this second person. They will all explain why they chose this animal. Go clockwise around the circle until everyone has told this second person which animal they thinks he would be and why they chose that animal. Now, the person sitting on the left side of the second person will be the third person about whom everyone will say what animal he would be and why. Continue until each person hears which animal the others think he would be and why.

.

Variations

1. In addition to animals, you can do the exact same exercise with other topics. For example: If you were a color, what color would you be and why? Or, if you were a song, what song would you be and why?

2. During the second round, after everyone told a person what animal they think he would be, he now tells them with what animal he agrees most and why. He can also tell with what animal he disagrees most and why.

3. During the second round, the participants can write their animal choices on pieces of paper and put them in a hat. They don't say their choices aloud. The person for whom they choose the animal draws a piece of paper from the hat. He reads the animal aloud and guesses which person wrote down the animal. If he guesses correctly, he earns a point. He also guesses the reason he thinks that person chose that animal. The person who wrote down the animal reveals himself and explains the reason. The recipient of these animal choices draws pieces of paper out of the hat until the hat is empty. He remembers the points he earned and it is the next person's turn to do the same. At the end of the game, the person with the most points wins.

4. Even if people don't know each other, they can play this exercise. The first round in which everyone comes up with an animal based on his own characteristics remains the same. However, in the second round, the participants come up with a characteristic based on their first impression of the person whose turn it is.

Why you should use this exercise

This is a fun exercise that can be in depth as well. Because each participant thinks of an animal that fits him the most, each person gains insight into how he perceives himself.
When, in the second round, they hear what animal others think matches their characteristics, they gain insight on how others see them. In a lighthearted way, these insights will teach them about their behavior and characteristics.
During this exercise, the participants will also have a lot of fun. The group will be very amused by the animal comparisons. Comparing compatible animals is a great way to raise positive energy. This exercise is an enjoyable way to let people get to know themselves and others better.

Scan this QR code to see an animated example video of this exercise:

You can also type: **team exercise 73 animals** into YouTube's search bar to find the video.

Team Exercise 74 - Values

"When your values are clear to you, making decisions becomes easier."
- Roy E. Disney

Necessities: A pen and twice the number of blank note cards as there are participants.

To start the exercises, you tell the participants to sit in a circle. Tell them that each participant can think about his most important value concerning teamwork. They also have to determine why that value is so important to them. Give them a minute to do this. Tell them it can be any type of value as long as they think it is an important value for teamwork. Tell them a value can be lighthearted such as accepting each other's humor, or a more serious value such as respecting each other's boundaries. You now start by pointing to a random person who will begin to share his value with the other participants. He also explains why that value is so important to him. For example, "When it comes to teamwork, the most important value for me is taking care of each other. I choose this value because I believe that teamwork only works if each team member feels that they are looked after." When this person is finished sharing his value and the reason that value is important to him, you write that value on one of the blank note cards. You don't have to write the reason. Now, the person sitting to the left of the first speaker will share his value and reason. When he is finished, you write his value on one of the note cards. Now, the person sitting to the left of the second sharer continues with the exercise in the same manner. Go clockwise around the circle until each person has shared his value and reason and you have written all the

values on the note cards. You now shuffle the notecards and pile them face down in the center of the circle. On the remaining empty note cards, you write the names of the participants. Shuffle them and pile them face down in the center of the circle next to the value cards. Now, the second round of the exercise will be played. You point to a first random participant who will pick a random card out of the name stack. Next, he will pick a random card out of the value stack. Tell him to think for thirty seconds how the person whose name is on the note card relates to the value on the other note card. For example, if he drew the name card with Jim on it, and he drew the value card with "being reliable" written on it, he will think about how Jim relates to being reliable. After thirty seconds, he shares his thoughts with the rest of the participants. For example, "I think Jim is really reliable. If he says he will finish a task at work, he will always do so. Also, he is always on time."

Now, Jim draws a name card and a value card and tells how the person whose name is written on the name card relates, in his perception, to the value written on the value card.

When this second person is done speaking, the person about whom he just shared his thoughts will now have a turn to pick two cards. He will follow the same procedure. Continue this until everyone has picked a name card and a value card and has told the team how, in his perception, these two relate to each other. Now you evaluate the exercise by letting each person share how he experienced the exercise. Ask them if they discovered new things about themselves and about others. And if they did, ask them to explain what they discovered.

Variations

1. Instead of each participant telling a certain person aloud how he thinks a value relates to him, you can tell them to silently write it on the back of the value card. They can then give it to that person. In this case, it stays private because no one hears it.

2. In the second round, you can let each person pick only a value card. He will then choose a person from the circle to explain how he thinks that person relates to that value. Because he chooses a person himself it might make it easier to explain the relationship between the value and that person. In this variation, you don't have to write down the names of the participants on the cards.

3. To shorten the exercise, you can write down certain values you think are important for the team. Write them on the note cards and pile them in the center of the circle. You write down the names of the participants on the other note cards, pile them up, and put them next to the stack of value cards. You now skip the first round and only play round two.

4. In addition to values, you can also execute this exercise with other topics. For example, you can use the topic "challenges". In the first round, each team member names what he thinks is the most important challenge the team is facing. For example "getting things done on time". In the next round everyone picks a challenge card and a name card and tells the rest of the team how he thinks these two relate to each other. For example how "Jane" relates to the challenge "getting things done in time".

Why you should use this exercise

During this exercise, the group will realize that everyone has different values concerning teamwork.
In the first round, each person will gain insight into his own most important team value.
They will also hear what others consider important team values. This will make them get to know each other on a deeper level.
In the second round, people will give each other feedback regarding a specific value. In this way, each participant will learn how other people see him regarding that specific value. This is an original way of giving feedback, because the value is predetermined. People might receive feedback regarding values about which they have never got feedback before. This will provide them new insights into how others see them.

Scan this QR code to see an animated example video of this exercise:

You can also type: **team exercise 74 values** into YouTube's search bar to find the video.

Team Exercise 75 - Acting

"To balance and take control of our emotions is one of the most important tasks in life." - **Dr T.P.Chia**

Necessities: None.

To begin the exercise, you tell the team to stand in a circle. Tell the group they are going to do an acting exercise. Tell them it is important for actors to show their emotions and that they are all going to practice this. Tell them that each person has to memorize the following sentence: "Today is my birthday". Tell them that using different emotions, they are going to say this sentence to someone in the circle. You now point to a first random person in the circle who will be the first actor. Tell him he will choose a random person from the circle, walk towards him, and stand still. He will say "Today is my birthday" to that person in a way the others can obviously see that he is happy. After he did this, the listener moves aside and the speaker takes his place. Now, the listener becomes the actor and gets a turn. He picks a new person from the circle, walks towards him, and says, "Today is my birthday" in a way everyone can see he is happy. Again, they swap places and the new actor now chooses someone from the circle and follows the same procedure. Continue until everyone has said "Today is my birthday" to another person in an obviously happy way.

Now, you point to a person who will say the same sentence in a way the others can obviously see he is angry. He will pick a random listener from the circle, walks up to him, and says the sentence. The actor swaps places with the listener and the listener now becomes the actor. He walks up to another random person and says the sentence in a way everyone can see he is angry. Continue doing this until everyone has

had a turn. Now, you point to a person who will say the sentence in a sad way. Again it has to be obvious to everyone that he is sad. They will continue doing this in the same manner until everyone has had a turn. Next, you will start the second part of the exercise. You tell the group that actors often want to show the audience that they are hiding an emotion. For example, an actor might have to act out a situation in which he is sad at a party, but he doesn't want the other people at the party to know. Nevertheless the audience should see that he is trying to hide his sadness.
Tell them that again everyone is going to say "Today is my birthday". Their performances should now convince people that they are hiding a certain emotion. Tell them it is important that it is still clearly visible to the others which emotion is being hidden. Tell them to start with the emotion of happiness. You point to a random person in the circle who will start the round. He will walk up to a random person in the circle and say the sentence. His performance should convince the others that he is hiding his happiness. Again, they change places. The listener becomes the actor and will now walk up to someone else from the circle doing the same. Continue until everyone has walked up to someone and said the sentence while showing he is hiding his happiness. Next, they will do the same in a way the other persons can see they are hiding their anger. And in the last round everyone will show they are hiding their sadness.

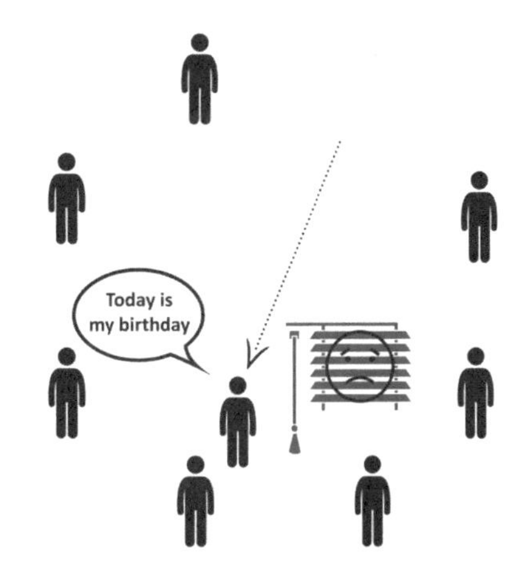

Now the participants evaluate the exercise. Ask them the following questions to encourage the discussion: Was it easier to show the others your emotion? Or, was it easier to show the others you are hiding your emotion? Was it always clear for everyone which emotion was being hidden?

Variations

1. You can play a third round in which each person can choose one of the three emotions he will be hiding. Let the others unanimously agree on what emotion he is hiding. If the others didn't see it correctly the actor will walk up to the same person again and do the same. Just as long it is clear to everyone which emotion he is hiding.

2. In addition to happiness, anger, and sadness, you can also utilize other emotions and feelings such as anxiety, jealousy, or intimidation. You play the exercise in the same way.

3. When they become proficient at the exercise, you can play a bonus round in which they are hiding an emotion with a specific other emotion. For example, someone shows he is hiding sadness by outwardly showing happiness. Let him say the sentence until the rest of the team can unanimously agree on what emotion he is hiding and what emotion he is using to cover it.

4. In addition to the sentence "Today is my birthday" you can play the exercise with other sentences as well. You can give them a sentence that relates to the group you are working with, for example, "Tomorrow we are going to move to another office".

5. You can also let participants create sentences themselves. The one who believes he has a good sentence can begin the exercise. In that round, the others will also use that sentence. For the second emotion, let someone create a new sentence. For each round, someone from the team can create a new sentence.

Why you should use this exercise

This is a fun exercise to allow the group to practice acting.
During this exercise, the participants will play with emotions in a lighthearted way. Each person will gain insight into what emotions are easy for him to display and what emotions are difficult to display. Even though this is an acting exercise, and the emotions are not real, it is still a safe way to practice revealing certain emotions. After they have conveyed emotions in this exercise, they will see that it will be easier to express these emotions in real life as well.
Hiding emotions in the second round will help them learn how to manage their emotions. If they hide an emotion too much, the others won't see which emotion they are hiding. However, if they don't hide it enough, the others won't see it as an emotion someone is trying to hide. They will see the difference between someone showing an emotion and showing that he is hiding an emotion.
The group will have a lot of fun and enjoyment while playing the exercise. This will contribute to a positive group chemistry.

Scan this QR code to see an animated example video of this exercise:

You can also type: **team exercise 75 acting** into YouTube's search bar to find the video.

Team Exercise 76 - A million dollars

"Compromise is what binds people together. Compromise is sharing and conciliatory, it is loving and kind and unselfish."
 - Ali Harris

Necessities: None.

To start the exercise, you tell the participants to sit in a circle. You ask them the following question: "If you won a million dollars, what would you do with it?" Tell them to think for a minute about what they would do with the money. Tell them also to think about the reason why they would spend it this way. Tell them they can decide to spend it all on one thing or to spend it on multiple things. They can come up with any expenditure as long as it is truly what they would use the money for. Tell them if they will would spend it on multiple things, they have to determine as precisely as possible how much money will be allocated for each expense. Give them an example to make it clear. For example, someone could say, "I would buy a luxury boat for two hundred thousand dollars because I love to sail. I will send my kids to college for one hundred thousand dollars so that they will have good jobs when they grow old. I will buy my own studio apartment in New York City for six hundred thousand dollars so I can go there occasionally to visit jazz clubs. The remaining one hundred thousand dollars I will give to a charity for homeless people because I think no one should live on the streets."

After the participants have thought for a minute about what to spend a million dollars on, you now point to a random person in the circle who will share what he would do with the money and why. After he has shared his story, the person sitting on his left shares what he would do

with the million dollars. Go clockwise around the circle until everyone has shared what he would do with his million dollars. Now you start the second part of the exercise.
You tell the group that in the next scenario, the whole group has won a million dollars together. Tell them they must unanimously decide how the money will be divided among the group members. They will do this based on what they just heard everyone say about how they would spend the million dollars. Tell them they can divide the money in any way they want as long as they unanimously agree on how the money is to be divided. Tell them they have ten minutes to discuss it. Of course, it can be easily determined by just dividing the million dollars by the number of participants, give each participant an equal amount and let each person decide what to do with it. However, most people will think differently about this. For example, someone may think that if a person doesn't want to spend it on himself but on a charity, he deserves more than someone who just wants to spend it on himself. After they have discussed this for ten minutes, and they have reached a unanimous agreement, they will tell you what they want to spend the money on. If they haven't decided how to divide the million dollars after ten minutes, you can give them another five minutes to discuss it.

After they finally come to a unanimous decision and they tell you how they will divide the million dollars, they will evaluate the exercise.
Ask them the following questions to encourage the evaluation: What worked in a positive way to help you come to a unanimous decision? What didn't work? What was the deciding factor that led you to the unanimous decision? Who was the leader of the discussion?

Variations

1. You can play a third round. In this round, instead of letting them decide how to divide the money, you can tell them that they can only spend the million dollars on one thing. In this case, they have to reach a unanimous decision on what they will spend the million dollars on.

2. When they can't come to a unanimous decision, you can give them a time frame and a warning. For example, you can tell them that if they don't come to a unanimous decision within five minutes, the money they have to share will be cut in half.

3. If they fail to come to a unanimous decision, tell them to try different options other than talking. For example, they can vote on different expenses. Or they can throw a dice to see what the expense will be. Maybe, if they have two options, they can flip a coin to see which one to choose. Tell them any method is fine as long as everyone unanimously agrees on the method they will use. Don't mention this at the beginning of the exercise. Only mention this if their discussion fails to yield a unanimous decision.

4. When they have successfully divided the million dollars, you can let them discuss issues they have to agree on in real life. For example, "How many times a year are we going to do a team building day?" Because they are already in the "unanimous decision mode", the real discussions will go smooth.

Why you should use this exercise

This is a great exercise to practice unanimous decision-making and compromising. In the first part of the exercise, each participant gains insight into what things in life are important to him.
The part in which everyone shares with each other what they would do with one million dollars is a fun way to get to know different aspects of each person.
In the second part of the exercise, they will practice unanimous decision-making. Decision-making is important in every group. It is important in a group of coworkers who have to solve a problem, or in a group of friends who want to decide where to go for a holiday. Unanimous decisions are the best decisions for creating a group vision. Through discussion, they practice determining what feels right and fair for everyone. They will learn using compromise to arrive at a unanimous decision.

Scan this QR code to see an animated example video of this exercise:

You can also type: **team exercise 76 a million dollars** into YouTube's search bar to find the video.

Team Exercise 77 - Mingle

"Each person you meet has something to teach you. Learn from each person!" **- Avijeet Das**

Necessities: Photos or pictures of animals equal to half the number of participants and a deck of playing cards with the jokers removed.

Before the exercise, you cut all the animal photos in half. Don't make straight cuts; make the cuts jagged so the two halves resemble puzzle pieces. You mix the pieces by shuffling them. To start the exercise, you give each participant one-half of an animal photo. Hand them out face down so no one sees who gets which half of which photo. Tell the participants that their goal is to find the person who has the other half of the photo that belongs to their half; this to make the picture complete. Tell them to do this as quickly as possible. There is one rule: Before two people are allowed to compare pieces, each person has to tell the other person something about himself. If they don't know each other, they can simply introduce themselves. If they already know each other, they can reveal something new about themselves. This should be information that they are sure the other person doesn't know. After they have shared information, they can compare their photo-halves to see if the two halves are from the same picture. If it is a match, they wait until the other participants have found their matches too. If it isn't a match, each person continues searching for the person who has the other half of his picture. They continue searching until each person has found the person with his matching photo-half.

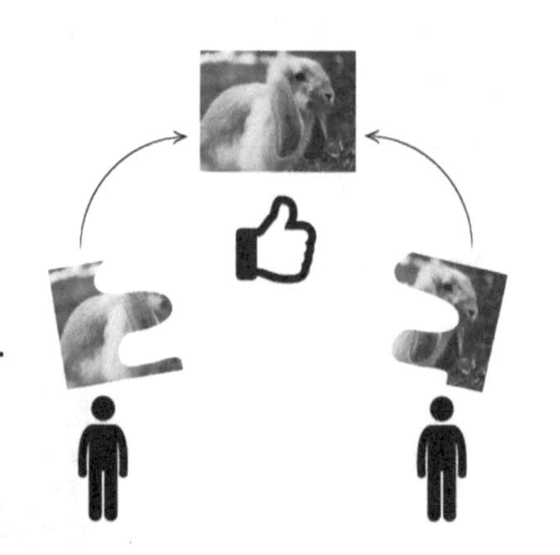

Now, you start the second part of the exercise. You give each person a playing card. Tell them that each number card retains its own value, for example, the three of spades represents the number three. Tell them that the jack represents the number eleven, the queen represents the number twelve, the king represents the number thirteen, and the ace represents the number one.

Tell them that the goal of each person is to find two other persons to form a trio in which the sum of their cards is an even number. For example, a three card, a queen, and a king equal an even number (3 + 12 + 13 = 28). The first group to form a trio that has cards equaling an even number wins the round. Each person from that group gets a point. Now, everyone returns his card and you give everyone a new card.

Now you play the second round. They will now form groups of three in which the sum of their cards is an uneven number. For example, a group of three people can have a five, an ace, and a three (5 + 1 + 3 = 9). The first trio that forms an uneven sum of numbers wins the round, and each person from that group gets a point.

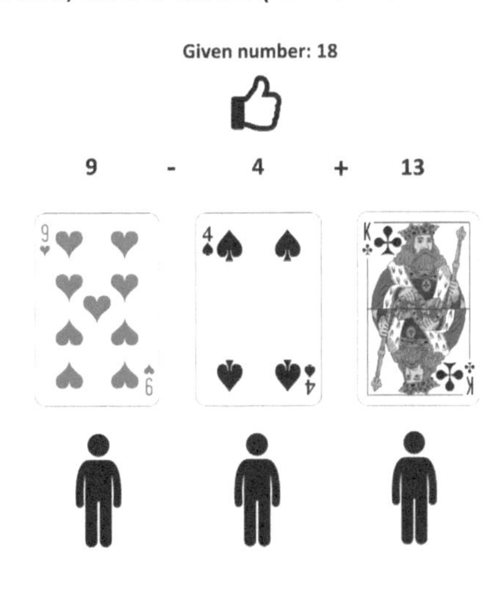

Now you play the final round. You give them a random number, for example, the number twelve. They will now form trios to form the number twelve. Tell them they can now add, divide, multiply, and subtract their numbers to let the outcome equal the number twelve. For example, if a trio has a king, a five, and a four, they can get the number twelve (king(13) - 5 + 4 = 12). The first trio that can reach the number 12 with their three cards wins the round. Each person in this trio gets a point.

Next, you give them another random number and they will do they same. Continue this with five different random numbers.

The person who has the most points at the end of all the rounds wins the game.

Variations

1. In the first part of the exercise, you can cut a photo in more than two pieces, for example, four pieces. Now everyone has to find his three matching people. Before comparing the pieces they all have to introduce themselves to each other.

2. In addition to introducing themselves in the first round before they can compare their puzzle pieces, you can let them reveal something. For example, the participants can reveal their biggest blunder, their biggest dream, or their desire for a team improvement.

3. Instead of animal photos, you can bring other photos, for example, photos of celebrities or famous buildings.

4. After the second part of the exercise, you can give the person who has earned the most points a fun prize. Tell the participants this before you play the exercise, so they will be more motivated to find the right people.

5. In the second round, instead of letting each person find two people to reach the given number, you can let them find three people to form a group of four. The first group of four who reaches the correct number wins the round.

6. If you are playing with a big group with more people than there are cards in a deck, make sure you take two decks. This way you can give each person a card.

Why you should use this exercise

This exercise is perfect for mingling large groups. It is also helpful as a warm up at the beginning of a team building day. Because this exercise involves a lot of walking, it energizes the group. Because they tell something about themselves before comparing the pieces of the photos, they get to know each other better in a casual atmosphere.
The second round contains a game element that will motivate the participants to mingle. Because everyone wants to find two other people to reach the correct sum as quickly as possible, they will have to communicate as efficiently as possible. In a lighthearted way, they are enhancing their communication skills.

Scan this QR code to see an animated example video of this exercise:

You can also type: **team exercise 77 mingle** into YouTube's search bar to find the video.

Team Exercise 78 - The orchestra

"No one can whistle a symphony. It takes a whole orchestra to play it."
- **H.E. Luccock**

Necessities: None.

You start the exercise by telling the team to form a straight line. You stand in front of the line and tell them that they will be an orchestra. Each person will be an instrument in the orchestra. Tell them you will do each part of the composition first, and if you point to someone in the line, he will copy your part. You begin to perform the rhythm by clapping your hands. After clapping the rhythm for a while, you point to someone in the line who will copy your rhythm by clapping the same rhythm with his hands. You and the person you pointed to now clap the rhythm together. When he has copied your rhythm correctly, you stop clapping so he claps the rhythm alone. Next, you perform the hi-hat by making the sound of a hi-hat with your mouth. Make sure it merges correctly with the clapping rhythm of the drum sound that the other participant is making.
So, now there are two "instruments" playing - the drum by someone in the line and the hi-hat by you. You now point to another person in the line who will copy your hi-hat sound. If he copied it correctly you stop the hi-hat sound. Now, one person in the line is performing the drum sound and another person in the line is performing the hi-hat sound. Next, you imitate a bassline sound with your mouth that merges with the sound of the drum and hi-hat. In the same way as before, you point to another person in the line who will copy your bassline sound. Now the drum, hi hat, and bassline are playing together. You now do the same for the strings. You make a high-

pitched "oeh" sound with your mouth to make a simple background string melody that merges with the other sounds. Again, you point to someone who will copy your string melody. Lastly, you whistle a short, repetitive melody that merges with the playing instruments and sounds. Make it a short, one or two measure melody that complements the other sounds. In the same way as before, you let someone copy your whistled melody. The team is now an orchestra performing a piece of music. Let them play the music for around thirty seconds.

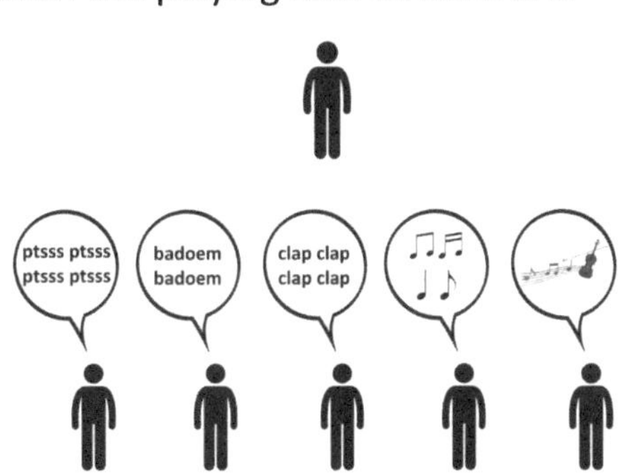

Now, you tell the team that if you point to someone, he will stop making his sound. However, if you will point to him again, he will start making his sound again. You now point to a random person who will stop making his sound. Continue pointing to people until they are all quiet. Now, gradually start the whole orchestra again by pointing to random people until everyone is making their sounds again. Next, you tell them that when you make a fist and point to someone, everyone must be silent except for the person you pointed to, so he will the only one playing his part. You now make a fist and point to a random person in the line who will keep on making his sound while the rest fall silent. Next, you point with your finger to random people who will start making their sounds again. Continue pointing with your finger and fist to random people to alternate the composition of the orchestra.

Now, you tell them that if you walk up to a person and take his place, that participant will take your place in front of the line and will be the conductor. You change places with a person, take over his sounds and let him conduct the orchestra in the same manner. Tell him that on a self-chosen moment he can walk up to a random person and switch places. That person will now be the conductor.

Continue with this until each participant has been the conductor once.

Variations

1. Start doing the exercise with well-known songs. This will make it easier for them to get back on track if they lose the rhythm or melody. A good song to choose is "The Lion Sleeps Tonight". The melody and rhythm of that song will work well with this exercise.

2. You can also let the participants make rhythms or sounds in other ways than with their mouth. You can for example instruct them to make a ritme by shaking their keys like a tambourine, or slapping their legs.

3. If the team becomes proficient and can perform and conduct a song easily, you can tell them to stand in a circle. You can let everyone be a conductor on a self chosen moment. Each person can now instruct anyone at any moment by pointing with his finger or fist to someone. They have to make sure just one person at a time gives an instruction. They have to sense together when it is someone's moment to make a change in the composition.

4. It can be the case that your instruction sound won't be heard because of the volume of the music that is already playing. In this case, you can walk up to the person you want to copy the sound, so he it can hear it over the music.

5. If you work with a big group, you can divide them into five subgroups. The subgroups stand next to each other with a small distance between them. The exercise will be the same, but instead of an individual performing a sound, a small group performs a sound together. For example, all the people from the "drum group" are clapping their hands. If you point to a subgroup, they will all stop making their sound at the same time.

Why you should use this exercise

This exercise is great to work on creativity and cooperation.
Each participant performs the sound of an instrument and has a responsibility to perform his sounds properly.
They have to listen very carefully to each other. It is important that all the instruments be aligned so they sound like a beautiful orchestra.
They will learn that next to taking responsibility on an individual level it is also important to listen to each other and work together to achieve the best result.
They will be amused because they will see that it is not always easy to sound beautiful together. There will be laughter when the inevitable glitches occur. When they are able to blend the sounds, they will be proud to hear themselves perform like a beautiful orchestra.

Scan this QR code to see an animated example video of this exercise:

You can also type: **team exercise 78 the orchestra** into YouTube's search bar to find the video.

Team Exercise 79 - The timeline

"Our memories are the only paradise from which we can never be expelled."- **Jean Paul Richter**

Necessities: A long cord and tape. Pieces of paper and clothespins twice the number of participants. And pencils equal to the number of participants.

To start the exercise, you hang the cord somewhere in the room so it is visible to everyone. The group sits in a circle next to the cord. You give each person a piece of paper, a clothespin, and a pencil. Tell each person to write his name on the paper. You now point to a random person and ask him to tell when and why he joined this group. After he has finished his story, he hangs his paper somewhere on the cord with his clothespin. After the first person hangs his paper on the cord, you tell them the cord is a timeline on which each person will hang his name regarding the correct chronological order. Tell them the timeline goes from left to right so the timeline starts all the way to the left side of the cord. Now, the person sitting on the left side of the person who just told his story does the same. He writes his name on the paper, tells when and why he joined the group, and hangs his paper on the cord. Where he hangs the paper is based on where the paper of the first person is hanging. If he joined the team later than the first person did, he hangs his paper on the right side of the first paper. If he joined the team earlier, he hangs his paper on the left side. The group will go clockwise around the circle until each person has told when and why he joined the group and has hung his name on the cord at the correct chronological place.

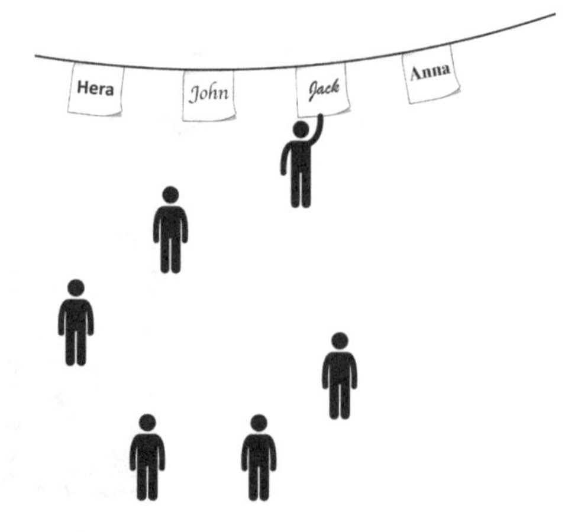

If everyone hung his paper on the cord in the correct place, the papers will create a chronological timeline of when each person joined the group.

You now give another blank piece of paper to each person in the group and you start the second round. You tell the team that each person can think of a memorable, positive moment that he experienced with this group. Using a few words, each participant will write down that moment on his paper. Tell them it can be anything. It can be something lighthearted and fun, or something emotional. However, it must be a memorable moment. You now point to a first random person who will tell the rest of the group about his memory. After he tells his story, he hangs the paper with his remembrance on the cord. He places the paper in the correct spot in the chronology. For example, if the memory occurred after Chris joined the group, but before Alice joined the group, he hangs his paper between the papers with Chris and Alice written on them. Now, the person sitting on the first person's left will do the same. He will relate his memory and will hang his paper on the cord in the correct chronological order. They go clockwise around the circle until each person has shared his memory and put his paper on the cord. There is now a timeline containing the moments everyone joined the group alternated with the memorable moments.

Lastly, if there are papers that are not in chronological order, they can be moved. Anyone who thinks his paper is in the wrong place can mention it and move the paper to the correct place on the timeline. Continue until everyone unanimously agrees that the timeline is correct. They now have a clear overview of when everyone joined the team and the highlights the team experienced together.

Variations

1. Next to letting them choose what kind of memory they would like to share, you can be more specific about what kind of memory you want them to share. For example, you can tell them that each person can share a memory about something that happened in the team that made an emotional impact. You can also tell them to share a funny memory or an educational memory. Any memory that could benefit the group will work.

2. In the first part of the exercise, you can let the participants place their names on the cord at the same time instead of individually. Tell them they can also change other papers if they think they aren't in the correct place. This can cause confusion and much laughter. This will create a lighthearted atmosphere. To complete this part of the exercise, the team must unanimously decide where every name should be.

3. If you don't have a good spot for attaching the cord, you can use the tape to attach the cord between two walls.

4. At the end of the exercise, you can take a picture of the timeline that the group can print out and hang somewhere in the workplace.

5. It is possible that there is no room to hang a cord that is long enough for all the papers. In this case, you can cut the papers in half, so they fit on the hanging cord.

Why you should use this exercise

This is a great exercise to remember when everyone joined the group and to reminisce about memorable moments.
The group members will enjoy sharing fond memories they experienced together. Talking about memories will form a bond because everyone is thinking about the same thing.
It is also fun for newcomers to hear other people talk about old memories, even if they didn't experience the memory themselves. Because the older members share their memories with them, the newcomers will feel a sense of inclusion and feel united with the group.
It is a good team building exercise because they are building the timeline together and agree unanimously about the chronological order. Seeing the final shared timeline will create a positive atmosphere.

Scan this QR code to see an animated example video of this exercise:

You can also type: **team exercise 79 the timeline** into YouTube's search bar to find the video.

Team Exercise 80 - Gifts

"For it is in giving that we receive."
- St. Francis of Assisi

Necessities: Enough wrapping paper for each participant to wrap two gifts. Extra paper in case some of the gifts are large. Tape and scissors.

To start the exercise, you divide the participants into random duos. You now tell the group that each person is going to buy or make two gifts for his partner. One gift will be an appreciation gift for an admirable characteristic his partner possesses. The other gift will be a motivational gift to help his partner change a certain characteristic. Give them examples to make it clear. For example, if someone appreciates his partner's sense of humor, an appropriate appreciation gift could be a notebook to write down his jokes. If someone thinks his partner is too outspoken, an appropriate motivational gift can be a pack of gum his partner can chew on instead of saying something that is better left unsaid.

Tell the team that everyone now gets fifteen minutes to buy or make the two gifts. Tell them they should not think about it for too long; their first idea is usually the best one. Tell them they don't need to spend much money on them; just two small presents are fine. If you think people may not want to spend the money, prior to the exercise you can ask their organization for money. If the organization is willing, you can give everyone a small amount of money to buy the two presents. Tell them they can also create gifts rather than buy them. Tell them they can be creative and look for available materials. Give them an example of a free gift to help them understand what you mean. For example, if someone is very shy,

his partner might want to give him a motivational gift to encourage him to be more outspoken. A handmade paper horn would be a good symbol for self-expression. This will cost nothing and is still a fun and meaningful gift.
You now place the wrapping paper, tape and scissors somewhere in the room, and tell them that they can wrap the presents if they want to. Each person will now go his own way to buy or to make two presents for his partner. After fifteen minutes, everyone should be back in the room.
They will sit in a circle again. You point to a first random person in the circle who will give his appreciation gift to his partner. Tell him to explain why he bought or made that gift. While he is talking, the others remain silent. After he gives his appreciation gift and explanation to his partner, the person sitting to his left gives his appreciation gift and explanation to his partner. Continue clockwise around the circle until each person has given the appreciation gift and explanation to his partner.
Now, you point to a random person in the circle who will give his motivational gift and explanation to his partner. While he is talking, the others remain silent. After he gives his motivational gift and explanation, the person sitting to his left now gives his motivational gift and explanation to his partner. Continue clockwise around the circle until each person has given the motivational gift to his partner and has elaborated on his choice.

You now evaluate the exercise. Ask them the following questions to encourage a conversation: Was it easier to buy an appreciation gift, or was it easier to buy a motivational gift? Was it better to give a gift or to get a gift? Why do you think that is?

Variations

1. Before the participants buy or make the presents, you can ask them if they want to give the presents to their partners publicly or privately. Some people might prefer to give the presents and feedback privately. It might make it easier for them to speak freely if there is no audience. After buying the gifts some persons wil give it privately and the others can just go back to the circle.

2. During the evaluation round, you can ask everyone where they bought the presents or how they made them. This can be fun for the others to hear.

3. You can also do the exercise without the presents being based on certain characteristics. Just tell them to buy a small gift for their partner that they think he will like and let them explain why they bought that present.

4. You can also let them form duos themselves. After explaining the exercise, you tell them to form a duo with someone they want to buy the two presents for.

5. If you think people need more time to buy the presents, you can extend the fifteen minutes.

6. You can do a bonus round; everyone buys or makes two presents for themselves. One of the presents should show appreciation for a characteristic he appreciates about himself. The other gift should be a motivational present that symbolizes a characteristic that he would like to change about himself. Everyone will show each other what presents they bought for themselves and tells why they bought them.

Why you should use this exercise

During this exercise people are giving and receiving feedback in a fun and creative way. Everyone will get feedback about a characteristic someone appreciates and about a characteristic someone would like to see improved. This will provide everyone with insight into how they are viewed by others.

This exercise generates positive feelings. Since the participants have to think about gifts that relate to their partners, the presents are very personal. This way everyone will feel special when they receive a gift. People will appreciate receiving thoughtful gifts and therefore will be more receptive to feedback.

Because everyone will have to think of gifts that coincide with their partners' characteristics, this is a great exercise to stimulate creativity.

At the end of the exercise, when everyone sees what everyone bought or made for their partners, many hilarious moments will occur. This will give the team a positive vibe.

Scan this QR code to see an animated example video of this exercise:

You can also type: **team exercise 80 gifts** into YouTube's search bar to find the video.

Team Exercise 81 - The riddle

"Problems are nothing but wake-up calls for creativity"
- Gerhard Gschwandtner

Necessities: None.

To start the exercise you tell the team to sit in a circle. Make sure everyone is listening and is paying close attention to you. You tell the group that they are going to solve a riddle. You will now tell them a story. Make sure you tell it in an intense and exciting way. Tell them they should imagine that they are walking through a big forest and that they are totally lost. It is getting dark and suddenly it starts to rain. They have to get home as quickly as possible. In the distance, they see a road that ends in a T-junction. They walk towards the T-junction. At the T-junction are two brothers and a sign. The sign says the following: One of the two roads leads to a dark place with wolves and witches and the other road leads back home. Tell them the sign doesn't say which road leads to which place. The brothers both know which road leads to the dark place and which road leads back home. Tell the participants that one of the two brothers always tells the truth and that the other brother always lies. No one knows which brother is the liar and no one knows which brother is the honest man. Tell them they can only ask one of the brothers one question. The answer to the question will have to tell them which road to take to get home. Now, you tell the group that together they have to develop the one correct question that will give them the answer they need to get home. The team will discuss together to develop the perfect question. They have to come

to a unanimous decision as to what the question should contain. They can discuss this for five minutes. Remind them that there is only one question that will lead them to the correct road and they can only ask one of the two brothers. The team now starts discussing the riddle.
The only correct question to know what road leads back home is: What would your brother answer when I ask him what way we should take to get home? No matter which brother they ask, the answer will lead them to the wrong road - the one with wolves and witches. If they ask the honest brother, he will tell them the lie his brother would tell him. Therefore, he will tell them to take the road that leads to the dark place with wolves and witches. If they ask the liar, he will lie about the right answer his honest brother would give him. Therefore, he will also tell them to take the road that leads to the dark place with wolves and witches. No matter which brother they ask, they will always get the answer that will lead them to the dark place with wolves and witches. Therefore, they should take the other way to get home safely.
After the group has developed a question they think will get them home, you tell them if it is the right question. If they have the correct question, you tell them that they solved the riddle. If the question is wrong, you tell them to continue discussing it for another five minutes. After five minutes, they share their question with you again. If they are correct, you tell them that they solved the riddle. If they still didn't come up with the right question, you can tell them the answer to the riddle.

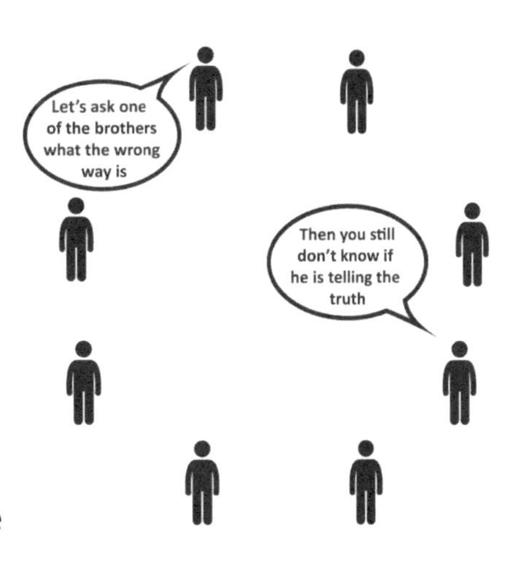

Now you evaluate the exercise. Ask the following questions to encourage the discussion: How did they come to the correct question? And who took the lead in the group discussion? What would they do different the next time they have to discuss a problem?

Variations

1. Ask the team if anyone already knows this riddle. If so, give these people a new riddle that they can solve together in another room. The riddle in Team Exercise 85 would be useful here.

2. If you are working with a very big group, you can split the group into smaller groups and make it a competition. You tell the story to all the groups at once and the first group that comes up with the correct question wins the game.

3. If they suggest a wrong question after their first attempt, you can give them a hint before they discuss the riddle again. For example: Tell them they should ask one of the brothers a question about his brother.

4. You can add details to the story to make it more exciting. For example, you can say that they went on a holiday to Africa and decided to take a walk in the forest. You can keep the story going for as long as you want, but end it with the same riddle.

5. You can change the characters in the story as long as the structure of the riddle remains the same. For example, you can tell them that there are two knights at the T-junction. One knight always lies and the other knight always speaks the truth.

6. You can write the riddle on a whiteboard at the beginning of the day and let everyone think about it during the day. At the end of the day, each person tells you his answer to the riddle. After everyone has told you their answers, you reveal the solution.

Why you should use this exercise

This is a great exercise to let the participants solve a riddle together. It is not an easy riddle, so they will need to coordinate their thoughts to get to the final correct answer. They will practice cooperatively reaching a conclusion to a difficult problem.
They will get insight into how the group chemistry works when they solve a problem together. They will become aware of who is prominent in the group and who stays in the background.
To get to the answer, they will need to think outside the box. This will stimulate their creativity, which will help with problem solving in real life.
When they reach the correct answer together, they will feel victorious. This will create positive group energy.

Scan this QR code to see an animated example video of this exercise:

You can also type: **team exercise 81 the riddle** into YouTube's search bar to find the video.

Team Exercise 82 - The four elements

"Everyone has different sides to them, and we're constantly changing."
- Bae Suzy

Necessities: Tape and four pieces of paper on which you write: earth, air, water and fire.

Before you start the exercise, you divide the room into four parts by making lines on the ground with the tape.
To start the exercise, you tell the participants to sit in a straight line on one side of the room. First, you will tell the group about the four elements: earth, air, water, and fire. Tell them that the element earth represents rationality and thinking. You then place the earth paper on the ground at the top of a random area you made with the tape. Now, you tell them that the element air represents amusement and lightheartedness. You now place the air paper at the top of another area. Tell them the element water represents emotions and sensitivity, and you put the water paper in a third empty area. Lastly, you tell them that fire represents passion and action and you place the fire paper in the last empty area. After you have created all four areas, you tell them that all people have each element inside of them. Everyone can be rational (earth), lighthearted (air), sensitive (water), and passionate (fire). Tell them each element is of equal importance. Everyone needs all elements in life. A life without rational thinking (earth) can be unorganized. A life without humor (air) can be boring. A life without emotions (water) can be shallow, and a life without passion (fire) can be flat. Tell them that people manifest different elements in different settings. For example, someone could be the funny one when he is at home with his family (air). He could be the rational one when he is with his colleagues (earth). He could be the sensitive one when he is with his friends (water). He could be the passionate one when he is with his soccer team (fire).

You now instruct each person to stand in one of the element areas that represents his behavior when he is with his friends. Give the participants time to decide which area best represents his behavior. After each person has made his choice, you point to a random person who will tell why he chose that particular element. After he has explained why he chose that element, you point to another person who will explain his choice. Continue choosing random people until each person has explained why he thinks he manifests that particular element when he is with his friends.

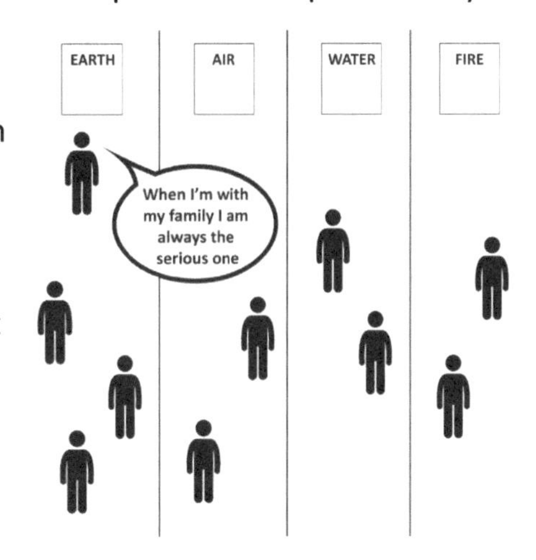

Next, you instruct the group that each person will now stand in the element area that represents him the most when he is with his family. When everyone chose an element you point to a random person again who will elaborate on his choice. Continue pointing to people until each person has explained his choice. Lastly, each person will stand in the element area that represents him the most when he is in the present group. In the same way as before, each person explains his choice.

In the final round, you tell the team that each person will now stand in the element area he wants to have more of when he is in this group. Give them an example to make it clear. For example, someone is standing in the fire area because he always motivates others. However, he finds it difficult to share his feelings. In this case, this person walks from the fire area to the water area.

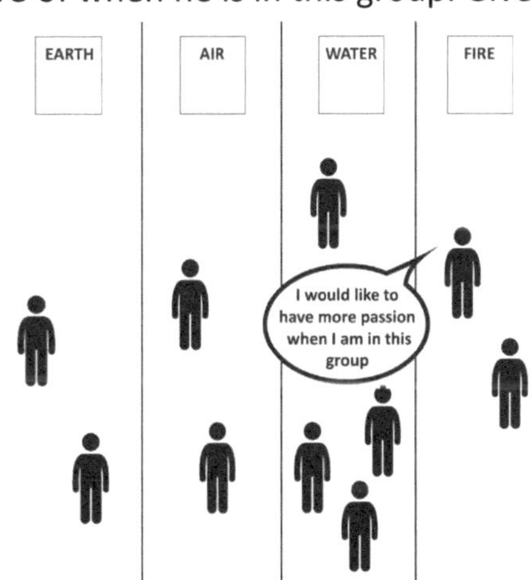

After everyone has changed areas, each person will explain the reason he moved from one area to another.

Variations

1. In addition to the elements they manifest when they are with friends, family, and the group, you can ask them what element they manifest in other situations. For example: at the dentist's office, in elementary school or on vacation. As they did in the original exercise, have them stand in an element area for each situation.

2. In addition to social situations, you can ask the participants which elements they manifest when they are in different states of being. For example, which element represents you when you are drunk, alone, or tired? Which element do you manifest when you are with people you don't like? As in the original exercise, they will stand an the element area for each state of being.

3. During the last round in which each person tells what element represents him in this group they can ask each other questions about their choices. Tell them that they are not obliged to answer the question if they don't want to. If you have enough time, you can do this for every round.

4. In the end, everyone is standing in an area which represents an element they would like to have more in this group. Tell them each person can think about a concrete action to increase that particular element within him when he is in this group. You ask each person to share that idea with the rest of the group.

Why you should use this exercise

This exercise is a fun and active way to teach a group about different personality elements.
Each participant will gain insight into himself and the others.
They will all learn a common "element language", so that they can talk about personality traits without judgement.
It might be the case that someone thinks that a person in the group can be "a bit too much". However, someone else might thinks that person is "amazingly motivating". Now, they can say without moral judgement that this person represents the element fire. They will see that each element has negative and positive characteristics.
The participants will also conclude that it is important to have all different elements in a group to achieve balance. In the last round, the team gets a clear overview of which person represents which element in the group.

Scan this QR code to see an animated example video of this exercise:

You can also type: **team exercise 82 the four elements** into YouTube's search bar to find the video.

Team Exercise 83 - The bluff game

"You can't bluff someone that's's not paying attention."
- Joe Mantegna

Necessities: A block of notecards and a number of pens equal to the number of participants.

Before you start the exercise, you put a row of tables in the middle of the room. To start the exercise, you tell the team to form duos. Each duo will sit facing each other on opposite sides of the table. You give each person a notecard and a pen. Tell the group that each duo is going to play a bluff game. During each round, two points can be earned. Each person will try to earn most points possible. There are three options each person can write on the notecards: split, steal, or you're a stealer. Tell them that no one knows what his opponent is writing on his notecard. It is a secret. Tell them that if someone writes "split" on his notecard, it means that he wants to split the two points with his opponent. Writing "steal" means that he wants to have both points. Writing "you're a stealer" means that he thinks his opponent wrote steal on his notecard and wants to have both points for himself. Tell them that after everyone writes one of the three options on his notecard, they will reveal to each other what they wrote. There can be six different outcomes: 1. Both people wrote split on their notecards and want to split the two points. In this case, the two points will be split and each person gets one point. 2. One person wrote steal, and the other person wrote split. In this case, the two points go to the person who wrote steal. 3. Both people wrote steal. In this case, no one gets a point. 4. One person wrote steal, and the other person wrote you're a stealer. In this case, the two points go to the one who wrote you're a stealer. 5. One person wrote you're a stealer, and the other person wrote split. In this case, the two points go to the person who wrote split. 6. Both people wrote you're a stealer. In this case, no one gets a point. Tell the participants that the moment the game starts they are allowed to speak with their opponent. Everyone will try to influence his opponent in order to get the most points out of the round. Each person is allowed to talk before, during, and after he wrote, split, steal, or you're a stealer on his notecard. For example, someone can lie about what he is writing on his notecard. He can tell his opponent he wants to split the points and promises him that he is writing split on his notecard. But in reality he wrote down you're a stealer. He hopes his opponent will believe him and will write down steal to steal the two points from him. If his opponent fell for the bluff and wrote steal, the bluffer who wrote you're a stealer wins the two points.

After each duo has played the game, each person remembers the number of points he has earned. Instruct the people in one of the lines to move one spot to the right. The person sitting on the far right moves to the far left chair. The people in the other line stay where they are. This way new duos are formed. You give each person a new blank notecard and the new duos will play the same game. After the points are divided, each person adds his new earned points to his previous points. Again, the people from the line that moved previously move one spot to the right so new duos are formed.

Continue in this manner until each person has faced everyone from the other line. The person with the most points wins the game.

Variations

1. You can also play the game without the you're a stealer option. This makes the game less complicated. In this case, there can be three outcomes: 1. Both cards have split on them, and both people earn one point. 2. One card says steal and the other card says split. In this case the one who wrote steal gets the two points. 3. Both cards say steal, and no one gets a point.

2. If there are two or more people with the same points, you can let these people play against each other until there is one final winner.

3. After the game, you can let the team evaluate the exercise. They can discuss which tactics worked the best. You can ask them the following questions to encourage the conversation: Was it easier to manipulate your opponent, or was it easier to discover your opponent's bluff? What was more profitable for you in the end - lying or telling the truth? Where you suprised by the bluffing abilities of your opponents?

4. If you don't have tables available, you can let them sit across from each other with no table between them. It can be a bit more difficult to write something on a notecard without a table; in this case, markers might work better than pens.

5. In addition to handing them blank note cards each new round, you can just give each person a block of notecards in the first round. When the people move, they will take their own block of notecards with them and get a new blank notecard themselves.

Why you should use this exercise

This is an exciting and interesting game to stimulate the group's interest in persuasion and influencing. Earning the maximum number of points requires the participants to be sharp and focused. This will train their concentration.
In order to win a round, each person will need to interpret someone's bluff. At the same time he needs to influence his partner trying to make him write down a particular option.
By trying to understand each other, they are improving their ability to read body language. By trying to influence each other, they are improving their negotiating skills.
The game element will create an exciting atmosphere and will keep the participants engaged during the whole exercise.

Scan this QR code to see an animated example video of this exercise:

You can also type: **team exercise 83 the bluff game** into YouTube's search bar to find the video.

Team Exercise 84 - Calling names

"Names have power." - **Rick Riordan**

Necessities: None.

During the exercise, the group stands in a circle. Make sure everyone stands at an arm's length distance from each other. You point to a first random person who will loudly calls out his own name. After he has announced his name, all the others repeat his name in unison. The person who announced his name doesn't repeat his own name and remains silent. Now, the person standing to the left of the first person announces his own name. All the others now call out the first person's name and the second person's name. The second person will now be silent. Now, the person to the left of the second person announces his own name. The rest of the group will now repeat in unison the first, second and third names while the third person remains silent. Continue clockwise around the circle until everyone has announced his own name. When the last person has announced his name, the whole group except for that last person announces all the names of the people in the group.

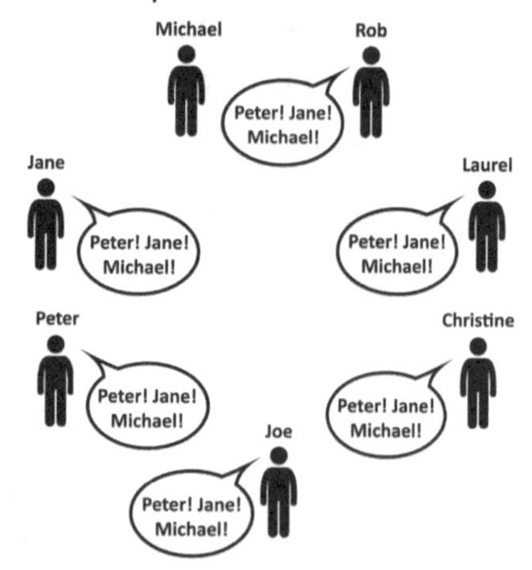

You now start the second round. Tell the team that each person will call out his name with an alliterative adjective before it. In the same way as in the first round the others then repeat the adjective and the name. You point to a first random person who announces his name and the alliterative adjective. For example, if someone's name is Hank, he chooses an adjective that starts with the letter H. For example, he could say happy Hank. The others, except Hank, say happy Hank in unison. Now, the person standing to the left of Hank does the same.

He announces his name preceded by an alliterative adjective. For example, if his name is Peter, he could say perfect Peter. The whole group, except Peter, now announces the name and adjective of the first person and the name and adjective of the second person. In this case, they say "happy Hank, perfect Peter". Continue clockwise around the circle until each participant has announced his name and adjective. When the last person has announced his name and adjective, the whole group except for the last person, announces the names and adjectives of all the people in the group.

In the third round, you point to a random person who will call out his name and adjective. Now, he also adds a movement. It can be any kind of movement as long it is uncomplicated and easy to copy. If the person you pointed to calls out "weird Waldo" while clapping his hands, all the others, except Waldo, will call out "weird Waldo" while clapping their hands. Now, the person standing to the left of Waldo does the same. He announces his name with an alliterative adjective, for example, "funny Fred". He also adds a movement such as pinching his nose. Now, the group announces the name and adjective and copies the movement of the first person and the name, adjective, and movement of the second person. In this case, everyone except Fred calls out ""weird Waldo while clapping their hands and then "funny Fred" while pinching their noses. Continue clockwise around the circle until everyone has announced his name and adjective and performed a movement. When the last person in the circle has called out his name and adjective and performed his movement, the whole group except for that last person calls out the names and adjectives and performs the movements of all the people in the group.

Variations

1. In addition to alliterative adjectives, you can instruct the group to add a descriptive adjective to their names that fits their personality. For example, they could say funny Sarah or caring Peter. In this case, it doesn't have to be alliterative, so it won't take long to produce an adjective.

2. After someone calls out his name, instead of remaining silent, he can also repeat his own name together with the others. In this way, everyone in the group will together be calling out the same thing at the same time.

3. In the second round, instead of an alliterative adjective, you can instruct them to produce adjectives that rhyme with their names. For example, sweet Pete is a good rhyme.

4. As a bonus round, you can instruct the participants to execute the exercise while walking crisscross around the room. In this case, they have to remember the order of the names without seeing it in the circle. This will make it more challenging.

5. If someone can't think of a movement, you can give him a few examples to choose from. Tell him he can wave, jump, or give himself a tap on the shoulder.

6. If someone can't produce an alliterative adjective, you can suggest a few alliterative adjectives for that person's name. He can choose the one he likes most.

Why you should use this exercise

This exercise is great to play with a group of people who don't know each other's names yet. During this exercise, all the names will be repeated. Therefore, after the exercise everyone will know each other's names. Knowing each other's names will create cohesiveness within the group.
It is also a great exercise to play with people who already know each other. It will be amusing for the participants to hear what adjectives everyone will come up with. Producing alliterative adjectives and movements will spark the group's creativity. Because of the physical movements in round three, the team will loosen up, which will bring a lighthearted and energetic atmosphere into the group. Therefore, this exercise can be used as an active energizer to start the day with.

Scan this QR code to see an animated example video of this exercise:

You can also type: **team exercise 84 calling names** into YouTube's search bar to find the video.

Team Exercise 85 - Thinking outside the box

"I have never understood the saying 'To think outside the box.' Why would anyone sit inside of a box and then think outside of it. Rather just get out of the box." **-Lawrence Anthony**

Necessities: None.

To start the exercise, you tell the team to sit in a circle. Make sure everyone is listening and is paying close attention to you. You tell the group that they are going to solve a riddle. They have to think outside the box to solve the riddle. Tell them that there is a man standing alone in an empty room with the door closed. There are no windows in the room and the walls are empty. On one of the empty walls are three switches: switch A, switch B, and switch C. At this moment, all the switches are pointing down which means they are turned off. Tell them that one of the three switches is connected to a lamp in another nearby room. The goal of the man in the empty room is to discover which of the three switches is connected to the lamp in the nearby room.

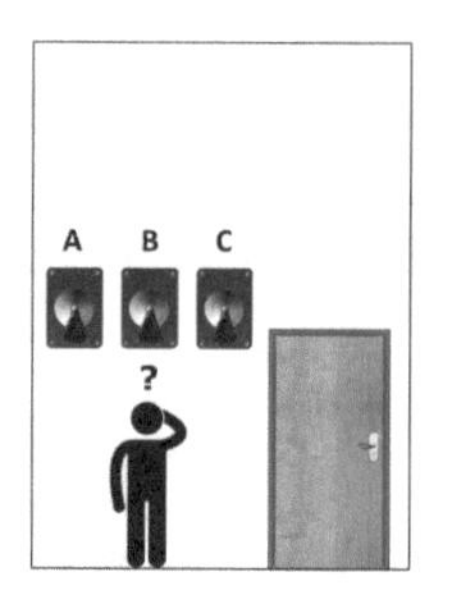

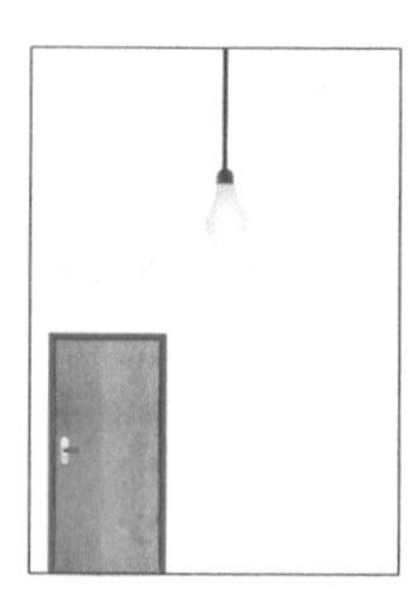

The man can turn the switches on and off as many times as he wants. However, he can only walk to the other room once, to discover which of the three switches is connected to the lamp.
You now ask them question of the riddle: How can the man discover which switch is connected to the lamp in the other room?
They can now decipher the riddle together. Tell them that a solution is possible if they think logically and outside the box. Tell them they should unanimously agree on the solution they develop.
There is only one correct solution to knowing which switch is

connected to the lamp: First, the man standing in the room should turn on switch A. After he turns on switch A, he waits for five minutes. After five minutes, he turns off switch A. He now turns on switch B and walks to the other room. If the lamp is on, he knows that switch B is connected to the lamp. If the lamp is off, he feels the lamp to see if it is warm. If the lamp is warm, he knows the lamp has just been on. Therefore, switch A is connected to the lamp. If the lamp is cold and off, he knows switch C is connected to the lamp. In this way, he will know for sure which of the three switches is connected to the lamp.
Give the group five minutes to develop a solution. For example, one person might say: "He can just turn on all the switches together and walk to the other room." Another person might say: "That doesn't make sense. If he turns on all the switches, of course the light in the other room will go on. However, he still doesn't know which of the three switches is connected to the lamp." After the group has developed a solution to knowing which switch is connected to the lamp, you tell them if they are correct. If they developed the right solution, you tell them that they have solved the riddle. If they developed the wrong solution, you tell them to discuss it again for five minutes. After five minutes, they tell you their newly found solution. If they are correct, you tell them they have solved the riddle. If they still don't know the right answer, you can tell them the answer to the riddle.

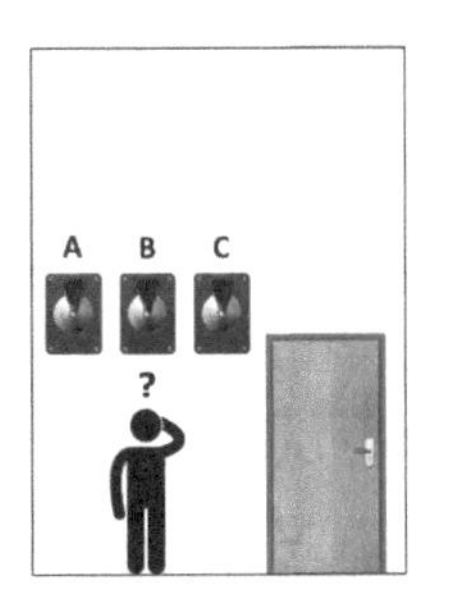

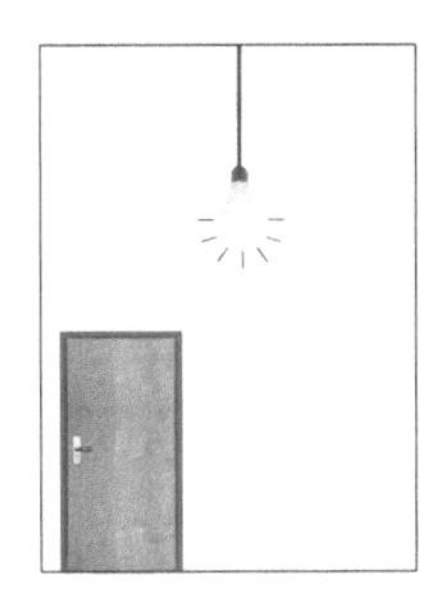

Next, you let them evaluate the process. Ask them the following questions to encourage a conversation: What process did you use to develop a solution? Was there adequate cooperation so that everyone had some input? What did you learn about problem solving during this exercise?

Variations

1. Ask the team if someone already knows this riddle. If so, give the people who know the riddle a new riddle that they can solve together in another room. For example, you could use the riddle of Team Exercise 81.

2. If you are working with a large group, you can split the group into smaller groups and make it a competition. You tell the story to all the groups at once and the first group that formulates the solution wins the game.

3. Before they start solving the riddle you can tell them the solution isn't something flimsy such as "he can just look under the door to see if the light is on", or "it is the right switch because that is the "right' answer". Tell them that the answer could be used as a solution if that situation were to occur in real life. Knowing this will motivate them to solve the riddle.

4. You can also write the riddle on a whiteboard at the beginning of the day and let everyone think about it during the day. At the end of the day, you ask who thinks he has the correct answer. After each person has shared his answer, you reveal the solution.

5. If they devised the wrong solution after their first attempt, you can give them a hint before they discuss the riddle again. For example, you can say, "To figure out which switch is connected to the lamp can take some time." Or, "You have more senses than just sight."

Why you should use this exercise

In order to devise a solution, the participants must use solution-oriented cooperation and communication. While they are trying to find the solution to the riddle, their minds will be focused on the same problem. This will make the group feel a cohesive energy because they will all be on the same page.
Because the answer to the riddle isn't obvious, they will need to think outside the box. Thinking outside the box will train their creative thinking skills.
Because it is a difficult riddle, the participants will be excited if they discover the solution together. The group will experience a eureka moment. If they don't find the solution, they will be surprised when you tell them what the solution is. This will create a cheerful moment in the group as well.
The part of the exercise in which they evaluate their processes will provide insight into how they communicate as a group. They can use this insight to improve their problem solving skills.

Scan this QR code to see an animated example video of this exercise:

You can also type: **team exercise 85 thinking outside the box** into YouTube's search bar to find the video.

Team Exercise 86 - Like, like, like

"We all need people who will give us feedback.
That's how we improve."
- Bill Gates

Necessities: None.

To start the exercise, you tell the participants to form two straight lines in the center of the room with an equal number of people in each line. The two lines will stand opposite each other at arm's length distance. Each person will face the person in front of him. You point to one line and tell them that everyone in that line will be person A and everyone in the other line will be person B. Now you instruct each person A to tell the person who is standing in front of him what he likes about person B's behavior. Tell them to say, "I like that..." and to finish the sentence with something they like about person B. They could say something lighthearted or something serious as long as they are being honest about their feelings. Tell them that just a few sentences will be fine. For example, person A says, "I like that you have such a great sense of humor. You make everyone happy with your jokes." Tell them that person B silently listens to what person A tells him. When all person A's are done talking, you instruct them that now each person A will tell the same person B what he would like to see differently regarding his behavior. Person A says, "I would like you to..." and continue the sentence with something he would like to see happening. In a few sentences, person A has to honestly tell person B what he thinks. For example, "I would like you to arrive on time for meetings. I think people would appreciate it when they can rely on

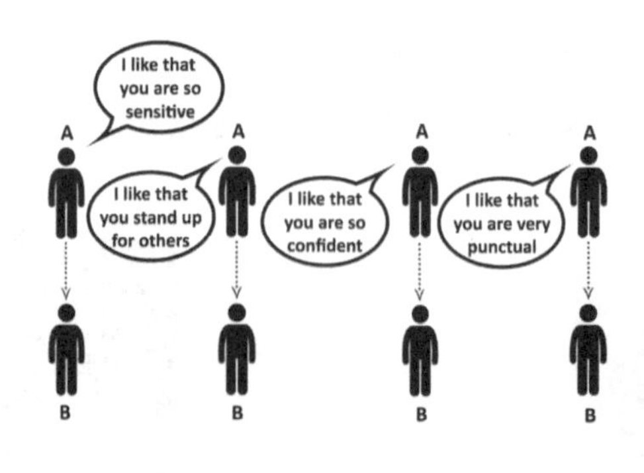

you." When all person A's are done talking, you instruct them that now each person B will respond. Person B tells person A what he thinks will happen when he implements this change in behavior. Person B starts with the words, "Then I would be like..."

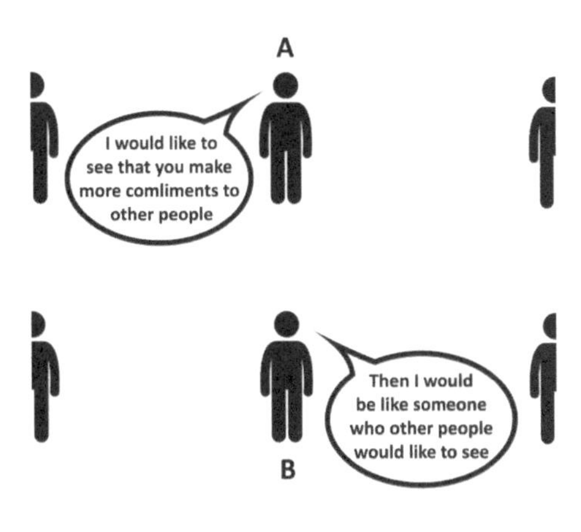

Using this "being on time" example, person B might reply, "Then I would be like someone who people can trust. People would take me more seriously and pay more attention to what I have to say."

When all person B's are done talking, you now tell the group to switch roles. Each person B will now tell the person A in front of him what he likes about him. He also starts the sentence with "I like that..." Person A will remain silent while person B is talking. Secondly, person B will tell person A what he would like to see differently regarding person A's behavior, starting with the words, "I would like you to..." Lastly, person A tells person B what he thinks it would be like if he made the suggested change, starting with the words, "Then I would be like..."

After all duos are done exchanging the three sentences, you now instruct people in line A to move one spot to the right. The person standing at the far right in line A moves to the far left spot. In this way, new duos will be formed. Now each new duo will do the same. When every duo is done, line A moves one spot to the right again. Continue this until everyone has faced everyone from the other line.

You now tell the participants to sit in a circle to evaluate the exercise. Ask them the following questions to encourage the conversation:

Was it easier to receive feedback or to give feedback? Do you think you are going to change your behavior due to the suggestions you have received? Give each participant the chance to answer the questions.

Variations

1. You can instruct each person to tell the person in front of him what he likes about this group in general. He starts with the words, "What I like about this group..." Next, he will say what he would like to change within this group, starting with the words, "What I would like to see in this group..." Lastly, the other person who just heard what the person across from him would like to change within the group says, "Then in the group it would be like..." and continues the sentence saying what he thinks it would be like if the group changed that way.

2. After everyone from line A has faced everyone from line B, you can instruct the group to form duos with people from their own line as well. Have them stand somewhere in the room and do the same exercise. Let them change duos until each person has faced everyone from the group.

3. You can also instruct the team to play this game while the group is standing in a circle. You point to a random person who will be person A, and he will choose another random person from the circle who will be person B. Instruct person A to walk towards person B and stand at an arm's length distance. They do the exercise in the same way while the rest of the group watches. After they have finished the three steps, they change places. Person B becomes person A and walks to another person in the circle who will be person B. Continue until everyone has been person A and person B once.

4. You can tell them to write down the "Then I would be like..." sentence. In this way, they can always review what they would be like if they changed their behavior in the way they have been told.

Why you should use this exercise

This is a great way for practicing giving and receiving feedback. During the exercise everyone will get insight into how other people see them.
Because people just say a few sentences while the others remain silent, the exercise won't turn into a discussion. In this way, the feedback process remains fresh and structured.
Because each person responds to the suggested behavioral change saying "Then I would be like...", it will make them understand the positive results the suggested change might bring. This will improve the chance that they will put the suggested feedback into practice.
The three likes - "I like", "I would like you to", and "Then I would be like" - will give the exercise a lighthearted and playful touch.

Scan this QR code to see an animated example video of this exercise:

You can also type: **team exercise 86 like, like, like** into YouTube's search bar to find the video.

Team Exercise 87 - The newspaper

"The strength of the team is each individual member. The strength of each member is the team." - **Phil Jackson**

Necessities: A printer you can connect to a laptop.

Prior to the exercise, tell the participants that they have to bring their own laptops. Make sure one out of three participants brings his laptop. If they have not enough laptops, you can take your own laptop and borrow some laptops from friends or the organization.
To start the exercise, you tell the team that during this exercise they will make their own team newspaper. You divide the team into random groups of three. Tell them that each trio has to create a category for the newspaper. Say that the categories can be anything they want as long as it is a category that can be found in a newspaper. To make it clear, you give them a few examples of categories that are found in newspapers. For example, entertainment, business, and gossip. You now point to the first trio that will unanimously decide on a category. The content they will use for their part of the newspaper will pertain to this category. For ten seconds, the trio can discuss which category they would like to work on. After they have shared their choice, you point to the next trio. Tell them that they have to choose a different category than the first trio chose. After this second trio decides on a category, you point to the third trio who will do the same. Continue until each trio chooses a different category. You now tell the group that each trio will sit somewhere in the building and work on their own category. Each trio must have at least one laptop. Tell them the stories should relate to this group. Each group will make at least one full letter-size page for the newspaper containing one or more articles about the topic of their category. Tell them that if they want to write multiple letter-size pages, that is also fine. However, five pages is the maximum. They can also use pictures in their article(s). They can download pictures on the internet, and if they have personal pictures on their phones they

want to use, they can include those as well. For example, if someone has a picture on his phone of the team at an art gallery and their category is art, they can use this picture. Tell them they can be as creative as they want. They can use several software programs to type the article and put the photos in. It doesn't have to be very fancy. Word Editor or a simple text editor will work. If there are laptops with fancier software like Photoshop or InDesign, they can be used as well.

After each trio has finished their newspaper article(s), tell them to email it to your email address. Take a laptop, log into your email account, and download the articles. You will now ask one or two volunteers to make all the articles the trios sent into one final newspaper. Encourage the two volunteers to make it look as much like a real newspaper as possible. For example, the front page of the newspaper has the most important article. Next to this article, will be quotes from the articles contained in the newspaper. Tell them that the editors can't change the content of the articles. The editors get a half-hour to finish the newspaper. While the editors are compiling the newspaper, the others can take a break.

When the editors finish the final newspaper, you connect the computer to the printer. Print all the papers and staple them together. Continue doing this until each participant has his own team newspaper.

Now, you evaluate the exercise by asking the participants how they experience the group process.

Let everyone share their findings with the other participants.

Variations

1. Tell the trios that if they want, they can choose creative symbolic categories as well. For example, they can choose weather as a category. They can use weather as a metaphor for the team's moods. For example, "On Monday, everyone was grumpy, so it was cloudy. On Tuesday, everyone was happy, so we had a lot of sun." They can continue their team mood weather forecast all week. If some trios choose such a category, it will bring a fun variety to the news paper.

2. When you are with a big group, you can tell one trio that they will be the editors-in-chief. The other trios will be the article writers just as in the original exercise. When a trio has finished their article(s), they show or email the first version to the editors-in-chief just as they would for a real newspaper. The editors-in-chief can provide comments and say what they would do to improve the article(s). When the editors-in-chief approve the article(s), the trio can email them to you. In the same way as in the original exercise two volunteers will make it into one final newspaper.

3. If you don't have a printer, you can make the newspaper into a PDF file and send the digital version to everyone by email. In this way, everyone still has his own newspaper. You can also do both; you give them all a paper copy and email the PDF file as well.

4. If you have a big group, you can instruct one trio to make a puzzle for the newspaper. Tell them the puzzle has to be connected to the group, for example, a word finder with all the names of the participants in it.

Why you should use this exercise

During the exercise, the participants work together to achieve the same goal: making their own team newspaper.
Each person in a trio will provide input that will add to their final article. All the articles the trios create will together coalesce to form the final newspaper. This will show the group that creatively joining their individual efforts can result in a superior product.
Because the articles are about the group itself, they will also get the chance to talk about the group and retrieve memories.
Creating their own team newspaper will boost their spirits and stimulate their creativity.
After the exercise, they will all have a pleasant memory to revisit any time they want.

Scan this QR code to see an animated example video of this exercise:

You can also type: **team exercise 87 the newspaper** into YouTube's search bar to find the video.

Team Exercise 88 - The right answer

"To know a very different person from ourselves is a great luck for us!"
- Mehmet Murat ildan

Necessities: Paper and pens equal to the number of participants.

To start the exercise, you give each person a piece of paper and a pen. You divide the team into random duos. Each duo will sit together somewhere in the room. Let the duos decide who will be person A and who will be person B. You ask the participants the following question: What is your favorite food? Person A now writes down his favorite food without showing it to person B. Person B writes down what he thinks person A just wrote. Then, person B writes what his favorite food is and person A writes down what he thinks person B just wrote. Next, they check each other's paper to see if they were correct about the other person's choice. Tell the duos that points can be earned in the following way: If they are both correct about the other person's choice, both participants earn two points. If one of the two participants guessed correctly, they both earn one point. If no one guessed correctly, no one earns any points. Each person now writes on his paper how many points he earned.

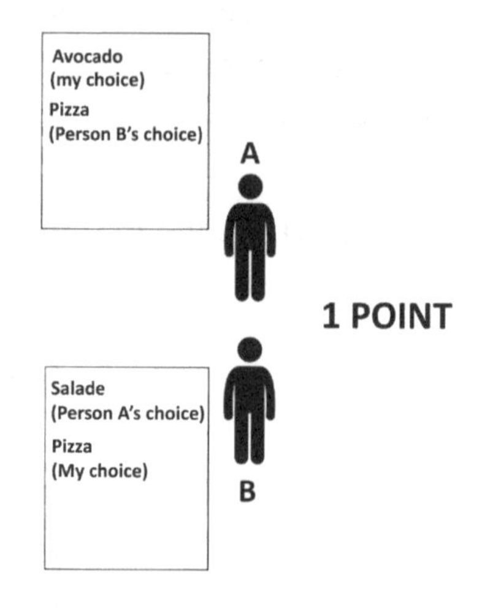

Now, everyone randomly switches partners. Each person sits somewhere in the room with his new partner. They decide who will be person A and who will be person B. You now ask them the second question. What did you want to be when you were a kid? Again, person A writes what he wanted to be when he was a kid without showing it to person B. Person B writes down what he thinks person A just wrote.

Then, person B writes what he wanted to be when he was a kid and person A writes down what he thinks person B just wrote. Using the same system, they compare their papers and write how many points they earned.
Everyone randomly changes partners again. You ask them the next question. What characteristic do you like most about yourself? Each duo plays the question in the same manner. Everyone writes their earned points on his paper and they change partners again.
Continue until each person has formed a duo with everyone from the team. For each round, you give them a new question. Some examples of questions are: What is your favorite music? What human characteristic do you think is the most annoying? What do you like about this team? What would you like to change within this team? Alternate light-hearted questions with more in-depth ones. Don't make the questions too serious. Make sure someone can always give a lighthearted answer to the question if he wants to.

After each person formed a duo with everyone, each person now adds up his points. The person who earned the most points during the exercise wins the game.
Now, tell the group to sit together in a circle to evaluate the exercise. To encourage the discussion, you can ask them the following questions: Were you surprised by the choices of your partners? What answer surprised you the most? Were you surprised about what your partners thought you wrote down? Give each person a chance to answer each question.

Variations

1. If there are multiple people with the same amount of points, you can let the winners play the game again. Each winner has to form a duo with another winner. At the end, the person with the most points wins.

2. It is possible that you are working with a big group and you need more questions. Some sample questions are: What is your favorite cartoon character? What do you consider your most annoying characteristic? What is your favorite movie? If you could be any celebrity, who would you be? What do people like about you? Which animal do you think is the scariest?

3. When you are with a small group, you can choose a duo to play the game in front of the audience. In this way, the others can watch and enjoy the answers. Continue putting duos in front of the group until each person has been in front of the group once.

4. As a bonus round, you can put one person in front of the group. Ask him the questions, and let all the others write what they think this person wrote down as an answer. The people who guess correctly earn a point. Give everyone a chance to answer a question in front of the audience. Let each person keep track of his points. After each person answers a question in front of the group, everyone adds up their points. The person who has the most correct guesses wins the bonus round.

Why you should use this exercise

This is a fun exercise to help people get to know each other on a deeper level. In a lighthearted way, this exercise provides insight into how the participants see each other.
You can play it with people who don't know each other yet. In this case, the participants will be guessing what the other could have written down, based on their first impression. Seeing what someone actually wrote, will help the group get to know each other quickly.
You can also play this exercise with people who already know each other well. In this case, it is possible that someone knows what the other wrote down. However, there are always things they don't know yet about their partner. Therefore new facts will be discovered during the exercise.
Because of the competitive element they will be motivated to guess their partner's answers correctly. This level of interest makes people feel important in the eyes of the others.
After a duo checks each other's paper, they will probably talk a bit about the outcome. This will help improve their bond.

Scan this QR code to see an animated example video of this exercise:

You can also type: **team exercise 88 the right answer** into YouTube's search bar to find the video.

Team Exercise 89 - The shoe tower

"A successful team is a group of many hands but of one mind."
- Bill Bethel

Necessities: A measuring tool like a tape measure, or yardstick.

During the exercise, the participants sit in a wide circle. To start the exercise, you tell the team they all have to remove their shoes. If someone isn't comfortable removing his shoes, it is not a problem. Tell him he can join the game in an advisory role. Now, you tell them that the goal of the exercise is to build a tower as high as possible using only their own shoes. All types of shoes can be used: flip flops, boots, sneakers, etc. They can use any part of their shoes to build the tower: shoestrings, shoe soles, and, of course, the shoe itself. Tell them that there are three rules. The first rule is that all shoes have to be used to build the tower. The second rule is that the lowest shoe has to touch the ground. The third rule is that each shoe has to touch another shoe. They can decide by themselves how to build their shoe tower; no further instructions will be given.
Tell them that a volunteer can start the first round by putting one of his shoes in the center of the circle. Tell them they can only put one shoe down at a time. The volunteer walks to the center of the circle, puts his shoe down, and walks back to his chair. After he returns to his chair, the second volunteer puts one of his shoes somewhere in the circle. It can be next to the first shoe, or on top of the first shoe. After the second person is done putting his shoe somewhere in the circle, he returns to his seat, and the third person now does the same.

After the third person puts his shoe

down, you tell the participants that there is a fourth rule. If the tower falls down, each person retrieves his own shoe or shoes and returns to his seat. Starting from scratch, the tower then must be rebuilt using the same rules and methods as during the first attempt.
Now, the fourth person puts his shoe down. One by one, the participants walk into the circle and put one of their shoes on top of or next to the shoes that are already there. Encourage them to help each other be inventive and creative. They will notice that the higher the tower is the more unstable it is. They have to be more careful each time they put a new shoe on the tower. Encourage them to take risks. Of course, it is very easy to just make two layers of all the shoes. In this case, all shoes are used and each shoe is touching another one, but it isn't a very high tower. Tell them that the higher they are trying to make the tower, the more fun and exciting the exercise will be.

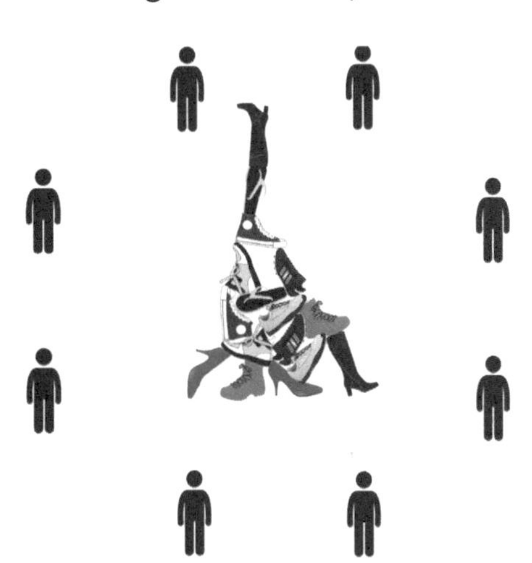

They continue putting shoes in the center of the circle until each person has used both of his shoes, and all the shoes are used to build the tower. When they have succeeded building a tower by using all the shoes, you now measure the height of the tower and share it with the group.
They will now try to break their own record by building a taller shoe tower. They will follow the same rules as before. When they finish building the second tower, you measure it and tell them if they broke their own record. If they didn't break their record, they can try again. If they broke their own record, they now play another round to see if they can build an even taller tower.
Let them play rounds until the team has broken their own record twice.

Variations

1. Between rounds, you can give them advice on how to build a big tower. For example, you can tell them to use a shoelace to tie shoes together. If it is possible, they can use a shoelace to hang a shoe from the ceiling. They can then use a shoelace to tie another shoe to the shoe hanging from the ceiling. In this way, they work from top to bottom.

2. If you are working with a big group, you can divide the group into smaller groups. Let each group build its own tower. The group that builds the biggest tower wins the game.

3. When they have succeeded in breaking their own record twice, you can play another game. In addition to a tower, you can now let them build a bridge. You place your own two shoes on the ground with a distance of six feet (2 meters) between them. Using their own shoes, they will now make a bridge between the two shoes. The same rules apply as in the original exercise. In this case, the shoes forming the bridge are not allowed to touch the ground.

4. Instead of building a tower by adding one shoe at a time, you can instruct them to put all of their shoes in the center at once. They can then build the tower together at the same time. This will demonstrate the roles each participant will play in the building process. It will be more chaotic, but it will also be a lot of fun.

5. In addition to building a shoe tower, you can tell the group to build a tower with their watches. This could be used as a bonus round. The same rules apply.

Why you should use this exercise

In this exercise, the group has the same common goal: building a shoe tower as high as possible. Working towards the same goal encourages teamwork and creates a cooperative atmosphere.
This exercise also stimulates creativity. Because they can use every part of the shoes to build a tower as high as possible, they can think outside the box to generate creative ideas.
The competitive nature of the exercise will engage the team. Every round they will be motivated to beat their own record.
The moment the shoe tower collapses will generate a lot of laughter and excitement. If they break their own record, the group will share a victorious feeling. This will create a lot of positive energy.

Scan this QR code to see an animated example video of this exercise:

You can also type: **team exercise 89 the shoe tower** into YouTube's search bar to find the video.

Team Exercise 90 - Admiring

"If you want to lift yourself up, lift up someone else."
- Booker T. Washington

Necessities: None.

To start the exercise, you tell the team to sit or stand in a circle. You tell the group that each person will think about the person that he admires most. Tell them it can be anyone - an artist (for example, Freddie Mercury), a family member (for example, their father), a historical figure (for example, Gandhi), or a friend. Tell them the reason to admire a person can be anything - appearance, success, characteristics, etc. Let them think about it for one minute. If they haven't thought of someone in one minute, give them another minute. When everyone has someone in mind, you point to the first person who will share with the rest of the group who he admires. He will also share why he admires this particular person. While he is talking, the rest of the group remains silent. When he is finished talking, the person sitting to his left will now do the same. Continue clockwise around the circle letting them individually share their admiration for the person they chose. After everyone has gotten a turn, you now start the second round of the exercise.

You tell them that each person will think of someone who he admires, but this time it has to be another participant sitting in the circle. Remind them that as in the first round the reason to admire someone from the circle can be anything. It can be something significant, for example, someone's leadership skills. However, it can also be something light-hearted such as someone's new shirt. Tell them they have to think of an honest reason; they are not allowed to just make something up. As in the first round, you give them a minute to think about it. When everyone has someone in mind, you point to a first random person who will share with the rest of the group which person sitting in the circle he admires. He also tells the group why he admires that particular person. Continue clockwise around the circle until each person shares his admiration.

Now, you start the third round. You point to someone in the group. Individually, the other participants will say what they admire about this person. Tell them they can say anything as long it is positive. It is permissible to repeat things that might already have been mentioned earlier about this person in the second round. To start, you point to the person sitting to the left of the person whom everyone will admire. He says what he admires about him. While he is talking, the person whom he is admiring remains silent. When he is done talking, the person sitting to his left now does the same. Continue clockwise around the circle until everyone tells why they admire this person.

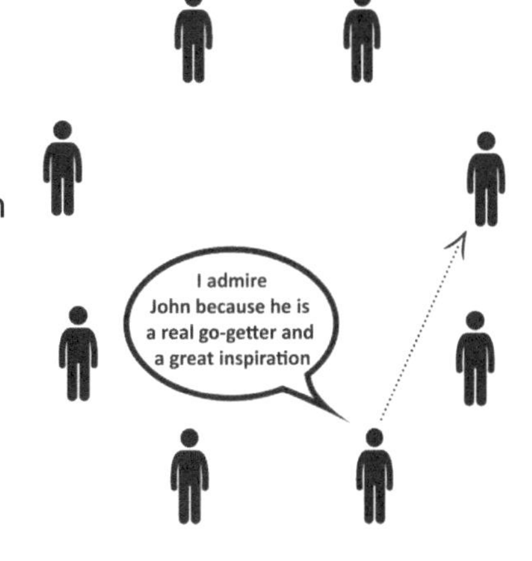

Now, it is the turn of the person sitting on the left of the first person. In the same way, they go clockwise around the circle until everyone tells this second person what they admire about him and why. Let them continue like this until everyone in the circle hears what each person from the group admires about him and why.

You now evaluate the exercise. Ask them the following questions to encourage the discussion: How does it feel to explain to another participant why you admire him? Is it easier to tell someone what you admire him for? Or is it easier to hear from others why they admire you?

Variations

1. In the first round, after someone mentions whom he admires and why, you can tell the group that the people who also admire that person can raise their hands. In this way, each person sees who else in the group admires the same person as he does. This shared admiration will create bonds among people who admire the same person.

2. During the third round, in which one person is told by everyone why they admire him, you can play a shorter version. In this shorter version, you choose a person and you point to another random person who will tell what he admires about this person. In this case, don't point to a person who already chose that person in the second round. Otherwise, he will hear the same thing again. Continue pointing to people until everyone hears from another person what he admires about him.

3. You can play a fourth round in which each participant reveals what he admires about himself. They will feel less embarrassed talking about personal admiration because they already have been talking about admiration for a few rounds.

4. If in the third round someone can't come up with something he admires about the person who has the turn, you can tell a few things that you admire in that person. The person who couldn't come up with something can now say with which thing you mentioned he agrees most.

Why you should use this exercise

In the first round of the exercise each participant tells who he admires in life and why. This will make the participants get to know each other better. The reason a person has admiration for someone reveals much about himself. Therefore, the participants gain new insight into their own and into each other's personalities.
Playing the second and third round will let the participants feel appreciated by the other people in the group. The mutual admiration raises the group's spirit. This will make the group form positive bonds which will create a positive atmosphere.
It is a great exercise to dispel negativity from the group. Of course, you can also use this exercise in a group that already has a lot of positive energy. It will just make the group stronger.
Playing this exercise will give the participants a positive boost and will therefore enhance group performance.

Scan this QR code to see an animated example video of this exercise:

You can also type: **team exercise 90 admiring** into YouTube's search bar to find the video.

Team Exercise 91 - Simon says

"The secret to success in any human endeavor is total concentration."
- Kurt Vonnegut Jr.

Necessities: None.

To start the exercise, you tell the participants to stand in a straight line. You will stand in front of the line and tell the group you are going to give them certain commands. Tell them the commands will be simple physical instructions. For example, "Clap your hands", or "Touch your nose." You tell the team they should only obey a command when you say the words "Simon says..." before the command. Tell them that if you say a command without the words "Simon says..." before the command, they shouldn't do anything. So if you say "Simon says jump," everyone should jump. However, if you say "Jump", no one should do anything. The moment someone obeys the command that didn't have "Simon says" before it you point to that person. This means he is out of the game and sits down. It can be the case that you spot someone accidentally starting to obey the command and then quickly holding back because he realizes he shouldn't be moving. In that case, you also point to that person and tell him he is out of the game. If someone obeys a command by mistake and you don't see him, he stays in the game. In this case, someone is just lucky and doesn't have to sit down. Tell them that it is important that they respond immediately when you say, "Simon says". If there are people who don't respond within two seconds after you said the command, you point to them and they are out of the game. If someone responds too slowly without being seen, he is lucky and doesn't have to sit down. After you explain these rules, you

now start announcing the first command. For each command you can decide whether you say, "Simon says" before the command or not. You can make it difficult for them by alternating the tempo between the instructions. In this way, they can't get accustomed to a certain tempo. You will notice that shorter pauses between commands confuse people. Since you are giving the commands quickly, it will be more difficult for them to only follow the "Simon says" commands. You can also make it difficult for them by saying many "Simon says" commands in a row and then all of a sudden switching to another command without "Simon says". Because they will be accustomed following up your command it will be difficult for them to do nothing when you suddenly give them the command without "Simon says" before it. They will have to be extra focused to control their impuls.

You can use all different kinds of commands. You can use simple commands such as jump, stoop or touch your nose. You can also add some creative variety, for example command them to smile, raise their eyebrows, or yell their own names.
The following is a possible command sequence: Raise your right hand (no one should do anything). Simon says smile (they should all smile). Spread your arms (no one should do anything). Simon says yell your neighbour's name (they should all yell their neighbour's name). Simon says clap your hands (they all should clap their hand). Clap your hands (no one should do anything), etc. If someone makes a mistake and sits down, tell him he can help you catch other people making mistakes. This will make it more difficult for the others not being caught when making a mistake. Continue giving commands until everyone except one person is out of the game. This person is the winner of the game.

Variations

1. Next to "Simon says", you can add more rules to the game. For example, when you say, "Carla says" before the instruction, they have to perform the instruction twice. The person who doesn't follow this rule correctly and has been spotted sits down.

2. When there is one final winner, you can play a second round in which that winner stands in front of the line. He is now the one who announces the commands and checks for mistakes. During this second round, you can either join the game or stay out of the line and help check for mistakes.

3. You can tell the group to stand in a circle and let one person at a time announce the commands individually. They go clockwise around the circle calling out commands. In the same way, if someone says "Simon says" before the command all the others in the circle execute the command. The one who announces the command doesn't have to execute the command himself. He will check if someone in the circle makes a mistake. If someone makes a mistake and the announcer spots the mistake, he points to that person. The person who made the mistake is out of the game. In this variation, only the announcer looks for mistakes.

4. Before you start the exercise, you can give everyone three points. When someone makes a mistake and has been caught, he loses a point. After someone has been spotted making a mistake three times, he is out of the game and will sit down. By doing this, the game lasts longer.

Why you should use this exercise

This exercise is great for raising energy. Therefore, it is a perfect game to play at the beginning of the day. Because the commands are physical, the team will feel energetic by performing all the movements.

This exercise also increases the team's focus and listening skills. They all have to listen intently to know whether they should carry out a command or not. Because they all focus on the same thing, the team will experience a common bond.

The game element makes the exercise exciting and will motivate the participants to be focused the whole time.

Scan this QR code to see an animated example video of this exercise:

You can also type: **team exercise 91 simon says** into YouTube's search bar to find the video.

Team Exercise 92 - Classifying

"Creativity is intelligence having fun." - **Albert Einstein**

Necessities: Pass out twenty random images of objects on a letter-size paper. You can do this with a photo-editing program, or you can manually cut out images and paste them on the paper. If you use a photo-editing program, you print out as many copies as there are participants in the group. If you paste the images onto the paper manually, you need to make as many copies as there are participants.
You also need blank letter-size papers equal to the number of participants, and scissors, glue, and tape for half the number of participants.

To start the exercise, you divide the team into random groups of four people. You give each group one of the copies. Tell them that there are twenty random objects on the paper. Each group is going to divide the objects into different categories regarding a topic they choose. Tell them they can make as many categories as they want. After they choose a topic and the corresponding categories, they will write the topic at the top of the blank paper. Next, they will cut out all the objects and paste them on the blank paper. The objects belonging in the same category will be pasted next to each other. They will write the name of the category above each group of items belonging to that category. Give them two examples of a topic and corresponding categories to make it clear. For example, they can choose the topic color and write "color" on top of the blank paper. Then they create categories that fit the colors of the items. For example, the categories could be gray, black, red, purple, orange, and brown. In this case, they cut out all the gray items and paste them next

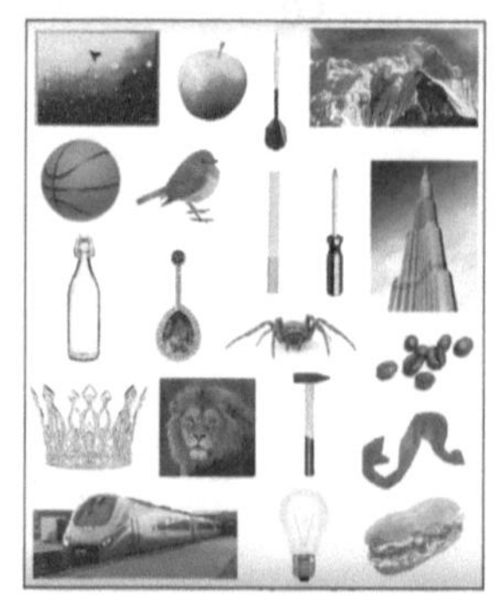

to each other on the empty paper. They write gray above these gray colored items. They do the same thing for the other color categories. A second example can be the topic: bigger or smaller in real life than in the picture. In this case, the items will be categorized into just two categories: bigger and smaller. All the items that are bigger in real life than in the picture will be pasted into the bigger category. The items that are smaller in real life go into the smaller category. Tell them that they can be as creative as they want in classifying the objects.
After you give the examples, each group executes the exercise: they choose a topic and categories, cut out all the items, and paste them onto the blank paper below their corresponding categories. When they are done, the groups merge. Each group now shows their paper to the other groups. They tell them what their topic is and describe how they classified the objects.
Now, you start the second round and tell them to form new groups of three people. You give each trio a new copy with the objects on it and a blank paper. Each group will do the same as in the first round. However, each group has to choose a new topic that wasn't used in the first round. After each trio has cut, pasted, and categorized the objects, the trios come together. They show the others their papers and explain their topic and categories.

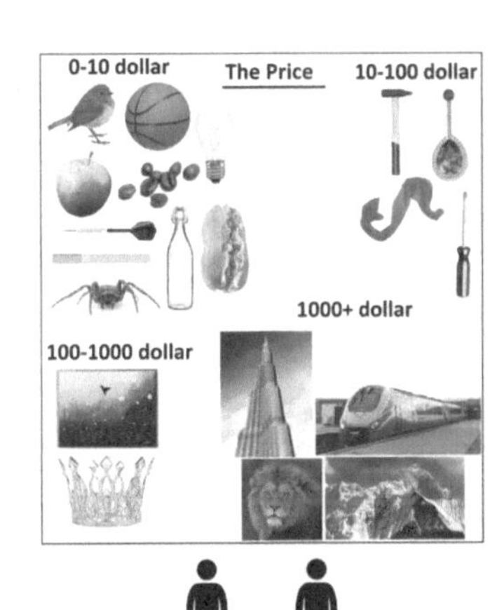

Now, you start the third round and tell the participants to make duos. Tell them that each duo has to choose a topic that has not been used before. You give each duo a copy and a blank paper. In the same way as before they make categories and divide the objects into the correct categories. Encourage them to be as original as possible. When each duo has executed the exercise, they come together and each duo shows their paper to the others.

Variations

1. When you are working with a small group, or if you want the exercise to be shorter, you can play two rounds instead of three. Start the exercise by letting them form trios and in the second round duos.

2. You can do a bonus round in which each participant works alone to categorize the objects. Tell each person to be as inventive as possible when choosing a topic and categories. After each participant is done, they merge, and each participant shows his paper to the rest of the group. The rest of the group now awards points for originality. Each paper is graded on a scale from one to ten. You calculate the average score for each paper by adding all the scores and dividing them by the number of people who voted. The person with the highest score wins.

3. If it takes too much time to let each group cut out all the items and paste it onto their empty paper, you can let them write the items under the proper category instead. They write the topic at the top of the blank paper. Below the topic, they write each category with below each category the objects that belong in that category.

4. After each round, you write the topics the groups choose for categorizing the objects on a whiteboard. This is a reminder for the new groups not to choose this topic again.

Why you should use this exercise

This exercise stimulates the creative mind. In each new round, they have to choose a new topic and devise categories in which to classify the objects. Therefore each round they have to be more inventive to find a topic that hasn't been used before. By coming up with new ideas each round, the participants have to think outside the box.

Because each group has to create the topic and categories together, their cooperation skills will be trained as well.

The composition of the groups changes each round. Therefore they get the chance to work with different people. This will have a positive effect on the group dynamics.

It is also a fun exercise because each round they are able to share their accomplishments with each other. In this way, they will inspire each other by showing their creative ideas.

Scan this QR code to see an animated example video of this exercise:

You can also type: **team exercise 92 classifying** into YouTube's search bar to find the video.

Team Exercise 93 - Imagination

"Imagination creates reality." - **Richard Wagner**

Necessities: An empty room.

To start the exercise, you tell the group to walk in a crisscross pattern around the room. Tell them to keep a normal pace and to walk silently. Tell them you are going to give them suggestions to create a fantasy. While they are walking around the room, you tell the group to imagine that they are not in that room anymore. Instead, they are walking on a sunny beach and they feel the sun on their heads. Let them walk around for a minute imagining the sunny beach. After a minute, you tell them to imagine they are walking barefooted on the beach. Tell them they feel the hot sand on their feet and between their toes. While they are walking, tell them that the sun and the hot sand become progressively hotter. Let the group walk around envisioning the warmth. After a minute, you tell them that it suddenly becomes cloudy. The temperature drops slightly and a light rain begins to fall. While they are envisioning walking in the rain, you tell them that the rain becomes heavy and a storm arises. The team now pretends to walk around in the storm. Next, you tell them that it is getting progressively colder and it begins to freeze. They now walk around for a minute envisioning the cold. You now tell them that the weather becomes moderate again and that slowly night is falling. Tell them to keep walking around with their eyes open. Every ten seconds, you tell them that it is getting darker. While walking around, they pretend to see less every time you say that it is getting darker. After telling them five times that it is getting darker,

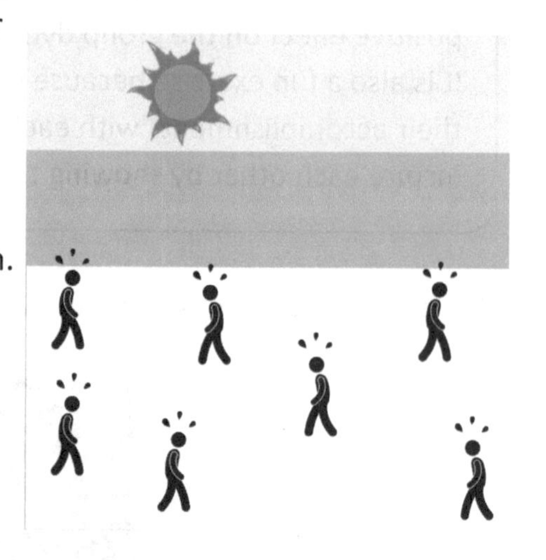

you tell them that it is now completely dark. They walk around with their eyes open pretending that they don't see anything. After walking around for a minute, you tell them to lie down on the ground and fall asleep. After a minute, you tell them to wake up. Tell them they are now in a forest. They hear animals everywhere. Let them listen to the animals for a while and then tell them to walk around the forest. After they walk around for a minute, you tell them that they see a river. They have to cross the river using the stones in the river. Tell the team to stand together on one side of the room and imagine that the river goes from that side to the opposite side of the room. The group now jumps to the other side of the room pretending that they are crossing the river by jumping from stone to stone. After they all have reached the other side of the room, you now tell them that they see a house in the distance. Tell them to walk towards the house. They now imagine that they are standing in front of the house. Instruct one of the participants to open the door. This person pretends to open the imaginary door and they all walk into the imaginary house. Instruct them to say aloud what they imagine. For example someone can say, "Oh wow, look at that clock!" Let them walk around the house announcing the things they see for a minute. After a minute you tell them that suddenly, the door locks and they are locked inside the house. Tell them they have to join forces and develop a plan to escape the imaginary house. Tell them that to create an exciting escape story, they can put obstacles in their path. For example, someone can pretend that he finds the key to the door. To create an obstacle they can pretend that when they try to open the door, the key breaks off in the lock. Tell them to act out multiple escaping scenarios until finally one of them works out. When they finally escape the house, tell them to celebrate their escape by cheering a loud.

Variations

1. During the exercise, you can use music to create the right mood. It will help participants become more engaged in the imaginary story.

2. You can join the group while giving the instructions. If the group has difficulty getting involved in the fantasy, it might be easier if you act things out with them. For example, right after you tell them it is getting cold, you can start to behave as if it is cold. Because you already broke the ice it is less awkward for the rest to act out that they are cold as well.

3. In the first part of the exercise when they are walking on the beach, you can tell them that each person has a butterfly sitting on his hand. All of a sudden, the butterfly starts flying. Each person follows his imaginary butterfly by chasing it around the room.

4. In the last part of the exercise, instead of telling them to walk into a house, you can create other imaginary situations. For example, they can walk into an imaginary dance club. Tell them to listen to imaginary music and dance. While they are dancing, tell them that a fire has broken out. They have to escape as quickly as possible. In the same way as in the original exercise, they come up with obstacles to make the escape story interesting. When everyone has escaped, they can celebrate their survival.

Why you should use this exercise

During the exercise you guide the team to use their imaginations. If everyone believes in the imaginary world they create, the group journeys together in the same fantasy. Fantasizing the same thing at the same time will bring the participants together.
At start, people might feel a bit weird walking on a pretend beach. However, the longer they share the same fantasy, the more comfortable they will be acting out made up suggestions. When they pretend to be in the house they come up with new imaginations themselves, without you telling them what to imagine. This will encourages the initiative to be creative.
At the end, the group will feel that they experienced a whole trip together without leaving the room. This shared experience will form a bond among the participants.

Scan this QR code to see an animated example video of this exercise:

You can also type: **team exercise 93 imagination** into YouTube's search bar to find the video.

Team Exercise 94 - The perfect team member

“Teamwork is the ability to work together toward a common vision.”
- Andrew Carnegie

Necessities: Blank papers equal to the number of participants divided by three plus one. Boxes of colored pencils equal to the number of participants divided by three.

To start the exercise, you tell the team to form trios. You give each trio a piece of paper and a box of colored pencils. You tell them that each trio will discuss which three personal characteristics they think the perfect team member should have. They have to be characteristics that will benefit the team. Tell them they can consider all kinds of characteristics as long as they aren’t physical characteristics. Give them a few examples of personal characteristics such as powerful, genuine, and funny. Tell them that they have to unanimously agree on the three characteristics. Let them discuss this for two minutes. When each trio comes to an agreement, they will write the three characteristics on the blank paper.

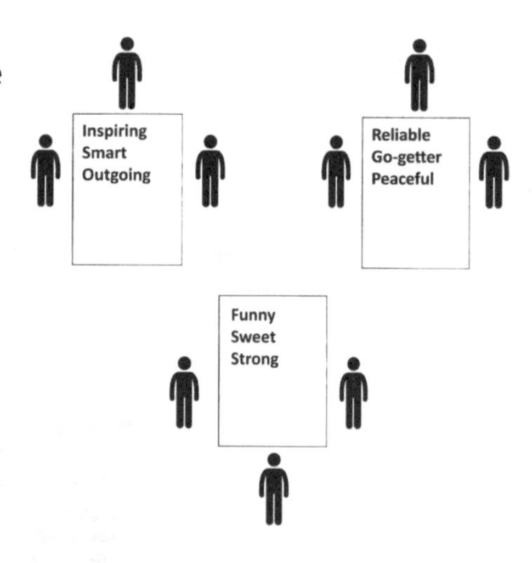

Next, you tell the group that each trio will discuss which three physical characteristics they think the perfect team member should have. Give them examples of physical characteristics. For example, the perfect team member should wear a hat, a normal sweater, and neat shoes. Tell them they have to unanimously agree on the three physical characteristics. Let them discuss this for two minutes.
When each trio comes to an agreement, they will write the three physical characteristics below the three personal characteristics they

wrote down earlier. Now you start the next round. You tell them to draw their perfect team member on the back of the paper using the colored pencils. Each trio can decide for themselves in what way they draw the perfect team member. They can draw it together by letting each person of the trio draw a part of the image, or one person can draw it while the others offer suggestions. Tell them it doesn't matter if they are not skilled artists. An impression of how they think the perfect team member looks like will do.

After all trios have completed their drawings they merge and sit in a circle. One trio at a time presents their perfect team member's personal characteristics, physical characteristics, and picture. After a trio is done sharing they also explain the reason they think this would be the perfect team member. After all the trios have shared their individual presentations, tell them they will now together create one final perfect team member. You give the group a new blank piece of paper. First, they all have to unanimously agree on three personal characteristics. Let them discuss this for two minutes and write them on the paper. They do the same for the three physical characteristics. When they are done writing, they will collaborate on the drawing of the final perfect team member. They will draw the final perfect team member on the back of the paper. They can decide if they want to draw it together, or appoint someone to do the drawing while the others give him instructions. If they disagree on certain aspects they will have to compromise just as long everyone agrees with the outcome. They keep on drawing until they unanimously decide it is the perfect team member.

You now can frame the drawing of the perfect team member so they can hang it somewhere in the workplace. This will remind them of what they think the perfect team member should look like.

Variations

1. You can tell them that the drawing of the perfect team member can also be an abstract drawing. In this case, they don't have to draw a person. They can draw creative things that represent that person. For example, if they think the perfect team member should be both caring and passionate, they can draw a heart with lightning around it.

2. In addition to drawing, you can tell the participants to cut and paste the perfect team member. In this case, you bring magazines, scissors and glue to the exercise. You distribute the magazines to the trios and tell them that they can cut out different parts of photos of people. They paste it onto their blank paper to make a collage of the perfect team member. In the last round, the whole group together can cut out parts from the earlier completed creations. They can then paste them onto a blank paper to construct the final perfect team member.

3. Instead of the perfect team member, you can also let the team construct the perfect manager, teacher, or someone else they work with. You play the exercise in the same way.

4. If you are pressed for time, or if you think the people don't like to draw, you can skip the drawing part. Just let the trios produce the personal characteristics and physical characteristics. In the last part of the exercise, they can come together and collaborate to produce the final six characteristics without making a drawing.

Why you should use this exercise

This is a creative exercise to discover what a group believes is the perfect team member. Each participant will gain insight into his own values and the values of others.
When the trios show each other their drawings, amusement, laughter, and a positive team energy will occur.
Collaborating on the final drawing will enhance their cooperation skills. They will explore what they all think is important in a team member and will compromise to come to the final six characteristics and a drawing.
When you frame the picture they created together and hang it in their workplace, the group has a fun memory to look at when they are working. Looking at the framed drawing will help them remember their shared team values. This will create a positive atmosphere in the workplace.

Scan this QR code to see an animated example video of this exercise:

You can also type: **team exercise 94 the perfect team member** into YouTube's search bar to find the video.

Team Exercise 95 - The moment I knew

"Knowing yourself is the beginning of all wisdom." - **Socrates**

Necessities: None.

To start the exercise, you tell the participants to sit in a circle. You tell them you will say the beginning of sentences which they will have to finish. You start by say the beginning of the first sentence: "I knew I was old when…." Tell them that the person you will point to will repeat that first part of the sentence and then create the ending. To give an example, you first end the sentence yourself. For example, "I knew I was old when I bought a beer and the bartender didn't ask me for my ID." Now you say, "I knew I was old…" while pointing to one of the participants in the circle. This person will repeat it and complete it with a past situation that made him realize he was old. For example, "I knew I was old... when someone asked me for directions and addressed me as sir." After he completes the sentence, the person sitting to his left does the same. He says the sentence, "I knew I was old…" and finishes it with a personal situation that made him feel old. Continue clockwise around the circle until everyone has finished the sentence, "I knew I was old…."

You now start the second round. You follow the same procedure, but now with the sentence: "I knew I was young…." You start by finishing the sentence yourself. For example, "I knew I was young when my grandma told me that I have my whole life ahead of me." Now you say, "I knew I was young…" again, while pointing to one of the participants in the circle. This person will repeat it and complete it with a personal situation

that made him realize that he was young. They continue clockwise around the circle until everyone finishes the sentence, "I knew I was young...." When everyone finished the sentence, you now tell the team to complete a sentence starting with the words: "I knew I fit into this team when...." You start by finishing the sentence yourself by honestly telling when you felt you fit into the group. For example, "I knew I fit into this team when you all laughed at my joke this morning when I introduced myself." You point to a random person who will also finish the sentence. Continue clockwise around the circle until everyone finishes the sentence "I knew I fit into this team when...."

Next, you begin the last part of the exercise. You point to a random team member, for example, John. The other participants will tell when they knew who he was. They will do this by completing the sentence: "I knew who John was...." You begin by completing the sentence yourself. If you know John, you tell the team when you really got to know him. For example, "I really knew who John was when we had beers together and he told me everything about his childhood." It is possible that you don't know John. In this case, you tell how this exercise helped you to know who John was. For example, "I knew who John was when he told us he realized he was young when he talked to his father about life." Next, you point to a random person who will also finish the sentence about John. Continue clockwise around the circle until everyone told when they knew who John was. Now, they follow the same procedure with the person sitting to John's left, for example: "I really knew who Kate was when...."

Continue clockwise around the circle until everyone told when they really knew who Kate was. This last round is finished when everyone told about each person in the group when they knew who that person really was.

Variations

1. In the first part of the exercise, you can add more sentences for them to complete. Some examples are: "I knew I was screwed when...", "I knew I was in love when...", "I knew I was funny when...", "I knew I was smart when...", "I knew I was stupid when...", "I knew what I wanted in life when...", etc.

2. In the second round in which they finish the sentence, "I knew I fit into this team when...", you can also let them share other team moments. For example, they could share the moment they knew they wanted to improve something within the team. In that case, you can tell them to finish the sentence: "I knew I wanted to improve something in the team when...." You can devise multiple team related sentences that would be beneficial to the team.

3. In order to ensure that the third round contains only positive sentences, you can start the sentence with: "I knew I liked (person) when...." As in the original exercise, you let everyone tell about each person when they knew they really liked him.

4. You can play a bonus round in which you let them finish the sentence: "I really knew who I was when...." Because this can be very personal, tell the participants they only have to finish the sentence if they feel comfortable doing so. Following the same procedure, you let everyone finish the sentence.

Why you should use this exercise

This is a great exercise to help the participants get to know each other better. In the first part of the exercise, everyone will share personal stories. In this way, they will get to know each other at a deeper level.
In the second part of the exercise in which everyone tells when they felt they fit into this team, they will sense a feeling of belonging. This feeling of belonging will initiate a common bond.
The last part of the exercise in which everyone tells each person when they really got to know him will make the participants feel seen and appreciated.
After playing this exercise, everyone will feel that they know each other on a deeper level and that they are part of the group.

Scan this QR code to see an animated example video of this exercise:

You can also type: **team exercise 95 the moment I knew** into YouTube's search bar to find the video.

Team Exercise 96 - Making a team logo

"A logo is the period at the end of a sentence, not the sentence itself."
- Sagi Haviv

Necessities: Boxes of colored pencils and white papers equal to half the number of participants plus one.

To start the exercise, you divide the participants into random duos. Each duo sits at a table somewhere in the room. You give each duo a box of colored pencils and a white paper. You tell each duo to design a logo that symbolizes this group. Tell them that they aren't designing the logo for their organization, but the logo they design will just represent the team itself. Tell them they can create the logo in any form they want. They can draw abstract shapes to symbolize the group, for example, circles, squares or stripes. They can also draw figurative things. Tell them they can be as creative as they want to reflect how they see the team. Give them examples to make it clear. Tell them that if high school teachers would do this exercise, they might draw a figure in the center of a circle with dots around the circle. The figure in the center of the circle could symbolize the teacher. The dots around the circle could symbolize the children the teachers teach all day. Another example could be social workers who draw a big heart with a star inside it. The heart could represent the love they put into their work. The star could represent their belief that their coworkers are stars. Create as many examples as you need until the group understands the purpose of the exercise.
After giving the examples, you now give the duos approximately ten minutes to create the logo. Tell them that both people of each duo should agree on the outcome of their drawing.
After all the duos are done drawing the logo, they merge and sit in a circle. You point to the first duo that will show their logo to the rest of the group. They tell the other participants what the logo symbolizes. Tell them to explain it as specifically as possible. If other people from

the circle have any questions about the logo, they are allowed to ask them. After the first duo displayed their logo, explained the symbolism, and answered the questions, you now point to the next duo that will do the same. Continue until each duo displayed and explained their logo and answered the questions.

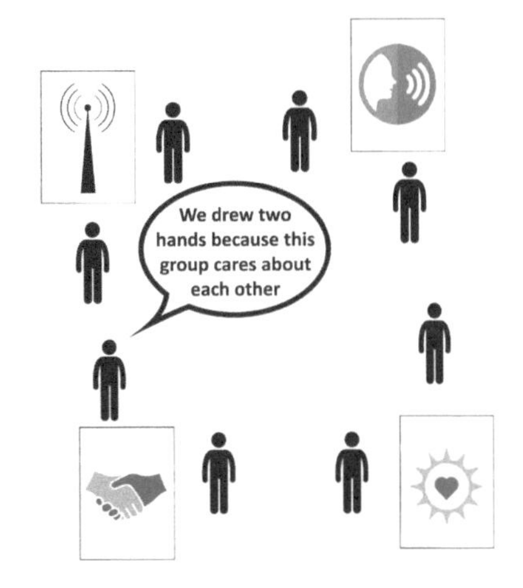

Now, you tell the whole group to sit somewhere at a table and draw a final team logo together. Tell them that the final logo should be based on the logos each individual duo made in the first round. They can combine some aspects of the earlier ideas and designs.

Tell them they can figure out themselves how to design the final team logo as long as they all agree unanimously. Give them a few suggestions on how to draw the logo. For example, one person could draw and the others could offer suggestions. They could also draw multiple versions of the logo and then vote for their final choice.

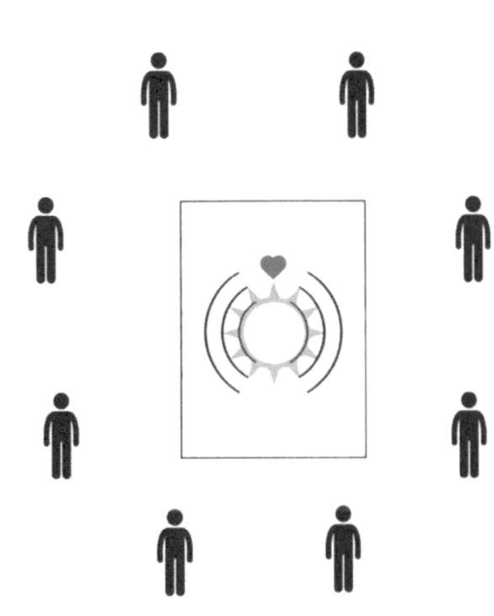

Give them approximately ten minutes to create the final logo. When they all agree on the outcome, they will show it to you. Now, they will explain why they drew this specific logo. You can ask them questions about the composition of the logo. For example, "What represents the sun?" or "What symbolises the little heart?" Let them answer your questions until you feel that you understand what the logo stands for.

After the exercise, they can frame the logo and hang it somewhere their workplace.

Variations

1. Instead of making a logo for the group, they can design a logo that represents the organization or school the group belongs to. The exercise will be performed in the same way.

2. If you play variation one, you can suggest adopting the logo as the actual logo of the organization. Their contributions to the new logo will help the participants feel important and appreciated.

3. In the first round, you can ask each duo why they chose certain colors for the logo. It is possible that they didn't even think about the significance of color choices. However, there might be subconscious reasons for this that weren't apparent until you asked.

4. Instead of using pencils and paper, you can let them design the logo on a laptop. As in the original exercise, both people have to agree to the final product.

5. Instead of drawing the logo, you can let them cut and paste pictures from magazines. In this case, you bring magazines, scissors, and glue. Distribute the magazines to the duos. They can cut out different shapes and figures and paste it onto their blank paper to form the logo.
In the last round, the whole group together can cut out parts from the earlier completed logos. They can then paste them onto a blank paper to construct the final team logo.

Why you should use this exercise

This is a fun and creative exercise to allow the team to think about and discuss their group identity. Putting the group's identity into a logo will enhance the creativity of the participants.
When the duos share their logos, they will all learn how the others feel about the group's identity. In this way, everyone will be inspired by the creations and ideas of the others.
During the final round, they have to reach a consensus on one final team logo. This will train the group to compromise.
In a playful way, this exercise will stimulate the group's creativity and cooperation skills.

Scan this QR code to see an animated example video of this exercise:

You can also type: **team exercise 96 making a team logo** into YouTube's search bar to find the video.

Team Exercise 97 - The lunch game

"There is something profoundly satisfying about sharing a meal. Eating together, breaking bread together, is one of the oldest and most fundamentally unifying of human experiences."
- Barbara Coloroso

Necessities: None.

This exercise is most suitable for big groups; the least you can have is nine people. You perform this exercise just before the group goes to lunch. To start the exercise, you tell the group to stand in a big circle. To form trios, you divide the number of people standing in the circle by three. For example, if you have twenty-one people, you would come to the number seven. Tell them that each person needs to remember the number you give him. You now point to a random person in the circle and say "one". You point to the person standing to his left and say "two". Continue clockwise around the circle giving each person a number. When you reach, in this case number seven, you start with number one again, so the eighth person in the circle will get the number one, and so forth. After you give everyone a number, you now tell all the number ones to stand together. This will be trio number one. After they form a trio, you tell all the number twos to stand together. This will be trio number two. Continue until everyone with the same number forms a trio. This way totally random trios have been formed. Now, you tell them that each trio will have lunch together. Tell them that it is going to be a special lunch. Each trio will now have to come up with an accomplishment or task to do during their lunch break. All three people have to unanimously agree on the task or accomplishment. Tell them they can be as creative as they want. The tasks can be serious, lighthearted, or funny. You can give them a few examples of tasks to stimulate their imaginations. For example, write a song, develop a business idea together, give each other nicknames and use these names during lunch, etc. Give each trio approximately one minute to think of a task. After all trios have decided on a task, you tell trio number one to share their accomplishment or task. Next, trio number two will share their accomplishment or task. Continue until each trio has shared their task.

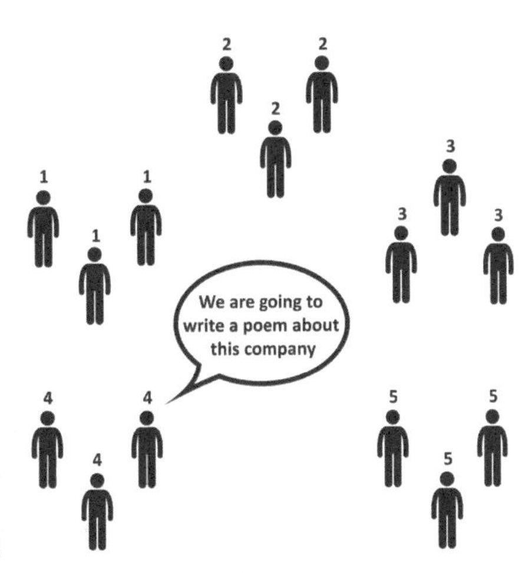

Now, you tell them that they are not going to keep their own tasks. Each trio is going to give their task to another trio. Trio number one is going to give its task to trio number two. In case trio number two doesn't understand the task, trio number one should explain it. After trio number two understands their new task, they give their original task to trio number three. Again, they can explain their task so trio number three knows what to do during lunch. Continue until the trio with the second to the last number gives their task to the trio with the last number. Lastly, the trio with the last number will give their task to trio number one. When each trio understands their tasks, they will go to lunch and perform the task they just received.

When everyone returns from lunch, each trio will tell the others if they completed the task. You point to a random trio and tell them to share their experiences and, if possible, to perform or show their task. For example, if they had to create a song, they can perform the song for the others. If there is nothing to present they just tell them their experiences of performing their task.

Variations

1. If there is a trio that can't think of a task, you can tell them to pick a task from your examples. If they don't remember these examples, you can repeat them.

2. If it is not possible to go out for lunch at a lunch place, they can also just bring their own lunch. Each group will sit somewhere together while each person eats his own lunch while they performing the task.

3. If the whole group eats at the same lunch place, you can put each trio at a different table. If they have to eat at the same table, make sure each trio is sitting together so that they can perform their task.

4. When there is a trio that really doesn't want to do the task they got from another trio, ask the other trios if they want to swap. If no one wants to swap, you can repeat the examples you gave in the beginning of the exercise and let them pick one. If they don't want one of these tasks either, they can just do their own original task. In this case, two trios do the same task.

5. If you have a very big group you can divide the group into groups of four. To form the groups of four, you divide the number of people standing in the circle by four. In the same way as in the original exercise you assign the numbers to the participants.

6. If you want to play this exercise with a small group, instead of trios you can divide them into duos. The rest of the exercise remains the same.

Why you should use this exercise

This is a great exercise to help a group of people mingle.
You can play this exercise with people who don't know each other yet. The tasks will give them something to talk about when there might be a lull in the conversation. This will add some levity to their lunch.
When they already know each other it is also a great exercise to do. Mixing people into random trios will make the participants have lunch with people they might normally not have lunch with. This will be good for group dynamics.
They will all be surprised when they learn that they won't perform their own devised tasks. This will add an element of shared excitement that will be good for group bonding.

Scan this QR code to see an animated example video of this exercise:

You can also type: **team exercise 97 the lunch game** into YouTube's search bar to find the video.

Team Exercise 98 - Music

"Music expresses feeling and thought, without language; it was below and before speech, and it is above and beyond all words."
- Robert G. Ingersoll

Necessities: A laptop, smartphone, or any other device that can play music. If you work with a big group you can bring extra speakers to connect with the device.

Prior to this exercise, you instruct participants to bring their favorite piece of music to the exercise. Tell them it can be any kind of music: modern music, classical music, or music that reminds them of their childhoods. Tell them that all kinds of music are fine as long as they engender emotion when they hear it. Tell them that if someone doesn't have a device to play it on, he can email the music file to you so that you can play it for him.
When everyone arrives with his favorite piece of music, tell the team to sit in a circle. Tell them that each person is going to let the others hear his favorite piece of music. While they are listening, he will tell them all about the music. Tell them he will share who the composer is, what it reminds him of and how the music makes him feel. Tell them to take long pauses between sentences when they talk, so the others can clearly hear the music.
You now ask a volunteer to go first. Tell this person that he can play his music for a maximum of five minutes. If the piece of music or song is shorter than five minutes, that is also fine. The volunteer now begins to play his favorite piece of music. Make sure that the music is not too loud or too soft. If it is too loud, people can't hear what someone is saying. If the music is too soft, people can't hear it. If you are working with a very big group, you can attach external speakers to the device that is playing the music so everyone can hear the music clearly.
While the music is playing, the volunteer tells the group about the

music. Make sure that when the music is playing, the rest of the group remains silent. When he is done, you now tell the group that they can ask questions about the music and the story they just heard. People who want to ask questions raise their hands. One by one, you point to someone who wants to ask a question, and the person who just played his music answers the question. Tell him he is not obliged to answer a question if he doesn't want to.

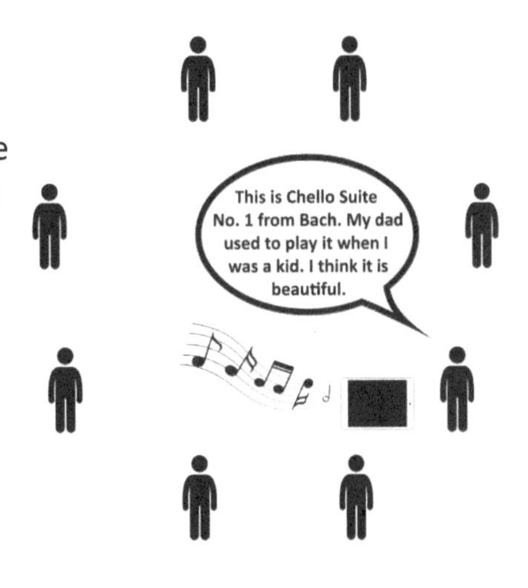

After all the questions are answered, you now ask for a second volunteer. This second person plays his music, explains why it is important to him, and answers the questions. It is possible that some people will bring the same kind of music. Tell them that isn't a problem at all. Everyone can have a very different experience with the same kind of music. Tell them that it can be quite interesting to hear different experiences with the same piece of music. Continue this procedure until everyone has played their music, shared their experiences with the music, and answered questions.

After the exercise you can make a team music album with all the numbers they played. Ask each participant to email you the name of the piece of music they played and you email everyone all the songs. They can play this playlist when they all get together. This will remind them of the exercise and will give them a shared positive feeling.

Variations

1. You can bring your own piece of music to the exercise as well. You start the exercise by playing your own piece of music while telling about it. Make sure you model taking pauses, so both the music and the explanations will be heard.

2. Instead of instructing the participants to talk during the piece of music, you can instruct them to talk after the song. By doing this, the audience can focus completely on the music and then focus completely on the explanation.

3. Instead of instructing the participants to talk during the piece of music, you can instruct them to talk before they play the music. The others will then listen to the piece of music with all the information about the music in mind.

4. Instead of their favorite piece of music, you can let them bring a picture of their favorite piece of art. Let them describe the artwork and describe what they like about it while the picture goes around the circle. The others can ask questions. In the same way as in the original exercise, everyone gets a turn to talk about their favorite piece of art.

5. Instead of a piece of music, you can let them bring their favorite movie scene. Each person will show the others their favorite movie scene on a laptop. After someone played the scene he describes what he likes about it and the others can ask questions.

Why you should use this exercise

This is a great exercise to help a group of people to learn more about everyone in the group. Music moves people and enables people to feel emotions. Because everyone is sharing both their music and their feelings, people will bond at a deeper level. When someone plays his favorite piece of music, the others will collectively listen to it. When the group is focusing together on the same thing at the same time, they will feel a shared bond. Because everyone will show their interest by asking questions, the one who played his music will feel seen and heard by the others. The exercise is also a great way to inspire people to listen to music that they normally don't listen to. If someone is passionate about a piece of music, the others will be positively affected and might be inspired to listen to that same kind of music again.

Scan this QR code to see an animated example video of this exercise:

You can also type: **team exercise 98 music** into YouTube's search bar to find the video.

Team Exercise 99 - Projecting

"Our minds influence the key activity of the brain, which then influences everything; perception, cognition, thoughts and feelings, personal relationships; they're all a projection of you."
- Deepak Chopra

Necessities: None.

To start the exercise, you tell the team to form two groups. You point to one group and tell them everyone in that group is person A. The persons in the other group are person B. Tell all A people to form a straight line. They should remain an arm's length distance between each person in the line. All A people now close their eyes. You now instruct them that each person B will stand in front of a random person A. They keep an arm's length from person A. They do this in silence so the A people don't know who will be in front of them. Tell them that each person A will open their eyes, and say the first thing that comes to his mind concerning the person B in front of him. Tell them it can be anything as long it is the first thing that comes to their minds. Give them a few examples to make it clear. Tell them they can say something about person B's personality, like "I see a strong person that can be kinder to himself". They can also say something abstract like: "I feel the warmth of a star". Tell them they should speak spontaneously without thinking too much about it. While they speak they will keep looking at person B. Tell them they have to continue talking for at least twenty seconds. All the B people will have to remember as much as possible of what the A people tell them.

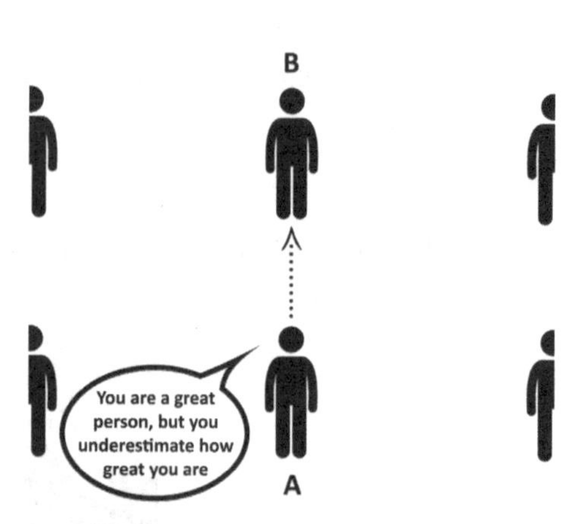

When all the A people are done talking, you now instruct all the B people to close their eyes. While all the B people have their eyes closed, you say aloud to all the A people that they should move to new B people. However, you immediately use body language to instruct the A people to stay where they are. If they have already started to move, you use body language to instruct them to return to their original spots. Make sure you do this in silence. You want the B people to be surprised when they open their eyes and see the same person.
Now, you tell the B people they will open their eyes and tell the person A in front of them the first thing that spontaneously comes up in their minds.
Tell them that now all the A people will have to remember as much as possible from what they just heard.
The B people continue talking for at least twenty seconds.

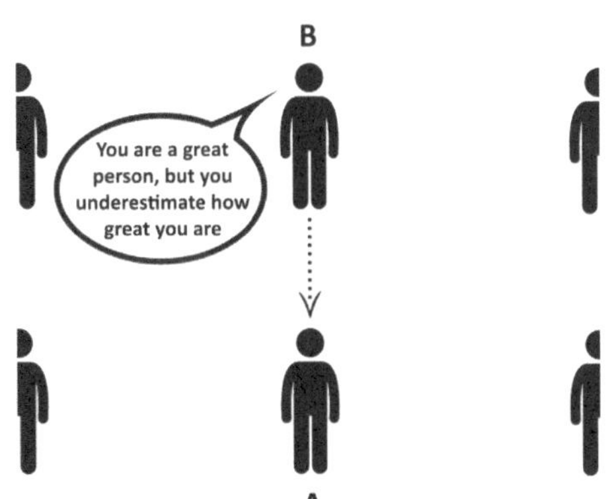

When all the B people are done talking, you tell them that each person A will now tell the person B in front of him exactly the same as what person B just told him. So he will repeat to person B what he just heard from him. So if person B just told person A "You are funny", person A will now say "You are funny" to person B.
When they are done repeating all the things, you tell the B people to think about how much of the things he originally told person A apply to himself as well. They share their findings with the person A in front of them.
Next, in the same manner, the B people will repeat to the A people what they said to them in the first round. The A people now determine if any of what they said to the B people were also about themselves. They share these findings with the person B in front of them.

Variations

1. After the exercise, you can tell the group about projecting. Tell them projecting is defined as feeling something and assuming that other people feel it too. For example, you feel grumpy so you assume everyone around you is grumpy. Another example is feeling happy and loving and believing that everyone around you is happy and loving also.

2. You can make the exercise more specific. Have them spontaneously share positive characteristics about the person in front of them. Alternatively, tell them to say what they wish for that person. In the same way the exercise will be performed. Indirectly they will now hear what they like about themselves, or what they wish for themselves.

3. After the exercise, you tell the group to sit in a circle and evaluate the exercise. Ask them if they agree that the things they told their partners were also applicable to themselves.

4. If you want, you can play two more rounds. You tell all A people to close their eyes. Tell the B people to stand in front of new A people. The A people open their eyes and start talking. When they are done, the B people repeat what they just heard to the A people. Now, all B people close their eyes and the A people stand in front of new B people. The B people open their eyes and start talking. When they are done, the A people repeat to the B people what they just heard.

Why you should use this exercise

In this exercise, each team member gives spontaneous feedback to a fellow team member. Therefore, each participant gains insight into how he is being perceived by someone else.
Because the participants will not know who will be in front of them and they have to speak immediately without thinking about it, the things they say will be spontaneous and genuine.
This exercise will also help with self-reflection. In an indirect way, each person is also giving feedback to himself. It will become apparent that the feedback we give others can reflect back upon ourselves. This is an eye-opening exercise because it teaches the participants that what we project onto others can be things we also need to tell ourselves.

Scan this QR code to see an animated example video of this exercise:

You can also type: **team exercise 99 projecting** into YouTube's search bar to find the video.

Team Exercise 100 - Self evaluation

"The more you know yourself, the more clarity there is. Self-knowledge has no end - you don't come to an achievement, you don't come to a conclusion. It is an endless river."
- Jiddu Krishnamurti

Necessities: None.

To start the exercise, you tell the team to sit in a circle. You tell the group that each person is going to evaluate himself. You tell them that each person has one minute to think of a personal characteristic of his that he thinks has a positive effect on the group. Tell them that the characteristic can be anything, for example, a good sense of humor, a positive attitude, good listening skills, or ambition. Instruct them to think about how this characteristic has a positive influence on the group. After they think about it for one minute, you choose a person to describe his characteristic and the positive influence it has on the group. Tell the other participants to remain silent while he is talking. When he is finished talking, you tell the other participants that they are going to show how much they agree with what they just heard. Tell them that they are going to demonstrate by raising one, two, three, four, or five fingers. The number of fingers represents how much they agree or not. Five fingers mean that someone totally agrees that this characteristic has a positive influence on the group. Four fingers mean that he agrees a little bit. Three fingers mean that he doesn't know whether he agrees or not. Two fingers mean he disagrees a little bit and one finger means that someone totally disagrees. In this way, each person will show how much he agrees or

disagrees on a scale from one to five. After everyone votes, you now tell the speaker that he can look around and see the scale at which others agree or disagree.

Now, you tell the participant sitting to the left of the person who just spoke to follow the same procedure. He tells everyone about his positive characteristic and the others raise their hands to demonstrate their levels of agreement. After he observes how others receive his comments, the person to his left now has a turn. Continue clockwise around the circle until each participant has had a turn. After everyone has described their positive characteristics and observed the responses, you start the second round.

You now tell the group that everyone will get a minute to think about what they can improve upon, regarding their behaviour in this group. They also think about why they think they can make this improvement. Give them examples of things that might need improvement. For example, participants might want to be less agitated, less curt, less indecisive, etc. After a minute, you choose a random person to tell the rest of the group what he thinks he can improve upon and why. When he finishes talking, the participants vote in the same way as in the first round. The person who just said what he thinks he can improve upon, looks around to see how much the other people agree. Now, the person sitting to his left does the same.

Continue clockwise around the circle until each participant has told what he thinks he can improve upon and why he thinks that is. Give everyone enough time to observe on what scale the others agree with him.

Variations

1. In addition to the previous topics, you can also let them share other things about themselves. They could share something they think they should stop doing or something they think they should do more. In the same way as in the original exercise, the others demonstrate their agreement by using the five-finger scale.

2. You can let the participants elaborate on their vote. While someone explains his choice, the person who has the turn listens to the explanation in silence. Only play this variation when you have enough time and you think it will be good for the group to exchange verbal feedback as well. Emphasize that no one should feel obligated to elaborate on the number of fingers he used.

3. You can turn the exercise around. You point to a random person in the group. Each other participant will share a characteristic of this person that has a positive influence on the group. After the recipient hears an opinion from someone, he agrees or disagrees using the five-finger scale. Continue until each participant has told him what characteristic of his he thinks has a positive effect on the group. After everyone shares, they now follow the same procedure for the person sitting to the left of the first recipient. Continue until each person has a chance to hear what the others think.
You can also let them play this variation for the improvement round.

Why you should use this exercise

This is a great exercise for self-reflection. Everyone shares what they think about their behaviour in the group. This will give them insight into how they see themselves.
They also see what others think about themselves. This way they all get to know each other at a deeper level.
After they shared how they see their own behaviour, the others show them on which level they agree with them. This way everyone gets insight into how others see them.
This exercise is very helpful for groups who talk a lot about each other's behavior. With this exercise, you can break that pattern. Because people only need to raise their hands, they don't have to verbally elaborate on their levels of agreement. This will allow them the freedom to be more honest.
After the exercise everyone gained insight into what he thinks his positive influence on the group is, what behavior he thinks he can improve upon, and on what level the others agree or disagree.

Scan this QR code to see an animated example video of this exercise:

You can also type: **team exercise 100 self evaluation** into YouTube's search bar to find the video.

Team Exercise 101 - Create your own workshop

"If your actions inspire others to dream more, learn more, do more and become more, you are a leader."
- John Quincy Adams

Necessities: This book.

Prior to the workshop day, gather all the participants together and give them the link to the YouTube channel that belongs to this book: www.YouTube.com/teamexercises. There are over a hundred team exercises on this channel. The exercises are divided into four categories: feedback exercises, communication exercises, cooperation exercises, and exercises that provide insight. Tell the group to scroll down on the channel and they will find the four categories. Instruct them that each person will choose a category in which he thinks the team needs improvement. Give them an example of a category and an exercise under that category to make sure they understand what they should do. For example, if a participant thinks the team needs to improve communication skills, he should choose the category "communication exercises" and an exercise from that category.
He should choose an exercise that he thinks works well with this group to improve the communication, for example:
"Team Exercise 66 - How to stop using filler words".
Each person should analyze why he wants to use that particular exercise. For example, "Team Exercise 66 helps people improve speaking by eliminating filler words. Because we all give a lot of presentations this exercise will be useful to us."
Tell them each person should study and memorize the exercise he chose before the actual workshop day, so he knows how the exercise needs to be performed.
During the day of the workshop, all the participants meet. You make sure you bring this book with you. You start the exercise by asking a volunteer to lead the exercise he chose.

Before he starts the exercise, he first tells what particular category he chose and why he thinks the team needs improvement in that particular area. Then he tells which exercise he chose and why he thinks this exercise will help them to improve.

After he finishes explaining, he begins the exercise. He can join the exercise or just remain the instructor. Tell the instructor that if he needs help or guidance, you are willing to assist. For example, if he forgets some part of the exercise, you could look it up in this book and remind him.

When the team has finished the exercise, you instruct them to sit in a circle. First, you ask the instructor what he experienced and learned while leading the exercise. After he shares his experiences, you ask the rest of the group to share what they learned from the exercise. Ask them if they think they will improve upon the topic of the category under which the exercise falls. Also ask them how the practiced skills are transferable to real life situations.

After they all share their experiences, the second volunteer leads his exercise. Before he starts the exercise, he explains why he chose a particular category and why he thinks this exercise is the best one for this group. Again, he can ask you for help. After the exercise, they conduct the same evaluation as they did after the first exercise.

Continue until everyone performs his prepared team exercise with the group.

Variations

1. If you don't like the idea of team members leading the exercises, you can instruct them to choose a category and exercise which you will lead yourself. Just as in the original exercise, they will explain during the day why they chose a certain category and exercise before you execute it. Instruct each person to email the exercise ahead of time. This will give you time to prepare.

2. If you are working with a small group, and you want the workshop to last longer, you can let each participant choose and prepare two or three exercises.

3. If you are working with a big group, you may not have time during the workshop day to let everyone lead an exercise. In that case, you can ask them who wants to be a volunteer to prepare and lead an exercise. Choose enough volunteers to fill the day.

4. You can tell the group prior to the exercise that you won't help the person who is performing the exercise. In this way, the person performing the exercise feels more responsible to lead the exercise correctly.

5. If you think it will be good for the group, you can join the exercises yourself as well. Decide for each exercise whether you will join or not.

Why you should use this exercise

This is a great exercise to let each person contribute to a team building day. Because the participants choose the exercises themselves, the team will improve upon topics they think are important. This will make the group motivated during the day.
Everyone will be the leader once and will be responsible for leading his own prepared exercise. This will enhance everyone's leadership skills.
Each person must evaluate how he guided the exercise and will be evaluated by the others. This will give them insight in how their leadership skills are being perceived.
Because it might be the case that people who aren't normally leaders will now lead the group, the dynamics of the group will change. Because a different person will lead each exercise, the group will experience fresh energy. This variety will keep the group engaged during all the exercises.
After this exercise, the group will be able to implement team exercises during a workshop day without an external trainer.

Scan this QR code to see an animated example video of this exercise:

You can also type: **team exercise 101 create your own workshop** into YouTube's search bar to find the video.

The End

"Every ending is a beginning. We just don't know it at the time."
- Mitch Albom

I hope you enjoyed the exercises and that you will put them into practise. I will work on new exercises on YouTube.com/teamexercises. There will be a new one each Sunday. When I created 202 exercises I will write 101 team building exercises part 2.
Please subscribe for free on my YouTube channel and let me know what you think of an exercise in the comments below the video.
I hope to see you there!

Did you like my book? Help me by writing a nice review on Amazon so others can find this book as well :)

Visit:

★★★★★

Thanks! :)

Made in United States
Troutdale, OR
11/09/2023